An Astonishing Discovery

The Seasons of our Lives

How They Alternate from Good to Bad One and Vice-Versa
And How You Can Benefit from this Knowledge
For a Better Life

George Pan Kouloukis

The Author

George Pan Kouloukis is a Greek attorney-at-law, a barrister. As a member of the Athens Bar Association, he has provided legal services to the Ionian Bank of Greece, the Greek Electric Railways Company and other corporations. Of course his book has nothing to do with law; it is the result of a series of observations that everybody could have made after extensive research, provided he or she had experienced the specific events and situations the author has experienced and described in the book.

E-mail: bm-iipafk@otenet.gr

Publishers note

Heart Space Publications
Australia: +61 450 260 348
South Africa: +27 11 431 1274
www.graysonian.com
pat@graysonian.com

Whilst editing this book, every effort has been made to preserve the voice of the author, that is, one of a Greek speaking nationalist, writing in a second language. As a result some of the tenses and manner of writing does not conform to normal English grammar.

In this book we have made use of numeric notations as opposed to the traditional text for values up to three figures. We have done this as we fell it will be easier for the reader to absorb the many numbers the author presents.

Copyright © 2009 by George Pan Kouloukis

Published in Australia by Heart Space Publication 2013

All rights reserved by the author.

ISBN: 978-0-9872816-5-4

The Seasons of our Lives

George Pan Kouloukis

Acknowledgements

I want to thank the following literary consultants, who helped to make this book publishable.

- Elizabeth Judd (Casco Bay Literary Services, U.S.A.), for evaluating, copy-editing and fact-checking thoroughly the entire book.

- Ashley Stokes (The Literary Consultancy, London), for his two successive editorial reports on the manuscript.

- Peter Gelfan (The Editorial Department, U.S.A.), for his evaluation of the manuscript.

- Cornerstones Literary Consultancy (London), for their final critique and encouragement.

Contents

Contents

The Author	i
Acknowledgements	v
The Astonishing Discovery	1
Ludwig van Beethoven	6
Giuseppe Verdi	15
Pablo Picasso	24
Napoléon	36
Victor Hugo	46
Winston Churchill	55
The Complete Picture	71
The Advantages	78
Mikhail Gorbachev	87
Nelson Mandela	94
Christopher Columbus	103
King Henry VIII of England	111
Margaret Thatcher	119
Queen Elizabeth I of England	127
Aristotle Onassis	136
John Glenn	153
Elizabeth Taylor	160
Maria Callas	168
Jacqueline Kennedy Onassis	180

The Dalai Lama of Tibet 189
Jimmy Carter 198
Sarah Bernhardt.. 206
Auguste Rodin.. 216
Josephine, Napoléon I's Wife 225
Confirmation 235
Practical Use 239
End Notes 249
Sources.. 255

 Chapter 1

The Astonishing Discovery

The moment you have finished reading this book, you will be able to know whether the years just ahead are good or bad for you and how long this season will last. Thus you will be able to act accordingly; if there is a storm on the horizon, you'll take shelter in time; if sunny days loom ahead you will take advantage of them before the opportunity passes. In short you'll be able to take crucial decisions regarding your career, marriage, family, relationships and all other life's issues.

This ability derives from the fact that the seasons of our lives alternate from good to bad and vice versa, according to a certain pattern. I explain the way the good and bad seasons have alternated in the lives of many famous men and women whose biographies I cite in the book.

From that pattern we can foresee how our own good and bad seasons will alternate *in the future*. This knowledge radically transforms the way we all live today and helps us to live a much better life. I will explain first in the book how our seasons alternate from good to bad ones and vice versa and how you can foresee how your seasons will alternate in the future. Then, I will cite all the advantages and benefits deriving from this ability.

Before continuing, we have to first clarify some terms we'll meet in the book. A "good" season tends to include both inner satisfaction and outer success, while a "bad" season is a season of anxiety with failure and disappointment. A good season is not always paradisiac, without any concerns or difficulties. Life is never like this. Similarly, a bad season is not necessarily a hell; it may contain moments of satisfaction. Conditions are especially mixed at the beginning of each season, which could be seen as a transitional period. The first part of each good season resembles spring and the first part of each bad season resembles fall. So there can be "storms" in spring and "Indian summers" in fall.

All of us have had good and bad seasons in our lives. Great German composer Ludwig van Beethoven, for example, went through a bad period around the age of 32 because he had become deaf. Contemplating suicide, he wrote his will. Then a good season returned. Beethoven overcame his hearing problem, was recognized as one of the greatest composers of all time – he wrote nine insuperable symphonies and became a celebrated member of Viennese society.

Napoléon provides another example. During a good season of his life, he conquered almost all of Europe, was crowned Emperor of France and lived a life full of grandeur, triumph and success. Then a bad season arrived; Napoléon lost all he had achieved, he was defeated at the Battle of Waterloo and he was exiled ultimately to the remote island of St. Helena.

The specific criteria that characterize a good or bad season usually include factors like money, fame, love and health. These criteria differ from person to person and can change over time. But usually there is only one main factor that shapes at a given moment the good and bad seasons of a person. For famous Greek ship owner Aristotle Onassis, for example, only money had any meaning throughout most of his life, as you'll see in his biography. But at the end of his life, when he fell seriously ill from an incurable disease, only his health counted – though he was the wealthiest person on earth, money meant nothing for him anymore.

Also for Beethoven, health and his hearing problem was of uppermost importance during one of his early bad seasons, but later when he overcame that problem his recognition as a composer became the main factor shaping his seasons. For Napoléon on the other hand, fame was the main factor shaping his seasons throughout his life.

Some of you may not have noticed that there are good and bad seasons in your life, so you might have a hard time believing these seasons exist. To be convinced, you only have to look back over your life the way I explain in this book. In the book I also provide scores of detailed examples of good and bad seasons in the lives of a lot of famous people, which fully confirm the existence of these seasons.

The Story of My Research

Before explaining the way our seasons alternate in life, we must first see what happened that led me to start a research regarding the alternations of the good and bad seasons in our lives and how I finally arrived at the discovery described in this book. This will help you to fully understand my discovery.

Like most of us, I had, too, observed in my life that an alternation of my seasons from good to bad and vice versa had occurred. Later, I asked myself whether these alternations happened according to a specific pattern and thus we could foresee how long each season would last or irregularly, without any pattern. But since it appeared to me too difficult to find the answer to this question, I abandoned the idea.

Suddenly, however, a book arrived at my hands (*The Universe*, published by Time-Life Books), which prompted me to continue trying to find whether our seasons alternate according to a certain pattern or irregularly.

That book mentioned that the magnetic poles of the sun reverse themselves every 11 years; the North Pole becomes the South Pole and vice-versa every 11 years. That reversal always occurs on certain dates; somewhere in 1957, in 1968, in 1979 and so on every 11 years. These solar alternations led me to a spontaneous thought; do the alternations of the sun's poles influence human behavior? Are the alternations of the good and bad seasons of life synchronized with the patterns of solar activity?

To test this hypothesis I reflected on my own life but my hypothesis proved to be wrong. My life's good and bad seasons hadn't alternated the way the sun's poles reverse – every 11 years. All I could come up with, however, was a turning point in 1957; a bad season had ended for me and a good one had started. But 11 years later – in 1968 – there was no reversal. On the contrary, my good season continued even better. I therefore realized that my idea was groundless and abandoned it.

Later, a new book caught my attention. It was its title that aroused my interest; *The Seasons of a Man's Life*. Its author, Daniel J. Levinson, a professor of psychology at Yale University, carried out a study showing that everyone's life has four seasons, each lasting 20-22 years. But he did not distinguish which of those seasons are good and which are bad. That book brought me back to the question of the alternations of the good and bad seasons in our lives. Do those alternations, I wondered, happen not on certain dates – say with the movement of the sun but at certain *points in* our lives, such as the intervals of 20-22 years suggested by Levinson?

With that possibility in mind, I decided to look back over my life again. But the outcome was again negative. My life's good and bad seasons hadn't alternated every 20-22 years. The only finding was that my life had taken a second turn at my age of 40; my previous good season then gave way to a bad season. However, between those two "turns" (1957 and age 40) there wasn't a period of 20-22 years, as I expected to find, influenced by Levinson's study. So, I abandoned the effort once more.

Some years later though, a new element appeared. A new turn had occurred in my life; the bad season I'd been previously experiencing had ended and a new good one had started. The above observation was of course, a starting point. So I decided to explore the subject further. I ought, I thought, to examine what happens in the lives of other people; have their lives alternated the same way as in my own life?

To find out what was happening in the lives of others, I examined many biographies. But since biographies on ordinary people usually don't exist, or they are very few, I realized that only biographies of famous people were available. The results derived from these biographies were amazing and they confirmed my initial findings. I found that the cycles of good and bad seasons occurred as in my own life.

At that point I said; "Okay, I can find patterns in the lives of famous individuals, but what about ordinary people? Is my discovery relevant for all of us?" There is no reason to think that the alternations of the seasons would happen any differently in the lives of ordinary people. To confirm this, I discussed the subject with friends and relatives as to how their seasons alternated. They all agreed with my findings. We can say therefore, that my discovery is valid for all. To confirm this, you can also examine your own life's good and bad seasons. I will explain later how you can find which your own seasons will be in the future.

I cite first, in brief, the biographies of famous people whose lives and seasons I have studied; ranging from Beethoven, to King Henry VIII of England and the Dalai Lama of Tibet. From the biographies cited, the way the famous people's seasons alternated is shown in startling clarity. In these biographies, you will discover that the people we think of being successful throughout their lives have had bad seasons and how their lives were radically affected by the cycles of good and bad fortune. I reveal my discovery *gradually*, step by step. We start with Ludwig van Beethoven, the great German composer.

Chapter 2

Ludwig van Beethoven

Beethoven was born in 1770. We don't know enough about the first 5 years of his life to know whether it was a good or bad season. But from 1776 on we know he had a pleasant childhood. Though his family was poor and his father was strict and severe, he was lucky enough to have a devoted mother and he spent happy hours in her presence. He also had many friends and opportunities to have fun.*

In 1778, little Beethoven recognized as "a child prodigy;" gave his first public concert in Bonn where he was born. The following year he began to study with a well-known musician, a director of the National Theater, who immediately recognized his talent and took him under his wing. After two years of instruction, in 1781, when Beethoven was only 11, he composed three sonatas and one concerto for the piano, all of which were published immediately. The same year he had another reason to be happy; he became acquainted with a family in Bonn that offered a supportive environment and nurtured his musical talent. Their home was a "refuge for happiness," [1] as he put it.

> *   *I have taken the facts and detail in this chapter from Gino Pugneti's* Beethoven, *published in Greek by Fytrakis Publications, Great Men of All Seasons series, Athens, 1965. There are also Beethoven's biographies in English that can studied; Barry Cooper's* Beethoven, *Oxford Press, 2001, or Maynard Solomon's* Beethoven, *Schirmer Books, 2001.*

In 1784 Beethoven became financially independent, while only 14 years old. That year he was appointed deputy organist in Bonn's court, with an excellent salary. Thus he could support his whole family. His father had become an alcoholic, his mother was seriously ill and there were two younger brothers to care for.

3 years later, in 1787, Beethoven's dream came true; he was able to leave Bonn for Vienna. Vienna was a cultural magnet at the time, where all the arts and especially music flourished. Bands "played in the streets and the whole city was awash in music,"[2] while "the theaters and the academies were always overflowing."[3] There, the young Beethoven met Mozart for the first time and received major encouragement from him. He improvised a composition on the piano, but Mozart was skeptical because he believed that the young man had previously memorized it.

Beethoven then asked Mozart to choose the theme himself and he improvised again. When Beethoven finished Mozart said, "This young man will surprise the world someday."[4]

However, Beethoven's first stay in Vienna lasted only a few months, as being the head of the family he had to return to Bonn. That year his mother died, his father remained an alcoholic. That unfortunate event didn't change Beethoven's good season as he managed to be granted a substantial allowance by the state with which to take care of his father, as well as his two younger brothers.

In 1789, Beethoven met Prince Maximilian, who held him in high esteem and mentored him. With the prince's help Beethoven enrolled, at the age of 19 in the university where he had an opportunity to study the works of philosophers and writers of his era; Kant, Schiller, Goethe and others. The next year, Beethoven's first important musical compositions were published and he began to be recognized as a composer.

At the age of 21, in 1791, he entered high society. He was received at the most exclusive salons and moved in fashionable court circles. A year later he met the great composer Haydn, who heard him playing a serenade on the piano. Enthusiastic, Haydn invited Beethoven to Vienna. A jubilant Beethoven again left Bonn for Vienna, this time as Haydn's student. Another dream had become a reality. He was now 22 years old.

The Season from 1792 on

In Vienna, however, Beethoven's experiences did not meet his expectations. Haydn, no longer young, had too many other preoccupations and turned out to be indifferent to his gifted student. Disappointed, Beethoven was forced to study with lesser-known musicians in 1793. The next year he was able to accept the hospitality of a prince but even that was short-lived, as the atmosphere in the palace was uncongenial. To support himself, he was obliged to give music lessons to a diverse array of students.

In 1794 Beethoven began to realize he had a hearing problem. He was only 24 and in 1795 another cause of concern arose. Beethoven gave his first major concert in Vienna, performing his Concerto No. 2 for piano and orchestra. It was a novel, stunning piece that made people think; Beethoven was bringing a more philosophical perspective to music. But the Viennese, accustomed to joyful music and entertainment had reservations.

Beethoven continued giving concerts in other cities: Nuremberg, Berlin, Dresden and Prague. But though he had great success, at the end of one of those concerts he realized with terror that his hearing had become worse. He began experiencing an incessant buzzing in his ears that sounded like a waterfall. In addition he couldn't always clearly understand speech. At first he kept quiet about his problem. But over the years 1797–1800, the situation became catastrophic; he became almost totally deaf. In 1801 he decided to confide to a close friend; "I am extremely distressed," he wrote, "the most vital part of myself, my hearing has become impaired and is steadily worsening. I do not know whether I will ever be cured."[5]

He also wrote to his doctor, "For the last two years I have avoided all social interaction. I cannot tell people that I am deaf. It is terrible."[6] In 1802, his doctor advised him to spend the summer recuperating in the countryside. But "it was a summer full of despair."[7] Beethoven composed a letter to his brothers that was meant to serve as a kind of will, with the proviso that it be read after his death. He was only 32 years old. The document said, among other things; "I want to end my life but music prevents me from doing so. For so long I have not felt any real happiness. I live as if I am in exile, since it is impossible for me to participate in the company of others, to talk with friends, to hear and be heard. I feel I am indeed a miserable creature."[8]

The same year, more despair was added to Beethoven's life. The woman he loved, Giulietta Guicciardi, said to have been "frivolous and self-centered"[9] abandoned him after a two year relationship. His despair over the lost relationship, combined with his illness, created the worst crisis of his life so far. Beethoven was on the brink of suicide. He didn't know that his bad season would be followed by a good one at a certain period.

Things were not much better in the musical arena, normally his only consolation. In 1805 Beethoven's melodrama *Fidelio* was performed, the only opera he wrote. Though it would later be considered a masterpiece, the initial production was a failure and closed after only three days. This failure was repeated the following year. *Fidelio* was presented again, in a new form, but only for two performances, the theater was almost empty, the earnings insignificant.

Things got worse between 1807 and 1809. Beethoven experienced another disappointment in love. He had fallen in love with a young, aristocratic Hungarian woman, Theresa von Brunschwick. Though they became engaged, her mother disapproved and did not allow them to see each other. Finally they broke off the engagement.

Beethoven was also beset by financial problems. In 1808 he decided to leave Vienna to accept a position as a choir director in Kassel. However, some of his friends interceded and helped him get a state allowance so he could stay in Vienna. But In 1809 the situation worsened; Napoléon's army seized Vienna, after a violent attack that convulsed the city. The "royal court and all the nobility abandoned the city, while in the streets chaos prevailed."[10]

Beethoven "found shelter in a pub, covering his aching ears with pillows to avoid the deafening report of the cannons."[11] Ordinary life in Vienna came to a standstill. The currency "became worthless, prices soared and inflation loomed."[12] Beethoven's state allowance almost evaporated and he often did not have enough money for food. At the same time he suffered "from excruciating abdominal pain."[13] Shabbily dressed, "ill and stooped over, he attended the funeral of his former teacher Haydn, under the menacing guard of armed French soldiers."[14]

At some point in 1809, his bad season finally ended.

The New Season from 1809 onwards

Just after this season began in 1810, Beethoven finally achieved a major goal; he became acquainted with a charming, clever woman, Bettina Brentano, who would devote herself to him and would make up for all the failed relationships he had experienced with other women. "Being close to Beethoven," she wrote in a letter to Goethe, "causes me to forget the world."[15]

The most important fact however, is that in this favorable season Beethoven managed to triumph over his cruel fate of his deafness. This allowed him to continue working as he found a solution; he held a wooden hearing aid with his teeth (a long, slim piece of wood) and touch it to the piano. This allowed him to perceive the sound of the music through the mouth to the inner ear.

In other ways too, the good days returned; In 1812 Beethoven became acquainted with Goethe and a friendship evolved between them, despite their age difference (Beethoven was 42, Goethe 62). When they strolled through the streets of Vienna, people would bow, something that annoyed Goethe but for Beethoven it was heaven sent; "Don't worry, Your Excellency," he once said to Goethe jokingly, "maybe the bows are only for me."[16]

In 1813 Napoléon began to lose power and Beethoven, full of enthusiasm, started to compose the *Victory of Wellington*, an immediate success. The following year Beethoven performed that work at the congress that took place in Vienna after Napoléon's downfall. The Czar of Russia, the emperor of Austria, the kings of Denmark, Prussia and Bavaria, "princes, ministers, diplomats and other statesmen" [17] were all present and they paid homage to Beethoven. It was a concert triumph.

From then on, Beethoven's life was glorious. In 1814, his melodrama *Fidelio*, a failure a few years earlier, was performed again in Vienna. This time because of his good season it was a tremendous success. Repeat performances of *Fidelio* were held in other European cities, including Prague, Leipzig and Berlin, always to great acclaim.

As Beethoven's reputation reached its apogee, he began to earn a great deal of money. His performances attracted audiences of thousands, among them many celebrities. The Austrian government offered state-owned halls for his performances and friends began to surround him and draw him into an active social life. He frequented the various cafés and restaurants of Vienna, where the previously gloomy Beethoven became unrecognizably gregarious, telling jokes and drinking champagne. He walked the streets of Vienna, stopping in shops to browse or buy things and talk with ordinary people.

In Vienna's central park, the Pratter, children would offer him flowers. After his walk Beethoven would meet his friends in the park's noisy cafés, where "amidst cigarette smoke and the smell of alcohol, all the artistic and intellectual problems of the times were solved."[18] To communicate, he would hand a notebook to his companions and have them write down their questions or comments. He would respond orally with ease and humor.

In this good season, women who had previously ignored him began to fill his life. They were young, beautiful and from the upper social echelons. His biographers report that there were at least fifteen of them; besides Bettina Brentano, they included Dorothy von Ertmann, Marianne von Westerholt, Eleonore von Breunig, Rachel von Ense and Josephine von Brunschwick (the sister of Theresa von Brunschwick, to whom Beethoven had been engaged in 1807, until her mother cut it off). Giulietta Guicciardi, the Italian woman who had abandoned him in 1802, leading him to contemplate suicide, she also returned. Beethoven was no longer interested.

In the professional arena, Beethoven had a prodigious musical output; he finished his 32 sonatas for the piano, composed his famous oratorio *Misa Solemnis* and finished part of the *Ninth Symphony*. The oratorio *Misa Solemnis* – "Beethoven's hymn to God"[19] was completed in 1820. From then on, Beethoven had a deeply spiritual outlook.

The same year (1820), the city of Vienna proclaimed Beethoven an honorary citizen of the city, an honor that thrilled him. In 1825, at the age of 55, Beethoven arrived at the high point of his life; his *Ninth Symphony* was performed in Vienna and was an unprecedented triumph. The audience went wild and Beethoven was profoundly moved. When the concert was over, several theater workers "had to carry him out; he had fainted!"[20]

The Season After 1825

Starting in 1825, Beethoven began facing serious health problems; arthritis and eye ailments. He remained at home, often in bed. He was forced to ask his brother for help and retreated to his brother's home in the countryside, staying in a small room and subsisting on an inadequate diet. The next year (1826), things got worse. Beethoven's friends abandoned him, he gave up composing and his works stopped being performed. After the Ninth Symphony's success in 1825, no other concerts featured his works. Deeply disappointed, he complained in his diary that "Vienna's high society seems interested only in dancing, horseback riding and attending the ballet."[21]

Beethoven tried to get all of his works published but without success. His bad season didn't allow it. The royal court that previously supported him now ignored him. Late in 1826 on a chilly December day he abandoned his brother's "lukewarm hospitality"[22] in the countryside and returned to Vienna on the "milkman's cart,"[23] because his brother, despite having his own coach, had not made it available to him. As a result, Beethoven arrived in Vienna seriously ill with pneumonia.

After a few days his health took a turn for the worse; his feet became swollen and he suffered from abdominal pain. On January 3, 1827 he wrote his will. Bedridden, he complained to two friends visiting him that he had been left alone in life without family members to care for him. Beside him was a portrait of Theresa von Brunschwick, the woman he had been engaged to two decades earlier.

On March 24, 1827, the end came. Beethoven asked the two friends attending him for Rhein wine. But it was too late. Two days later, on March 26, 1827, the great Beethoven died at the age of 57, while a violent storm battered Vienna.

Conclusion

This biographical sketch has shown that in 1776 a good season emerged in Beethoven's life. Then a bad season started in 1792. A new good season began in 1809, while another bad season started in 1825. Based on these dates of his seasons' alternations and combined with the dates of the other biographies' that follow, you can determine *your own* good and bad season's cycles.

Chapter 3

Giuseppe Verdi

We continue our trip with the life of Giuseppe Verdi, the great Italian composer. Verdi was born 14 years before Beethoven died. We do not know much about his childhood and youth years until the age of 18 and so we cannot say whether these years were good or bad. We only know that he was born in 1813 in a small village near Parma, Italy. His father was a grocer and when Verdi was 8 his father bought him a piano. At the age of 12 he was appointed organist in the village church.*

But we can see that from 1832 on, when Verdi was 19, he was in a bad season of his life. A wealthy merchant friend of Verdi's father's was aware of his great talent and offered him a music scholarship in Milan. Accompanied by his father and his teacher, Verdi arrived in Milan in May 1832. However, a great disappointment awaited him there; he applied to the Milan Conservatory but after hearing him play the piano, the school rejected his application.

---

* All the facts and details in this chapter derive from Gino Pugneti's Verdi, published in Greek by Fytrakis Publications, Great Men of All Seasons series, Athens, 1966. There are also Verdi's biographies in English, as for example; a) Mary Jane Phillips-Matz's Verdi; A Biography, Oxford University Press, 1993, or b) William Weaver's Verdi; A Documentary Study, W.W. Norton and Company, 1977.

He was a "foreigner" they said, he was above the age of 14 and he had a "rural look."[1] He also seemed inadequately trained. Deeply disappointed, the young Verdi "felt uprooted and lost in the city."[2] Finally, he enrolled in a different private school. The same year (1832), he experienced another blow; his beloved sister Josephine died. It was the first great sorrow of his life.

The following year, 1833, Verdi encountered one more injustice. The Philharmonic Orchestra of Busseto, a small town near his village was without a conductor and invited Verdi to take that position. The church authorities rejected him and "appointed a candidate of their own choice."[3] The scandal attracted the attention of the local government where a major uproar ensued. Though Verdi finally got the job in 1835 the incident caused him great sadness.

Two years later in 1837, a great misfortune befell Verdi. From his marriage to Margherita Barezzi (in 1836), he had a daughter, Virginia, whom he adored. Virginia died when only a few months old, in 1837. Dispirited Verdi isolated himself in his home and he resigned from his position with the Philharmonic Orchestra of Busseto, a position he had fought so hard for. Later in 1838 he left for Milan.

In Milan, Verdi faced tremendous difficulties; he was jobless, had no money and often could, "only eat once a day, usually in miserable inns."[4] As if all that were not enough, in 1839 his second child, a young son, died. Verdi was devastated with his loses, but despite all his sorrow he still had to earn a living and so composed lighthearted music. In 1840 he was commissioned to write *Un Giorno di Regno (King for a Day)* for the impresario Merelli, a famous Italian manager.

The bad season was not yet finished for Verdi. In 1840, he received the most tragic blow of all; his beloved wife Margherita Barezzi died. Grief stricken, Verdi fled Milan for Busseto so that he could find solace. But impresario Merelli reminded him of his obligation to complete *King for a Day* so Verdi had to return to Milan.

He would have been better off not returning. *King for a Day* was performed in La Scala on September 5, 1840, but it was a catastrophe. After pandemonium broke out with the audience whistling and shouting its disapproval, the opera was abandoned. Verdi was devastated. He became reclusive and lost his desire to compose music.

In late 1840, Merelli, who never lost faith in Verdi, asked him whether he would like to compose the music for a work titled *Nabuchodonosor*. Verdi refused but Merelli insisted, putting the libretto for that work in Verdi's pocket. Half-heartedly he started composing. But "the notes weren't appearing"[5] or if they were, they were full of sorrow, like the composer's soul. However, he finished it in 1841.

The Second Season from 1842 onwards

Rehearsals for the opera *Nabuchodonosor* or *Nabucco*, as it came to be named, in the meantime, started early in 1842. Immediately it became clear that Verdi had composed a masterpiece. Nabucco was performed for the first time in La Scala in Milan on March 9, 1842. What followed was an unprecedented triumph. The enraptured audience responded with a standing ovation, "demanding with a frenzy of applause, repeated encores of the moving chorus song "*Va, pensiero, sull' ali dorate,*"[6] which still causes shivers of emotion.

Verdi, now 29, had suddenly become famous. People were singing the chorus song from *Nabucco* in the streets, while "hats and neckties with Verdi's name inscribed on them"[7] were sold everywhere. Milan's wealthiest families opened their homes to him. The same year (1842), the composer became acquainted with a famous soprano, Josephina Strepponi. They developed a lasting relationship that persisted until her death in 1897.

During the next nine years, between 1843 and 1851, Verdi composed thirteen operas, which were performed in the big cities of Italy; Milan,

Rome, Venice, Naples, Trieste as well as London and all with great success. The first of those operas was *I Lombardi*, which was performed at La Scala on February 11, 1843. The day of its premiere, enthusiastic crowds mobbed the theater and the success of that opera was similar to *Nabucco*.

Ernani followed in 1844, based on Victor Hugo's work of the same name. It premiered in Venice on March 9, 1844, to great acclaim. Exuberant Venetians "lifted Verdi to their shoulders and carried him triumphantly around Saint Mark's square."[8] With the money he earned from *Ernani*, Verdi was able to buy a small farm near his village.

Jeanne d'Arc (Giovanna d'Arco) followed in 1845, with equally great success. Verdi had now so much money that he acquired a mansion in Busseto. Other accomplishments included *Attila* in 1846 and *I Masnadieri (The Bandits)* in 1847. *The Bandits'* premiere was held in London with great fanfare; Queen Victoria and almost all the members of Parliament present. The opera was a huge hit and Verdi made staggering amounts of money. He bought a large farm with woods and vineyards near Busseto and an apartment in Paris, where he retreated from time to time to relax with his companion, Josephina Strepponi.

Tension between Italy and Austria was mounting in this period and to stir up patriotic sentiments, Verdi composed *La Battaglia di Legnano (The Battle of Legnano)*. That opera was first performed in Rome in 1849. Tickets for the premiere were sold out. It was another smash hit. Ecstatic, the audience demanded as an encore "the repetition of the entire fourth act."[9] Verdi had become a national hero. At the end of that year, another Verdi opera was performed. This was in Naples and called; *Luisa Miller*, which was based on Schiller's tragedy of the same name.

During the next eight years (1851–1859), Verdi composed his extraordinary masterpieces *Rigoletto, Il Trovatore, La Traviata, Les Vêpres Siciliennes, Simon Boccanegra, Un Ballo in Maschera* and others. He arrived at the culmination of his glory. He finished the first of those masterpieces, *Rigoletto*, early in 1851 and its premiere was staged in Venice on March 11 of the same year. All night, Venice's canals resounded with "the voices of gondoliers' singing *Feather in the Wind*,"[10] a song well known even now. After 21 performances in Venice, *Rigoletto* began to be performed all over the world.

In 1851 Verdi began to compose his next masterpiece *Il Trovatore*, which he completed the following year. The premiere was held in Rome in January 1853, again to great acclaim. Two months later his third masterpiece, *La Traviata* premiered in Venice. It was another instant hit and was even performed in America.

In 1855, Verdi finished *Les Vêpres Siciliennes*. Its premiere was held in L' Opera de Paris; then in 1856 it was performed in La Scala in Milan with tremendous success. Its ardent patriotism stirred the souls of Italians. In 1857, *Simon Boccanegra* was performed in Venice and the same year, Verdi composed *Un Ballo in Maschera*. The latter opera was performed in Rome in February 1859 with great success – "the ticket prices were seven times the normal price."[11]

Verdi had arrived at the pinnacle of his career; at the age of 46 he was considered Europe's greatest composer. To make his success complete, in early 1859 he married the woman with whom he had lived for the last 17 years, Josephina Strepponi.

The Third Season from 1859

From 1859, Verdi lapsed into a crisis that lasted for a number of years. He isolated himself on his farm in Busseto and became preoccupied with ordinary farm chores. He rose "at daybreak, took care of the farm animals (horses, dogs and so on), bought cows and other animals at the local market and looked after the harvest."[12]

"There is not a place uglier than this one," he complained in a letter, "but where else can I find solitude for thinking?"[13] Especially during the winter, time stood still and the tediousness was unbearable. Verdi's connection with the larger world was through the mail. To alleviate his boredom he took interminable walks in the area around his farm, accompanied only by his dogs, his precious assistants, as he called them.

Verdi did spend some time composing music during that season, managing to compose one work every four or five years in contrast to his previous output of one work a year. For a while he was distracted by politics and was elected to the Parliament of Turin in 1861. But by now, being in a bad season of his life, political wrangling left him disillusioned and so he stopped attending the sessions.

The next year Verdi finished his work *La Forza del Destino (The Power of Destiny)*, which the Russian Theater of Petrograd had commissioned. But when the opera was performed after many obstacles and delays, in November 1862 in Petrograd, it had little success. More than five years passed before Verdi finished another work. In March 1867, *Don Carlo*s was performed for the first time in Paris. What followed, however, was a major disappointment for the composer; the critics accused him, unjustifiably, of borrowing from Wagner's music. Deeply wounded, he closeted himself in a hotel before he could face the public again.

The same year Verdi suffered two more blows. His father died, which had a devastating effect on the composer. Soon afterward, his father-in-law (his first wife's father), his benefactor Antonio Barezzi to whom Verdi owed so much also died. At the funeral, the eulogy was extraordinarily moving; "My second father, who loved me so much and whom I loved dearly, is gone,"[14] Verdi lamented.

4 more years would pass before Verdi was able to finish another work. At the end of 1871, after numerous delays, his opera *Aïda* was performed in

Cairo. The performance lasted more than eight hours, from 7:00pm to 3:00 am, and was attended "by odd and variegated audience members ranging from Christian Coptics and Jews to women from the harem."[15] But the composer wasn't satisfied with his work. For the first time in his life he had decided not to be present to conduct the performance himself.

The same year, the great conductor and Verdi's close friend, Angelus Mariani, who had conducted many of Verdi's operas, abandoned him and joined the ranks of Wagner's supporters. The Wagner camp was antagonistic toward Verdi. Mariani's decision to conduct Wagner's opera *Lohengrin* in Bologna was a blow to Verdi. He now felt an immense loneliness and sorrow, expressing these feelings in his next work, the mournful *Messa da Requiem*, performed in May 1874, in the church of St. Mark in Milan. Finally, this bad season for Verdi ended.

The Fourth Season from 1875 onwards

In 1875, Verdi's sorrowful *Requiem* suddenly realized enormous success. After having conquered all of Italy it did the same in the rest of Europe, while in London an "unbelievable chorus of 1,200 voices"[16] would participate in the performance, a fact that moved the critics to write rave reviews.

Verdi had shaken his loneliness and now aged 62, again began to enjoy the delights of life. He became acquainted with a young intellectual, Arrigo Boito, who shared the pleasures of culture with him, exposing him to the new intellectual currents and fashions. Verdi acquired a new lease on life and a prolific new period began.

In 1876, Verdi conducted – personally this time, his *Aïda* in Paris and soon the opera was performed triumphantly all over Europe. From now on the composer began writing new works, though each now took him many years to complete because of his advancing age. In 1881 he rewrote *Simon Boccanegra*, which was performed that same year in its new form with great success.

From 1879 he had started setting the music for Shakespeare's Otello, which he finally finished in 1886. The premiere took place at La Scala in 1887. Celebrities from all over Europe arrived for the performance and tickets prices reached unprecedented heights. At the end of the performance the audience's cries of joy could be heard blocks away. When Verdi came out of the theater overcome with emotion, the people "unhitched the horses of his carriage and drew it themselves to his hotel."[17]

Between 1888 and 1892, Verdi composed another masterpiece, *Falstaff*, again based on Shakespeare. But now he worked only a few hours a week. It was "as if he was in a long summer vacation,"[18] his biographers say.

The Season After 1892

In 1892 Verdi was 79 years old. The idea of death was often on his mind. Two years later, when *Falstaff* was performed in La Scala, he reiterated Shakespeare's words; "Everything has finished, old John. Go away now."[19] More disturbing was the fact that Verdi's romanticism was losing its luster in Italy. Verdi found himself increasingly dismissed as old-fashioned. He began to question the quality of his early works and discouraged their revival. Many of his works had virtually vanished from the stage; many of his greatest achievements were unknown.

In 1897, Verdi was left alone in life; his beloved companion, his wife Josephina Strepponi, the "divine gift"[20] as he called her, died. From then on, his health crumbled and the year 1900 found him confined to a wheelchair. In 1901, the great composer, one of the greatest in the world, departed from this life at the age of 88.

Conclusion

Verdi's biography reflects that his first bad season ended in 1825. A good season followed around the same year. The next bad season started in 1859, followed by another good season that begun in 1875. Verdi's last bad season of his life started in 1892. Combining Verdi's dates to those of Beethoven we've seen in the previous chapter, we arrive at a series of dates as shown in the accompanying graph. The upper dates in the graph indicate transitions from good to bad seasons; the lower dates indicate the reverse. This is true for all the graphs in the book.

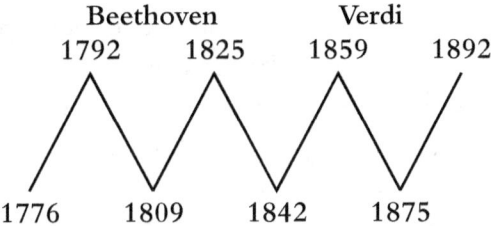

You may recall Beethoven's dates of his life's alternations of seasons were 1776, 1792, 1809 and 1825; Verdi's alternations were in the years 1842, 1859, 1875 and 1892. Between each one of these dates is a constant *16 -17 years*. This is the *first* observation of this book. We'll see the second soon. In the meantime, I will further extend the first observation.

Chapter 4

Pablo Picasso

In this chapter we'll continue the revelation of our discovery by exploring how the good and bad seasons alternated in the turbulent life of Pablo Picasso, the famous Spanish painter.* Picasso was born in Malaga Spain, in 1881, 68 years after Verdi. When he was 11 years old in 1892 a bad season was underway for him. Picasso's family moved to La Coruña, a town on the Atlantic Ocean where they lived for about four years. There, rain and fog prevailed almost every day, in contrast to sunny and hot Malaga. "The rain… and the wind," Picasso wrote in a melancholy tone as a young child, "have begun and will continue until Coruña is no more."[1]

After 1895, Picasso's family moved to Barcelona. There, Picasso, now 14 entered art school and started producing his first drawings. Almost immediately, conflict with his father arose. The father, also an amateur painter felt his son's drawings were not up to par. Not surprisingly, Picasso wanted to get away from his father's influence. In 1897, with financial help from one of his uncles he left for Madrid. There he enrolled in the School of Fine Arts

---

* *My source for Picasso's biography is Lael Westenbaker's (and the editors' of Time-Life Books)* The World of Picasso, *Time-Life Books, Library of Art series, Amsterdam, 1976, European edition. For further reading you can see Patrick O'Brian's* Pablo Ruiz Picasso; A Biography, *Collins, 1976.*

but almost immediately dropped out. His uncle then stopped supporting him and Picasso became penniless. He didn't have enough money for food and in 1898 he became seriously ill from scarlet fever.

A year later, Picasso was forced to return to Barcelona, where his moods fluctuated between joy and despair. In 1900 he resumed wandering and he left Barcelona for London. He didn't get farther than Paris, a town he was only going to explore for a few months. In the Christmas season of 1900, he returned to Barcelona. It was a disastrous homecoming. Picasso's unkempt hair, his "bohemian" attire and especially his paintings, aroused his father's ire. To escape his father's wrath he fled back to his uncle's home in Malaga.

The situation there was equally bad; his uncle demanded that Picasso cut his hair and begin painting "naturally." Not able to find peace anywhere, Picasso went back to Madrid. There he found a friend from Barcelona, an anarchist named Francisco de Asis Soler and they both decided to publish a magazine for which Picasso would provide the illustrations. But after a few issues the magazine folded.

Picasso again left Madrid in the spring of 1901, heading for Paris. On the way he stopped in Barcelona to say goodbye to his family but his father had become extremely hostile; the rift between them would never be bridged. Not long after that the son stopped using his father's name Ruiz and kept only the name of his mother; Picasso.

In Paris Picasso faced extreme hardship. He was unable to sell any of his paintings and became more desperate from day to day. At the end of 1901, the prodigal son's life continued; he was forced to go back to his family in Barcelona again so he would at least have something to eat.

Picasso stayed in Barcelona for three years. Those years were full of depression, which was reflected in his work. He painted beggars, prostitutes and other lonely and dejected street people. These paintings were dominated by the color blue, which suited their themes and Picasso's mood.

In the spring of 1904 Picasso became restless again so he returned to Paris. He stayed in a miserable ground floor room with a rotten floor, without ventilation or heat. He was as poor as many of the "bleu people" he was painting. He tried to sell some of his works but the results were disappointing. He made contact with an agent who handled artworks, an unscrupulous former circus' clown named Clovis Sagot, who used him and bought his works for almost nothing. He had another bad experience with the owner of a furniture shop who wanted to sell some of his paintings. This man who had a drinking problem and knew nothing about art bought Picasso's drawings, "wholesale", for a penny.

In the meantime Picasso got involved with a young woman who lived next door, Fernande Olivier. Now he tried to make his works "commercial" in an effort to sell them. Two years after arriving in Paris, in 1906, he produced *Les Demoiselles d'Avignon*, featuring five nude women with deformed bodies and animal-like faces. When he showed the painting to his friends, it caused a stir. No one had a good word to say about it. Matisse, the great French painter, said that that painting "would sink Picasso."[2] Deeply disappointed he put the painting in a corner so nobody could see it.

Still, Picasso continued with his bizarre paintings. In the summer of 1908 he went to the countryside near Paris and on his return brought some paintings with country scenes. They were, however, all distorted landscapes in which you couldn't tell "where the grass ends and the sky begins."[3]

The Season from 1908 onwards

From the first year of this season Picasso at last began to earn a good income from his paintings and he could in 1909 go for a summer vacation with Fernande to a small village in Spain. In the fall of the same year he abandoned the miserable room he had lived in for the past five years and moved with Fernande to "a large apartment… with a living room, dining room, bedroom and room for a studio"[4], in one of the best sections of Paris. He furnished this in luxury and decorated it with expensive carpets and statues. He also hired a maid and started receiving wealthy friends and others at receptions on Sunday afternoons.

In 1909 Picasso inaugurated a new kind of painting; cubism. This was a bizarre kind of painting; his works emphasized objects and faces divided into squares and other geometric forms. But as he was in a good season these paintings soon made him world famous. The following year he produced a great number of these works, which were snatched up immediately by collectors. In 1911, Picasso's paintings were exhibited in the Salon des Indépendants in Paris. The cubist movement spread rapidly and collectors from New York, Munich and London proudly showed off their collections of Picasso's cubist works.

The same year, Picasso ended his relationship with Fernande, after they'd been together for seven years. He immediately became involved with another woman, Marcelle Humbert (or Eva as he called her). At the same time that he was beginning a new life with her, he moved his studio to a more exclusive section of Paris; Montparnasse.

In 1914 World War I began. Though the wartime situation was very difficult for many people, for Picasso it was not. Most of his friends went to the army and he never saw many of them again but because he had Spanish citizenship, he was not required to serve in the military. On the contrary, he spent the summer of 1914 with Eva at Avignon, where he continued with his cubist paintings, usually with vivid colors.

In 1915 Eva became seriously ill, probably with cancer and died the following year. Picasso soon found a substitute, Olga Khokhlova, a Russian ballet dancer and a general's daughter, whom he had met while doing the costumes and set design for a ballet performance. In July 1918, Olga and Picasso were married.

The ballet not only brought Olga to Picasso; it also brought him huge profits and fame. His works were now eagerly bought up and his income was so substantial that he and Olga could move to a luxurious apartment in the fashionable Champs Élysées area. Their apartment was decorated according to the latest fashion and paintings by Renoir, Cézanne and other famous artists hung on the walls. Picasso rented another similar apartment upstairs for his studio.

He could no longer be described as a bohemian; by the age of 37, he had become bourgeois. He wore tailored suits, with a handkerchief tucked into his breast pocket, sported a gold watch with a chain attached to his buttonhole and had meticulously groomed hair. He could often be seen walking his wife's Russian wolfhounds while she spent freely on whatever pleased her.

World War I ended in 1918. The next year, Picasso accompanied the ballet to London. London was a triumph for him, the English were fascinated by his decorations for the ballet and he was invited to receptions everywhere. With his morale at a high point in 1920, Picasso depicted whatever pleased him; painting his old love and his new one, clowns, dancers, bathers by the sea and the peasants in the countryside. He employed a variety of styles, ranging from realism to cubism.

For Picasso the next five years between 1921 and 1925 were full of money, comfort and pleasure. He was deprived of nothing during those years while he was constantly invited to the receptions and dances of the Parisian nobility. He spent the summers in the most expensive French resorts, for example, at Cannes on the Riviera.

The New Bad Season from 1925 onwards

According to his biographers, beginning in 1925 Picasso became, "possessed by some great inner rage."[5] He began painting nightmarish works, depicting figures with the faces of monsters, rotten teeth, naked human bones and twisted limbs and for no apparent reason. The first of those works was done in 1925. It was *The Three Dancers*, showing figures with dislocated bodies and displaced noses, mouths, hands and breasts, a work that revealed his own fragmented mental state, a state of perpetual nightmare.

That situation continued into the next years. In 1927 he painted the *Seated Woman* depicting another disconnected, menacing figure, while in 1929 he produced the *Woman in an Armchair* having only a "suspicion" of a human head, with displaced breasts, a gaping jaw, jagged shark-teeth and a confusion of limbs that made it impossible to tell "which of these limbs are arms or legs."[6] In 1930, he painted another seated woman (seated women were the subject of most of his works in this period), called the *Seated Bather*. This painting again shows a nightmarish, distorted figure, with pincer-like jaws and sharp teeth. In short, the theme is brutal.

That violent treatment of women, Picasso's biographers say, was not unrelated to his own family life. In those years his relationship with his wife Olga had become very difficult and in 1931 their marriage began deteriorating. She was a strong woman and they argued constantly. As their marriage fell apart, the 50-year-old Picasso became involved with a German woman in her early twenties, Marie-Thérése Walter.

Despite this new relationship his works continued to emphasize violent images of women. In 1932 he painted the *Girl before a Mirror*, with Marie-Thérése as his model; this was another dislocated and inconceivable figure. The other two works he painted the same year, the *Figure in a Red Chair* and the *Yellow Belt* were even more disturbing. The subjects were again seated women, fragmented and dislocated.

In 1933, the "winter" of this season definitely entered Picasso's life; the great painter ceased painting. In 1935 he produced some portraits of Marie Thérése but he would not show them to anyone for many years. And the summer of that year was the first summer of his life, in about 30 years in which he didn't go away on vacation but stayed in Paris. "I am alone in the house," he wrote a friend, "[and] you can imagine what has happened and what is waiting for me."[7] His marriage to Olga had ended definitively that year; she had left, taking their 14-year-old son Paulo with her.

Marie-Thérése was living in an apartment elsewhere in Paris, with their daughter Maya, who was a few months old. Picasso visited them regularly and sometimes also helped with the care of the baby, by washing diapers and performing other tasks. But though he wanted to marry Marie-Thérése, he couldn't do that; his Spanish citizenship did not permit a divorce from Olga.

Picasso was at a complete loss. He was given to bouts of anger, isolated himself in his house, refused to see anybody and he became lethargic. He didn't finish any of the paintings he had been commissioned to do; instead he started writing surrealistic poems, without rules of grammar or form, which "he tried to keep… secret."[8]

That situation persisted in 1936 and 1937. In 1937 new problems emerged when Spain began to be torn apart by the civil war. Picasso was deeply afflicted and he did what he could, offering financial support to those who were loyal to the Spanish government – the Loyalists. To express his personal feelings, he painted a huge work, Guernica that movingly depicted the horrors of fascism and of war.

When that work was shown at the Paris World Exhibition in 1937, it provoked a terrible reaction. Critics called it "vulgar", "debasing "and the like. It was indeed another of Picasso's nightmarish works, again with dislocated bodies, distorted eyes, noses, ears, twisted feet, hands, menacing teeth and with faces that were a cross between those of bulls, dogs and humans.

The French patriots reacted cruelly. Instead of wasting his energy on that work, they said, Picasso would have been better off going home and serving in the army. **

Picasso didn't want to give up his surrealistic works. Another young woman, Dora Maar from Yugoslavia had replaced Marie-Thérése in his life and he began to use her as his model. In 1938 and 1939 he produced more ghoulish paintings, including one of a woman who had the head of both a person and a dog and another of a menacing cat with huge sharp teeth devouring a bird.

In September 1939 World War II broke out. Frightened, Picasso abandoned Paris and went with Dora to a small town on the Atlantic coast, Royan. He wasn't able to bring most of his art supplies with him and had to use whatever was available. He even made his own brushes. Picasso stayed in Royan until August 1940 when the Germans arrived. Unable to do anything else, he was forced to return to Paris, where the German troops were in control.

In that disturbing atmosphere, 1941 began.

The New Good Season from 1941 onwards

To Picasso's surprise, the Germans treated him with great politeness and respect. Officers frequently visited him at his home, admiring his works; including *Guernica* and sometimes offered him coal for fuel during the chilly 1941 winter. But he refused with grace and humor. In 1942 a new Picasso was born; his anger dissipated, giving way to a calm and joyful disposition that was reflected in his works.

** *Guernica was a small Spanish town bombed by Hitler's planes in 1937. The town was leveled and most of its inhabitants, men, women and children were killed. Picasso's* Guernica *is now considered one of his masterpieces.*

The first of those works was a statue (the first time that Picasso was involved with sculpture), called the *Man with a Sheep*. This was a serene, natural work like those of the great Italian Renaissance painters. Picasso started the statue in 1942 and finished it in 1943. Also in 1943, he painted another joyful and calm work, the First Steps, in which a mother with a radiant expression guides her small child as he takes his first steps.

In June 1944, the course of the war changed after the Allies landed at Normandy. A new spirit of hope spread through Paris and Picasso began to paint Paris scenes. These are beautiful and romantic scenes from the Seine bridges, showing Notre Dame, Montmartre, Sacré Coeur and other landmarks. In August 1944, sharp, vivid colors returned to the painter's palette for the first time in many years.

The same month, the Allies triumphantly entered Paris. Filled with joy the crowd ran through the streets. Picasso's old friends and acquaintants, together with soldiers and others, flocked to his studio in a celebration that lasted for days. Picasso had suddenly become a new kind of hero, a symbol of passive resistance to the enemy during the oppressive days of the occupation. In the fall of 1944 it seemed that "Picasso loved everybody and everybody loved him."[9] He was one of the most popular people in France. The only person who could be compared with him was General Charles de Gaulle, the great hero of the war.

Picasso accepted that approbation with warm words and deeds; his house was always open at any time of the day or night. Even exhausted soldiers arrived to sleep during the night; sometimes as many as 20 people were accommodated in his studio. Around that time, the big "Salon d' Automne" once again opened its doors after four years of enforced idleness. Until then no foreign painter had been invited to participate, now Picasso was the honored guest. A whole gallery was made available to him and he sent 70 of his paintings and 5 of his sculptures, all made after 1940 and unknown to the public.

But there was a "spring rain shower." On the third day of the exhibition an infuriated crowd of young men invaded the gallery screaming "Take his paintings down." They tore Picasso's pictures from the walls until the officials controlled the riot. It was a reaction against Picasso's affiliation with the Communist Party, which he quit a little later. The next day however, a group of pro-Picasso students and friends moved in to guard the gallery.

From 1945, Picasso's "storm and fury" evaporated forever. He turned to cheerful and vivid subjects and to a new art form; lithography. The same year, another woman entered his life; Françoise Gilot, 21 years old, beautiful, clever and vivacious. (Picasso was 64). He painted his new model in a deft, cheerful manner; like "a flower with… a face surrounded by leaves or petals."[10]

He continued with the same style in 1946. On the Riviera, where he again spent the summer, he painted more than 30 lighthearted works, all multicolored with delicate rosy, blue and green hues. One was Joie de Vivre, again depicting Françoise as a dancing flower. When he returned to Paris in the fall of 1946 he suddenly faced a tremendous demand for his works, all the museums wanted to acquire them.

The next year Picasso and Françoise had a child, a son named Claude and settled in a village on the Riviera where they acquired a house. Picasso got involved with a new art medium, ceramics. From then on a period of unprecedented calmness and happiness began for him. He produced some clay masterpieces, like the *Pregnant Woman* (1950) and others, with Françoise as his model.

In the summer of 1953, his relationship with Françoise ended and another woman, number six, came into his life. She was Jacqueline Roque, a beautiful and self-possessed young woman. He was 72 years old. She became his second wife and would be with him until the end. The following year Picasso painted her and created a picture of insuperable beauty and grace.

Invigorated by his new life, Picasso left the village on the Riviera in 1955 and bought a villa in Cannes, where he created some of the most beautiful portraits of Jacqueline. In 1957, he arrived at the distillation of his life's work; he painted a series of variants on his compatriot Velazquez's works titled *Las Meninas*, which remain unsurpassed.

But this good season finally ended here.

The Season from 1957 onwards

From the very beginning of this season, Picasso felt old; he was 76. His main concern at that age was, of course, his health. He wasn't feeling good; he also felt disappointed and his mental condition was bad. He soon withdrew from the world's stage. In 1961 he bought a villa on the Riviera surrounded by lush trees that screened the house from the outer world. Frustrated, he isolated himself for the rest of his life. His days of innovation and of surprising the public with his works were over. In 1973, he left this life at the age of 92.

Conclusion

Picasso's biography shows that a bad season started for him in 1892, which was followed by a good season that begun in 1908. A new bad season started in 1925, then a new good one begun in 1941. Picasso's last bad season of his life started in 1957. Combining Picasso's dates to those of Beethoven and Verdi's we've seen in the graph of the previous chapter, we arrive at a longer series of dates that extends over a 181 year period (from Beethoven's era – 1776 to 1957), as shown in the accompanying graph.

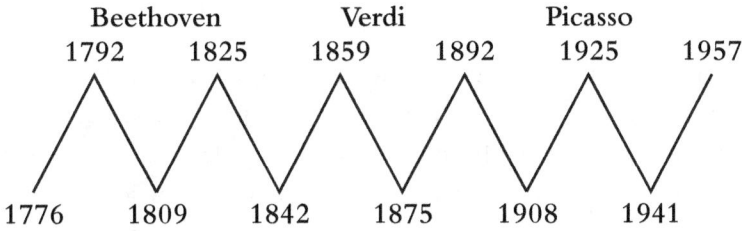

Notice that in 1892 the *last* bad season in Verdi's life started, as you may recall, while at the same year Picasso's *first* bad season began in his life. Again, between each one of these dates there is a constant 16 -17 years. We've found that the seasons in the lives of the people we have studied so far have alternated every 16 -17 years and at the dates shown in the above graph over a period of 181 years. Now surprise awaits the reader, in the next chapter.

Chapter 5

Napoléon

Based on what I had learnt I decided to study a biography of a person who lived *at the same era* as someone whose biography *I had already studied*. For this purpose, I took the biography of Napoléon I, who was almost an exact contemporary of Beethoven. Napoléon was born in 1769 while Beethoven in 1770 and Napoléon died in 1821 while Beethoven died in 1827. But then, a surprise came up. We'll start seeing its revelation by exploring first how the good and bad seasons alternated in the life of Napoléon I (also known as Napoleon the Great).*

The Season from 1776 to 1792

The available biographical facts for Napoléon's childhood are less detailed than we would like. But the limited information we have suggests that the period from 1776 to 1792 was a bad season for him. Between the ages of

---

* *All the details in this chapter derive from Mario Rivoire's* Napoléon, *published in Greek by Fytrakis Publications, The Great Men of all Seasons series, Athens, 1965. There are also Napoléon's biographies in English, a) André Castelot's* Napoléon; A Biography, *Rombaldi Publishers, 1971 or b) Frank McLynn's* Napoléon; A Biography, *Arcade Books, 2003.*

10 and 16, Napoléon was enrolled in a military academy. After graduating, he was appointed as a young officer in an artillery regiment in the provinces of France. But he hated life there and repeatedly asked for leave so he could get away.

In 1789 he abandoned the army out of disillusionment and returned to his home, the island of Corsica, where he became involved in politics. But he was entangled in a dispute with local party leaders there, who accused him of disloyalty, so he abandoned politics and returned to the army, where he hadn't any significant success, until 1792.

The Good Season from 1792 to 1809

In 1793 Napoléon participated enthusiastically in France's military invasion of the Sardinia's island of Mandalena. Though the undertaking failed, Napoléon's brilliant season had started. He left Corsica with his family, mother, brothers and sisters and returned to France. There he was promoted to captain and participated in an expedition to expel the English from Toulon. On this expedition, his exceptional abilities were acknowledged and he was promoted to major general. Later the same year (1793), the French Parliament promoted him to the rank of *brigadier-general* at the age of only 24.

The promotions continued the following year. Napoleon went over to the political party of Robespierre and was appointed commandant of the artillery and sent to the Italian front where he soon distinguished himself and won the esteem of his superiors. But a storm descended; Robespierre was expelled from power and suspicion fell on Napoléon. He was arrested and imprisoned. However his superiors needed him and ordered his release. Napoléon thus returned triumphantly to his position in the army.

Further advancement lay ahead. In 1795 Napoléon was brought back from Italy to Paris where he was commissioned to defend the French

Parliament against the rebellious mob. He carried out the task so successfully that the French government officials appointed him major-general and supreme commander of the army of Paris – aged 26.

The next year Napoléon took another important step; he married Josephine, the widow of a French general, thus cementing relations with the military regime (we will see Josephine's biography later). Napoléon's military acumen and his connections soon led him to his appointment as supreme commander of the army of Italy, turning a fantastic dream into reality.

He lost no time defeating the Austrians at Genoa and triumphantly entered Milan. There, he created a royal court for himself where he took up residence in a tower and surrounded himself with nobles and servants, living like royalty. Though he had learned that his wife Josephine, who had remained in Paris, was "unfaithful to him,"[1] that fact didn't distress him. He immediately brought Josephine to Milan and so things settled.

In 1797 the successes continued. After a victorious campaign Napoléon forced Italy to surrender. When he returned triumphantly to Paris, "crowds congregated into the streets to welcome him."[2] Napoléon had become a hero. Soon afterward, in 1798, he persuaded the government to entrust him with "the conquest of Egypt,"[3]. He crushed the Egyptian army at the Battle of the Pyramids and took over as a monarch and a "modernist" in that country, surrounded by a team of lawyers, civil employees, artists and others he had brought from France.★★

★★ *While in Egypt, Napoléon learned again that Josephine continued being unfaithful. He decided to divorce her, but when he returned to France, Josephine stayed all night weeping and begging him, so he finally forgave her.*

In 1799 Napoléon had a new success; he "abandoned his army in Egypt to the command of one of his generals,"[4] and returned to Paris. He made the trip from Egypt to Paris (without the government's permission) and despite the risk of being captured by the English ships that dominated the Mediterranean. His good season held out and he managed to cross the Mediterranean unscathed. When he arrived in France Napoléon received a hero's welcome and though he had abandoned his post in Egypt without the authorization of the government, the regime did not dare bring charges.

On the contrary, in November 1799 in a period of political turbulence, when the Directory was overthrown in France and replaced by the Consulate consisting of three consuls, Napoléon was appointed by the Senate as the third consul. From now on he and the other two consuls conducted the destiny of France. Napoléon's political career had begun. Jubilant crowds rushed into the streets to celebrate. Napoléon's first act was to abolish the Parliament – with the intervention of Paris's military forces which were under his command. This brought "the French Revolution of 1789 to an end."[5] Now a period began in Napoléon's life, which would bring him unmatched success and worldwide fame. In the first year of this period (1800), Napoléon was appointed at the age of 31, *first* consul of the French government, that is, head of state. His selection was confirmed by a referendum in which he received 99 percent of the vote. He settled in the royal palace with Josephine and his mother and became "the absolute monarch of France."[6] From that position he created real miracles in the public life of the country; he "codified all the laws and reorganized the administrative machinery, educational system and judiciary into a new system"[7], which acquired his name and was destined to last almost until to the present day.

In the same year (1800), Napoléon also became commander-in-chief of the army. He set in motion the great expedition against Austria. Leaving Paris he crossed the Alps as Hannibal had done, an undertaking that "captivated the imagination of the French people"[8] and arrived on the outskirts of

Milan. There, in two great battles, he routed the Austrians. When news of the victory reached Paris, "jubilation broke out throughout the city."[9] In 1801 the Austrians were forced to sign a humiliating peace treaty.

The same year (1801), Napoléon signed another treaty, this one with the Pope, thus bringing much needed religious harmony to France. In 1802 the summer continued. Napoléon signed another peace treaty, this time with England. The French were so appreciative that Napoléon was appointed by the Senate a consul *for life*, supplanting his previous ten-year term. The following year (1803) reflected the same climate of achievement and satisfaction.

The biggest event came in 1804 where the Senate proclaimed Napoléon Emperor of France. The decision was confirmed by a referendum with a crushing majority. At his coronation in the church of *Notre Dame* in Paris by the Pope, who "had come to Paris just for that purpose"[10], Napoléon took the crown from the Pope's hands and he put it on his own head and then on Josephine's. That was an indication of his sense of superiority.

As emperor, Napoléon began to live an exalted life. He created an imperial court with a large staff of servants for himself as well as for Josephine, while at the same time surrounding himself with a new aristocracy of princes and princesses (among them his sisters) and other dignitaries. Women who had often slighted him in the past, swooned at his feet.

Napoléon's ascent in Europe continued. In 1805, Great Britain, Austria, Russia and Sweden formed an alliance and they prepared to attack France. But Napoléon preempted them by attacking first. He resoundingly defeated the Austrians at Ulm. Marching on, he delivered a crushing defeat to the Austrian and Russian forces at Austerlitz. This was Napoléon's most brilliant victory and the primary basis for his military glory. Three weeks later the Austrians were forced to sign a demeaning peace treaty.

Napoléon was on the move. In 1806 he attacked the Prussians, destroying their army at Jena and nearly captured their king and queen. He entered Berlin where he took possession of the royal palace. From Prussia, Napoléon invaded Poland, attacking the Russians who occupied that country. There he became acquainted with a Polish countess, Maria Walewska, who later gave him his first child. Chasing the Russians from Poland, Napoléon clashed with them at two decisive battles in 1807 and then forced Czar Alexander I to enter into a peace agreement.

The two emperors met to work out the details of the peace treaty at Tilsit, Prussia. The czar was enchanted by Napoleon and Napoléon confessed later that this was the happiest moment of his life. At the top of his form, he returned triumphantly to Paris, where his arrival was celebrated with unprecedented processions and parades.

Napoléon's summer continued. In 1808 he captured the king of Spain in battle; he "replaced the deposed king with his own brother, Joseph."[11] When the Spaniards rebelled, Napoléon invaded Spain, crushed the revolt and entered Madrid triumphantly. He then revolutionized the whole social and political system of the country; he abolished by decree the notorious Inquisition, as well as the feudal system that had prevailed for centuries.

The Season from 1809 onwards

From the first days of 1809, the situation began to turn against Napoléon. During his absence in Madrid some of his generals in Paris plotted to overthrow him. Napoléon hastened back from Spain and neutralized the conspirators, but he could not punish them because Austria had declared war on France and he needed all his generals for the battles that lay ahead.

Napoléon attacked the Austrians and made headway but he did not succeed in destroying their forces. He himself "was shot in the foot."[12] He tried again to overcome them near the Danube, but failed. Though a month later Napoléon managed to defeat the Austrians but his casualties were huge, he lost his best warriors and his army was in disarray.

Meanwhile, the conditions in France had become tragic; a severe economic crisis was underway and the public was showing alarming signs of unrest. Unemployment was skyrocketing, while French products were accumulating unsold in warehouses. For a time, there were no more battles for Napoléon to fight and thus no victories either.

This situation continued in 1811. In 1812 the clouds began to thicken; in April 1812, the Russian czar sent an ultimatum to Napoléon demanding the withdrawal of the French army from Prussia. Instead of replying, Napoléon decided to attack Russia. The Russian army pulled back in order to draw the French further in. When "Napoléon entered Moscow, without any resistance from the Russians, he found the city deserted and in flames."[13]

Embarrassed, Napoléon sent a letter to the czar proposing peace but did not receive an answer. The severe Russian winter arrived and the French army could no longer hold out in Moscow – Napoléon's bad season was against him. He decided to retreat but as his soldiers trudged through the ice and snow, without provisions, "the Russians decimated them."[14] When his army crossed the frozen Berezina River, the Russian artillery smashed the ice in the river and what followed was total destruction. Most of Napoléon's forces – the famous "Grand Armée"[15] included were exterminated.

Napoléon abandoned the remnants of his troops in disgrace and disguised as a Russian peasant wrapped in fur on a sledge, headed back toward Paris, escorted by a handful of men loyal to him. After having traveled through all of Europe under such miserable conditions, he arrived at last in Paris totally humiliated.

The failures mounted. In 1813, the Prussians decided to shake off Napoléon's yoke and declared war. In the battles that followed, Napoléon initially won in Saxony, but then was defeated in Leipzig where he faced the united Prussian and Austrian forces. A united Europe now marched against Napoléon; "the Russians, Austrians and British invaded France from every side."[16] The French army – composed "mainly of young boys"[17] after the loss of the experienced troops in Russia, the famous "grenadiers" included, were unable to pass muster. Napoléon won some battles but the end was near.

The definitive defeat came next year (1814). The "allies", the British and Germans invaded France. Napoléon was defeated in the battles that followed and within two months the allies entered Paris which "Napoleon's army had already abandoned."[18] Empress Marie-Louise whom Napoléon had married in 1810 after divorcing Josephine and their son, had already gone. Napoléon's generals pressed him to quit, he asked them to continue the war, they refused and then he attempted suicide but the poison he took did not do the job. Napoléon was forced to resign unconditionally.

Immediately after that the allies arrested him and exiled him to the island of Elba. When he was en route, infuriated Frenchmen tried, many times, to lynch him, but he was protected by his guards. On Elba Napoléon was forgotten by all. He was visited only "by his mother and by the Polish countess Maria Walewska and their son."[19] Empress Marie-Louise was dancing and being entertained at receptions all over Europe. Josephine had died soon after Napoléon was exiled to Elba.

After a stay of ten months on Elba, Napoléon decided on a desperate deed that led him to his end. He escaped in February 1815 and made his way to Paris. He again settled at the royal palace, resumed leadership of the army and mobilized against the English and Germans. But because this was his bad season, he was unable to reverse things. In the historic battle of Wateloo, Napoléon was defeated and suffered total destruction.

Disgraced, he returned to Paris, where the infuriated citizenry demanded his resignation. He abdicated for a second time and tried to escape but finally was forced to surrender. He "hoped for asylum in England."[20] But the British government, having learned a lesson from his escape from Elba, banished him to the remote Atlantic island of Saint Helena, where he arrived in October 1815.

In Saint Helena Napoléon lived a miserable life. He slept in a wooden shed built to serve as a stable, while at same time he suffered from stomach ailments and could eat almost nothing. His skin was yellow and swollen, he was in severe pain and he couldn't sleep on the narrow bed provided. He woke at night and recalled, as he confessed to his guards, how far he'd fallen. He was nostalgic for his childhood in Corsica and suffered unbearably at the thought of not leaving Saint Helena. He said he would rather have died in the Russian campaign or at Waterloo.

Finally, on May 5, 1821, the greatest military leader of modern times died, as a terrible storm was battering the island of Saint Helena. He was only 52 years old.

Conclusion

Napoléon's biography shows us that his good and bad seasons alternated at the dates 1776, 1792 and 1809 every 16 -17 years. These dates are relevant in unraveling the promised surprise which also happens in the other biographies we have seen. Napoléon's *last* season didn't last the complete 16 -17 years period from 1809 to 1826, since he died before the end of that period, in 1821. This is true not only for the last seasons of people whose the lives we've seen – Beethoven and Verdi but also for the last seasons of many other people whose biographies we'll see below.

We continue the unraveling of the promised surprise by seeing in the next chapter the biography of Victor Hugo, the great French author, poet and playwright who was born 33 years after Napoléon.

Chapter 6

Victor Hugo

From the few known facts, Hugo's early years seem to have been bad years.* His father, an army officer had to move incessantly during the campaigns of Napoléon and at the same time he had taken up with another woman whom later he married. For the young Hugo, his father was thus a shadowy and somewhat unreliable. The situation worsened in 1814, when Hugo was 12 years old, his father asked his wife for a divorce, which was granted 4 years later. Hugo, together with his mother, brother and sister, went to a poorhouse where years of misery followed.

In that setting, the 17-year-old Hugo fell in love, in 1819, with a girl younger than him, Adela Fouché but his mother disapproved and broke up the relationship. After two years, in 1821, his mother, who was everything to him suddenly died of the flu. In despair, Hugo ran to Adela for consolation and a year later they were married. The young couple had no means of support so they lived with her parents. In one respect their marriage was

---

* *I have based Hugo's biography in this chapter on Cesare Giardini's* Hugo, *published in Greek by Fytrakis Publications, The Great Men of All Seasons series, Athens, 1966. There are also Hugo's biographies in English; a) Matthew Josephson's* Victor Hugo; A Biography of the Great Romantic, *Telegraph Books, 1992, or b) Graham Robb's* Victor Hugo; A Biography, *W.W. Norton & Company, 1999.*

shrouded in sadness; Hugo's brother Eugene was also in love with Adela and his jealousy ended in madness which led to his confinement to a mental asylum, where he died after a few years.

The Season of 16-17 Years from 1825 to 1842

From 1825 on, things improved for Hugo's when his first good season began. At first, he was awarded a royal grant of 3,000 francs per year, allotted to him for his novel *Han the Icelander*, published two years earlier. With this money the couple could face the future with more security and so they moved to a bigger house. Around the same time, the novel, Han the Icelander attracted the attention of a famous literary critic, who opened his house to Hugo. Thus Hugo suddenly found himself mingling with many other novelists, poets and artists.

The same year, the young writer who had just published another work, *The New Odes*, a poem, was named by the king of France, "Knight of the Legion of Honor,"[1] at the age of 23. He was also invited to be present as a distinguished guest at the coronation of King Charles X which took place with great splendor at the Cathedral of Rheims. After the ceremony Hugo described his impressions in his *Ode on the Coronation*, which was published by the royal printing house. His reward; a porcelain serving set from Sévres.

In 1827 Hugo published his first drama, *Cromwell* but it was too long to be performed. In 1829, his second drama, *Marion Delorme*, was performed and aroused great interest, though "the government soon banned it for political reasons."[2] In 1830, Hugo's drama *Hernani* was performed and its premiere created "a turning point in the history of the French theater."[3] It aroused mixed reactions; some people were in favor, while others were critical. Nevertheless, the play was a milestone for Hugo. It ran for "a hundred performances and brought him huge earnings; collecting more than 6,000 francs."[4]

In the meantime Hugo's family had increased in size; he and Adela now had four children, two sons and two daughters. However, his earnings from Hernani allowed him to purchase a mansion big enough both for his family and to entertain large numbers of writers, artists and other creative people. Things improved even more. In 1831 Hugo published his works *Ruy Blas* and *Notre Dame de Paris,* as well as his collection of poems titled *Autumn Leaves*. Notre Dame de Paris, a novel of about 700 pages with unforgettable characters like Esmeralda and Quasimodo, sold out almost immediately.

In 1833 his work *Lucretia Borgia* was performed with great success in Paris. Hugo formed a close relationship with the actress Juliette Droué that would last more than 50 years. She remained devoted to him for the rest of her life. At the age of only 30, Hugo was recognized as the greatest living author. His literary output was prodigious. In 1833 he published *Maria Tudor*, simultaneously with *Lucretia Borgia*. In 1834 he published his books *A Study for Mirabeau, Literature and Philosophy and Claude Gué*. In 1835, his A*ngelo, the Tyrant of Padua* was performed with great success and at the same time he brought out his poems *Songs of Twilight*. In 1837 his collection of poems titled *Inner Voices* was circulating.

In 1838 Hugo's drama *Ruy Blas* was performed and in 1840 he published his collection of poems *Rays and Shadows*. The following year Hugo reached the apex of his career when he was elected, at the age of 39, a member of the French Academy. At the ceremony that followed all of France's high society "gathered under the dome of the Academy."[5] When in 1842, Hugo published his book *Le Rhin*, containing his impressions from a trip on the Rhine two years earlier, the book achieved great success; Honoré de Balzac, the novelist, found it a masterpiece.

The Bad Season of 16-17 Years from 1842 to 1859

At the beginning of this season, Hugo published his play *Les Burgraves* (1843), inspired by the ancient German castles on the banks of the Rhine. This work did not have the success that *Le Rhin* had. The critics pronounced *Les Burgraves* "the beginning of Hugo's decline."[6] Cruelly, they suggested "that at the age of 41, Hugo had said all he had to say."[7] From "a literary perspective, he was considered dead."[8]

The same year Hugo suffered a second blow. Theater critic Charles Sainte Beuve published a book in which he revealed that he had been the lover of Hugo's wife Adela for about ten years. They had apparently met secretly at her home as well as in other places all those years. The humiliating news became widely known and, of course, wounded Hugo's ego and prestige.

The worst blow was to follow. His beloved oldest daughter Leopoldine got married in 1843 – at the age of 19 to the son of a wealthy ship owner. But seven months later she and her husband drowned at sea. Hugo learned the news "as he was returning home from a trip he and Juliette had taken to Spain, from a newspaper that lay on the table of a provincial café."(9) As Juliette said, "she saw a man thunderstruck, with eyes that looked but did not see."[10] The pain his soul suffered remained for many years and was imprinted on several of his works.

To forget, Hugo tried to find consolation in his work. In 1845 he began his great social and historical novel *Les Misérables*. But he soon put it aside and he didn't take it up again for ten years. The same year he became embroiled in a scandal; he was "caught in the act" [11] with the wife of a painter named Biarre. She was escorted to jail, while Hugo avoided persecution. His title as a Peer of France, which King Louis Philippe had just granted him, helped decidedly, but he was forced to leave Paris for several weeks.

Soon the situation worsened. Hugo stopped writing and got involved in politics, trying to bring about reforms. In 1848 he was elected a deputy of the right wing of the French Parliament and with a newspaper he published, he supported the bid of Louis-Napoléon (nephew of Napoléon I) to become president of the French Republic. But when Louis-Napoléon finally became president, he disappointed Hugo by dissolving the French Parliament. He also eliminated democracy and restored the monarchy, proclaiming himself Emperor of France and taking the name Napoléon III.

Hugo's enraged reaction was to be expected; he assailed Napoléon III openly in 1851, calling him "Napoleon the Small."[12] As an immediate consequence, both of Hugo's sons were confined to prison. At the end of 1851, the situation for Hugo became even more unpleasant. He joined the mobs demonstrating against Napoléon III in Paris and spoke out openly against him. As the season was against Hugo, he couldn't reverse things. Soon the rebellion turned bloody. With the aid of a forged passport, secretly escaped from Paris in 1852 and went into exile. He did not return for 19 years.

Hugo's first stop was Brussels, Belgium. With only Juliette with him, he began writing about the events he had just lived through in Paris, but soon gave up though he continued attacking Napoléon III with a libel titled *Napoléon the Small*. He and Juliette left Brussels for the British island of Jersey, in the English Channel, where the rest of his family joined them. His wife Adela had come to accept Juliette's presence and they all lived there together.

On Jersey, Hugo became acquainted with other exiled French citizens and they published a newspaper with a revolutionary slant. Because of this, Hugo was expelled from Jersey in 1855 and was forced to go to the island of Guernsey, also in the English Channel. There he completed his collection of poems titled, *The Contemplations*, published in 1856. With the money he made, he bought a house on Guernsey. This attempt to put down roots was a sign of his disillusionment with conditions in France. He felt the monarchy would last forever and that he would never return.

He furnished the house in a heavy, oppressive style with chunky armchairs, huge tables and inscriptions on the walls like "Exile is Life."[13] In that environment of disappointment, Hugo worked on various writing projects from 1856 to 1859 including the novel *Les Misérables*.

The New Good Season of 16-17 Years from 1859 to 1875

In 1859, Hugo's bad season finally ended. In August 1859, Napoleon III gave general amnesty to all French exiles. Hugo could now return to France but he couldn't tolerate the regime that still prevailed in France. Thus, he replied to Napoleon III that "he would go back to France only when democracy returned too."[14] Besides, he had now come to love Guernsey. He would go for walks on the beach, swim and work in a room he had built at the top of the house with large windows that provided a beautiful ocean view. He was thus reluctant to leave the island.

In 1861, he wrote that "though people assumed he was depressed, he was in fact very happy."[15] In the island's pleasant environment, Hugo returned to *Les Misérables*, finishing most of the book in 1861. Only the description of the Battle of Waterloo remained. To write this piece, he left Guersney and set foot for the first time in nearly ten years on Continental Europe. He went to the Waterloo battleground in Belgium to relive the details of the battle. Returning to the island, he threw himself into his work. He wrote at night; in the morning Juliette organized the manuscript pages and copied them neatly. The work was completed in about a month.

Les Misérables was published in 1862, initially in Brussels and then in Paris. Triumph followed; the bookstores in Paris were mobbed by crowds and Hugo's profits amounted to sums huge for that era. The characters in the novel, Jean Valjean, Javert, Mario and Cosette immediately became familiar to everyone and they remain unforgettable. A new Hugo emerged at the age of 60 and beyond.

Enjoying the island's tranquility, he continued the new phase of his literary work with undiminished intensity and he published his *William Shakespeare* (1864), *Songs of the Forest* (1865), *The Workers of the Sea* (1866) and *The Man Who Laughs* (1869). In 1870 his dream was realized; Napoléon III's monarchy in France collapsed, the country was again proclaimed a democratic one and Hugo returned to Paris. His arrival attracted crowds of doting admirers who welcomed him at the railway station. Deeply moved, he greeted them from a balcony.

Soon Hugo became as prosperous as he'd ever been. In September, 1871, a brilliant era began for him. His drama *Ruy Blas* was performed again and after that, "all the theaters of Paris asked to perform his works."[16] Because of the rehearsals, Hugo was obliged to attend, he had no time to write anything new. To find some peace he left Paris in August 1872 and went to his beloved Guernsey, where he wrote his new work Ninety-Three.

He returned to Paris a year later, in July 1873. An astonishingly productive period followed. In 1874 his works *Ninety-Three* and *My Sons* (dedicated to them) were published. He also wrote a three-volume work on his experiences in exile. His other publications in this period included the second volume of *The Legend of the Centuries* and *The Art of Being a Grandfather*, as well as the first and second volumes of *The Story of a Crime*. The poet Paul Valéry said that during the last period of his life, Hugo also wrote verses '*incomparable*' in conception and imagination.

But what most vividly characterized this good season of Hugo's life was his social life. His home in Paris was frequented by the best representatives of the arts and politics in Paris. The 70-year-old Hugo also had many women admirers; among them were the novelist and playwright Judith Gautier, as well as a young, later famous actress, Sarah Bernhardt. (We'll see Bernhardt's biography later).

The Season After 1875

In 1876 Hugo decided to reenter politics, for the first time since 1848. Even though he was elected a senator he faced tremendous disappointment. He tried again, through intervention in the Senate and by means of public speeches, to bring about political reform but in vain. In 1878 at the age of 76 Hugo experienced a major blow. After eating and drinking too much and engaging in heated debate he suffered a stroke. The doctors prescribed rest and Juliette took him to Guernsey.

Hugo would not write any more. Nor would he feel joy again. In 1881 a huge birthday celebration was organized under the windows of his home in Paris. Despite the cold weather, a huge crowd gathered to wish him well. But "the bouquets of flowers the people brought remained on the street, frozen; Hugo was sitting in front of his fireplace and for the first time in his life, remained silent."[17]

Two years later he lost the most precious asset he had in life. Juliette, after spending 50 years with him, died of cancer. After Juliette's death, Hugo wrote in his will; "I wish to be carried to the graveyard on the cart used for paupers' funerals. I do not wish any prayers in church, I ask for private prayer by everyone. I do believe in God."[18] Two years later, in 1885, France's most prolific writer was dead – at the age of 83.

Conclusion

It can be seen from Hugo's biography that his seasons also alternated every 16 -17 years, in 1825, 1842, 1859 and 1875. Note that these dates synchronized with Napoléon's dates. Combining the two men's sets of dates, we get a series of dates as shown in the accompanying graph;

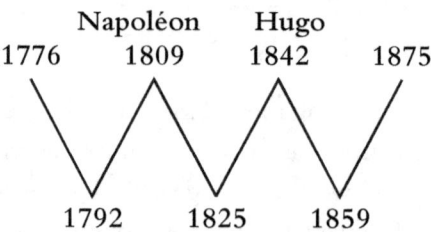

Though you may have realized, that a new row of dates, every 16 -17 years begins with Napoléon and Hugo's dates, we must, however, continue our trip and see what this new row reveals. This is not simply one more row showing the same thing. On the contrary, it consists of the *second* base of our discovery, as mentioned earlier. We have to keep on and see in the next chapter how the good and bad seasons alternated in the stormy life of Winston Churchill, the great British politician and what is revealed from his alternations of seasons. Churchill was born 11 years before Hugo's death.

 Chapter 7

Winston Churchill

As Churchill wrote in his memoirs, the years of his childhood and youth until the age of 18 were the worst of his life. They formed, he wrote, "a somber grey path upon the chart of my journey... [and they were] an unending spell of worries... a time of discomfort, restriction and purposeless monotony."[1] ★

Young Churchill went to school at the age of seven, in 1881 as a boarder. The school atmosphere was one of extreme cruelty as was typical of elite English schools at that time. His first traumatic experience was with a Latin teacher. When he asked him why it was necessary to say "Oh, table!" in Latin, since we never address tables, the teacher retorted that, "if you are impertinent, you will be punished... severely."[2]

That threat was realized many times over and with great cruelty; Churchill was often beaten. The situation was so unbearable that he began to stammer and developed health problems. His parents then sent him to another

---

★ My main source for Churchill's biography of this chapter is Sebastian Haffner's Churchill, Haus Publishing Ltd, London, 2003. Other biographies on Churchill are; a) Stuart Ball's Winston Churchill, New York University Press, 2003, or b) James C. Humes's Winston Churchill, DK Publishing, 2003.

school but the damage had already been done. The new school was equally unbearable. Churchill was not disposed to study and he failed his exams again and again. His biographers say he was essentially "on strike"[3] at school for 12 years! He also formed few friendships. When he finished school in 1892, at the age of 18, he was "profoundly ignorant," as he himself said later.

Something else made those years among the worst of Churchill's life; his relations with his father, Lord Randolph Churchill, were poor to nonexistent. The senior Churchill had high expectations for his son and condemned him for his poor performance as a student, considering him incompetent and a failure. Whenever he dared approach him, the son said in his memoirs, he made young Winston feel frozen "into stone."[4] That contempt poisoned young Winston's soul.

Churchill's relationship with his mother was not much better. In that era in England, children became completely acquainted with their parents only after reaching adulthood. Not long after birth, upper class children were given to nannies, who would raise them. Churchill's nanny meant everything to him. When she died, he was 20 years old and people said they saw him crying at her funeral. Her photograph hung on the wall of his office even when he was prime minister during World War II.

After the end of his studies, in 1892, Churchill took the entrance exams for Sandhurst, the Royal Military Academy. His father had decided he was fit only for the army. But there was more disappointment when he failed the exams.

The Season of 16 -17 Years from 1892 to 1908

The next year, Churchill retook the Sandhurst exams and passed. At first the year was something of a cool springtime for him. Since he had entered Sandhurst with a poor academic record, he was placed in the cavalry, not in the infantry where the best students were assigned. The cavalry cadets had to buy their own horses and the horses were expensive. Churchill's father didn't have enough money to buy one. His father was furious about this expense and lashed out; "If you continue on that path," he wrote him, "you will end up a zero."

The situation soon changed. The same year, Churchill's father, already in his last days, reconciled with his son, asking forgiveness and expressing his unqualified love. In his life, he said, many "things… [didn't] always go right with me."[5] That is why he asked young Winston to show understanding toward him. That unprecedented show of emotion remained in Winston's memory for the rest of his life.

In the following five years, the situation improved even more. These years, Churchill would later write, "Were the happiest time of… [my] life."[6] In 1895, at the age of 21, he graduated from Sandhurst and was named an officer. From now on, there were no obstacles in his path. From the age of 21, his biographers say, Churchill was, "like a coiled spring that was suddenly released." He himself wrote later that from 1895 on, "I was… the master of my fortunes."[7]

In 1896, while peace prevailed throughout Europe, Churchill found a way of doing what he most wanted to do which was to go to war and for that purpose he went to India. There, he was overcome by a desire to learn and began studying furiously; Plato, Darwin, Schopenhauer and many others. He also began to write. In 1897 Churchill returned to England and then left in 1898 to participate in an expedition to the Sudan. In the same period, his mother, who had previously shown little interest in him – finally entered his life. She gave him money and introduced him to London's high society where she had various connections. As a result, Churchill was now present wherever anything important was happening and more crucially, he managed with his mother's connections to be sent everywhere that a war was taking place.

In the same period (1895–1899), Churchill discovered he had another talent besides fighting. His literary prowess would soon make him famous and would net high earnings; later it would bring him the Nobel Prize for Literature. Churchill started as a reporter and went as a war correspondent to Cuba in 1895 (army officers were not yet prohibited from writing for newspapers). The articles he sent from Cuba were successful and his income was rising steadily.

In 1897 he began to write books. His first book, on military history, received favorable reviews because of the detailed descriptions of battles it contained. His next book also on military themes was equally successful. The primary benefit Churchill reaped from these publications was that they brought him to the attention of England's most powerful statesmen. Ministers and deputy ministers, even the prime minister himself sought him out.

Churchill then discovered he had a third talent – politics, a talent that would give him a brilliant future. In 1899 he left the army and became a Conservative candidate for Parliament, representing a small workers' electoral district (constituency). But his time hadn't come yet and he lost the election. Success however, was waiting for him the same year in another sphere; war. At the end of 1899, Churchill became a national hero. The opportunity came with the Boer War that broke out that year in South Africa. Though he had resigned from the army Churchill sped to the war and was one of the first to arrive on the scene as a war correspondent.

Things were not going well for the English; one defeat after another and an oppressive psychological climate had begun to prevail. Then news spread of an incident in which Churchill was the protagonist and reversed everything. In a battle that was going badly for the English the young former army officer assumed leadership of the fighting force. In the midst of general confusion and to save them from certain capture; he loaded the wounded onto a train and sent them to safety. He also tried to free the other prisoners on the train, but was taken prisoner. However, he managed to escape from a prison camp in the enemy's capital. After wandering for several days in unfamiliar territory and without understanding a word of the language he finally arrived, hidden in a train loaded with coal, in neutral Mozambique. His good season had caused a miracle.

That heroic achievement convulsed England. Churchill became a national hero and the government restored him with honors to the ranks of the army. As an officer now, Churchill returned to South Africa, where he continued his military feats. In 1900 he led an invasion of the capital Pretoria and with the help of his good season again, he freed all the English prisoners from the prison camp. All of England was now talking about Churchill.

At the end of the same year it became clear that the war would end victoriously for the English. The government, wishing to take advantage of the jubilant atmosphere, proclaimed general elections. Also taking advantage of the glory he had attained Churchill again resigned from the army and declared his candidacy for Parliament in the same electoral district he'd tried to represent previously. This time he was elected a Member of Parliament by an overwhelming margin. He was only 26. When later Churchill traveled to the United States to give some lectures, Mark Twain addressed him as the "future Prime Minister of England."[8] Indeed, from that point on, Churchill's political career took off, a career that would culminate in his taking the country's highest political office.

From 1901 to 1904 Churchill served in Parliament. But he aspired to a cabinet-level position. The Conservative Party, to which he belonged had been losing ground – after 18 years in power, Churchill anticipated that the party would lose the next election. Chances were slim that, as a Conservative, he could get a ministerial position. Thus, he did something that shocked the political world; in May 1904, he switched to the rival Liberal Party. His good season again helped him. As a famous young man who had left the Conservatives, Churchill was treated well and assured he would get a good position.

Indeed when in the next election, in 1906, the Liberal Party came to power, Churchill was appointed undersecretary of the colonies at the age of 32. Two years later, he became president of the Board of Trade (minister of state economics). In only a short time, he'd had a meteoric career. In 1908 he took another important step, this one of a personal nature. He married a woman of excellent character, beautiful, clever and polite, not rich, with whom he would live "a lifelong and exemplary union."[9]

The Bad Season of 16 -17 Years from 1908 to 1924

Soon after the happy event of his marriage in 1908 Churchill faced his first failure in politics when he lost his seat in Parliament in the elections of that year. The newspapers of the rival Conservative Party exulted; "Churchill is out [of Parliament,] Out, OUT!"[10] But the season was still "fall"; another electoral district was soon found that reelected him. The descent, however, had begun. Churchill now started to slide toward the extreme left of the Liberal Party, almost too radical a position. That tendency would eventually cause him serious problems.

The cause of that turn was David Lloyd George, the famous politician from Wales, a member of the Liberal Party and a radical. He was a "political genius, demagogue, incomparable… [speaker]."[11] Seeing Lloyd George as the future prime minister of the country, as he later became, Churchill decided to become his principal ally and supporter. That alliance, however not only horrified the Conservatives but also the Liberal Party leader, Prime Minister Herbert Asquith, who decided to break up the alliance.

For that purpose Asquith appointed Churchill First Lord of the Admiralty in 1911, at a time when war was imminent. World War I got underway three years later in 1914. In that position Churchill was forced to ask for more and more money for military purposes, in spite of other pressing financial needs in society. That fact caused a rift with Lloyd George and the two men parted company.

Though Churchill's position was unpopular, he realized that England was not prepared for war; more preparations and more resources were necessary. Neither Prime Minister Asquith nor Minister of War Horatius Kitchener, with whom Churchill had particularly tense relations, saw his point of view. Even his assistants were disdainful. The public was against him as well. He was considered an extremist and a warmonger, as well as an opportunist for having changed political parties. When he submitted a memorandum to Parliament predicting the bad consequences of the war for the English no one paid any attention.

Churchill spent the next two years (1912 and 1913) in that difficult atmosphere and in 1914 he experienced his first humiliating defeat. World War I had begun and the Battle of the Marne was underway. Churchill, as First Lord Of The Admiralty, saw that the only salvation for England was to land at Antwerp, Belgium. But no one agreed with him.

Then he did something unbelievable. He went alone to Antwerp, assumed leadership of a small body of sailors and ordered two divisions "of recruits still in training"[12] to be transferred from England to Antwerp. The season was against Churchill and what followed was a catastrophe. The operation was a complete failure and the sailors were all captured by the Germans. The anger that swept through England because of that senseless sacrifice was explosive. Churchill's prestige was wounded.

He was involved with an even greater calamity in 1915. Churchill believed that a second front behind the German troops in the Balkans should be opened so that the war could be won. Minister of War Kitchener, however, again disagreed. Then Churchill, First Lord Of The Admiralty, decided to do what he had done the previous year, to open that front himself with the navy alone, without the support of the army.

For this purpose he ordered British naval forces to land at Gallipoli, in Balkan Turkey. But again what followed was another disaster. Although Kitchener later sent troops there, the Turkish resistance could not be overcome. The campaign was lost. Prime Minister Asquith dismissed Churchill from his admiralty post on May 17, 1915. To punish him further, he appointed Churchill a member of a "Committee for Gallipoli", whereas in fact Churchill was the accused. "I am done," he said over and over; "I am finished."(13).

The situation worsened. In the same year, idle and distraught, Churchill asked to return to the army. His petition was accepted and as a lieutenant colonel he left for the front in France. But he wasn't able to reverse his bad season. His hopes for a meaningful role in the army were dashed, all he was allowed to do was to take part in procedures to rid the soldiers of lice. As a result, the other officers in the regiment treated him contemptuously. As if that was not enough, "members of Parliament and diplomats touring the front… came to inspect the miraculous beast," (14) a former minister in such a bad state and he was obliged to stand at attention before them.

Naturally Churchill could not endure that situation for long. In 1916 he left the army and returned to England. His resignation was accepted with the humiliating stipulation that he never again would be permitted to resume an officer's duties during the war. In England, Churchill returned to his Parliament seat but there, too, the situation was no better. The prime minister was now Lloyd George who, knowing Churchill's value but also weaknesses, decided in 1917 to bring him to the government but placed him under close supervision to prevent him from making false steps. He did not permit Churchill to take any serious initiative and always insisted on having the final say. For the next five years (1918–1922), Churchill was only "Lloyd George's shadow,"[15] as he himself said.

As a result, Churchill was deeply displeased with the Liberal Party. He was trying to find an opportunity to return to the Conservatives where "by tradition" he belonged. Yet he did not dare do that. Besides, Lloyd George had warned him during an intense discussion; "A rat could desert a sinking ship," he told him, "but it couldn't climb back if the ship didn't sink after all."[16] So when in 1922, Lloyd George fell, Churchill also fell with him; for the next two years was not even elected a Member of Parliament.

The New Good Season of 16-17 Years from 1924 to 1941

In the first year of this season (1924), Churchill accomplished the daring deed he had hesitated to do for so long; he went over again to the Conservative Party. While that action would have had destructive consequences for any other person, Churchill escaped unscathed. Stanley Baldwin, the new leader of the Conservative Party, not only opened the party's doors to him, and thus Churchill was reelected a member of Parliament, but he also gave him a ministerial position immediately after the election.

As the season was still "springtime," the ministry to which Churchill was appointed was Chancellor of the Exchequer, a financial position, not to his liking. For that reason, in the five years he stayed at that ministry (1925–1929), Churchill was occupied more with his other great love – literature and less with politics. During those years, he wrote his renowned five-volume work World Crisis, a history of World War I, which was recognized immediately as a wonderful achievement and brought him enormous profits.

In 1930 Churchill left his government post but retained only his parliamentary position, which he kept for the next nine years. A new life, free of worry, filled with social pleasures and envied by all, now began for him. First, with the money he had earned from his book, he bought a luxurious mansion in London where he was preoccupied with the garden, the goldfish, the exotic butterflies and with painting. The mansion resounded every evening with the sound of visitors, politicians, writers and others who listened to him with respect until late in the night.

Churchill now began smoking expensive cigars from Havana (which later became his trademark) and drinking exquisite liquors and wines. He was also preoccupied with his children, three daughters and a son as a strict but magnanimous father. "In the last few days," he once said to his son, "we have spoken together more [things]… than [I discussed with my father] in his entire lifetime."[17]

In this period, Churchill continued his involvement with his great love, literature. At first he wrote newspaper articles about international politics, articles that were published in other countries and was well paid for them. He also produced a colossal work, the four-volume biography of his ancestor, *Marlborough*. As soon as he finished that study he began writing the multivolume *History of the English-Speaking Peoples*.

Of course Churchill was still a politician. In Parliament during that season he gave some of his most famous speeches where all listened with politeness and admiration. His speeches were mainly cautionary. He saw World War II (as he named it later) approaching and believed that England was not prepared to face it. He was warning his fellow citizens to arm themselves. Initially they could not see the threat he perceived from Nazi Germany, so when war finally broke out in 1939 England was caught off guard. Churchill, the prophet, the great man, the only one that could save them was "back"[18] in favor. On September 3, 1939, Prime Minister Neville Chamberlain invited

Churchill to enter the government. Churchill resumed his old post as First Lord Of The Admiralty.

The situation became increasingly precarious. Chamberlain was forced to resign then died. The crucial moment arrived on May 10, 1940. Parliament appointed Churchill, then 66, prime minister. He had become the most powerful person in England. He ruled everything, he later wrote in his memoirs and "had the authority to give directions over the whole scene."[19]

Churchill's first objective as prime minister was the removal of all pacifists from the government. Next, he created a new Ministry of Defense, making himself a Field Marshal. After that he mobilized the country's industry and thus converted England, in 6 months into a fully armed war machine. His third concern was the forging of a firm alliance with the United States, an alliance that he established through a secret personal correspondence with President Franklin Roosevelt, without going through diplomatic channels.

By 1941 Churchill was at the zenith of his power; Hitler and Stalin were embroiled in a war in the depths of Russia, Rommel had been defeated in the Mediterranean and Africa and the British airplanes were hammering Germany. When America entered the war that year Churchill celebrated. The only thing that remained now was the great leap to victory, a leap he was planning to start from the Mediterranean.

The Season After 1941

Though some people may think that the years from the middle of 1941 to 1944 were something of a triumph for Churchill, this is not so. The truth is that while in 1941 Churchill was preparing the great leap forward, the landing of the Allied forces in a Mediterranean country. In1942 everything began to go wrong; Japan had entered the war and occupied Burma in Southeast Asia. They in the meantime threatened India, still a member of the British Commonwealth, while Rommel defeated the English in Egypt. Further, Singapore, a British colony, surrendered to the Japanese with 100,000 British soldiers, while Tobruk in Africa also fell into German hands. The British Navy was decimated; in the Pacific, the Indian Ocean, the Mediterranean, even in the Arctic.

This situation naturally had unfavorable consequences for Churchill. In July 1942 a loss-of-confidence motion against him was submitted to Parliament. Though with much effort he managed to overcome it, in September a government crisis loomed again and Churchill's position as prime minister was threatened. Another Member of Parliament, Stanford Cripps, prepared to challenge him for the position. However, the season was still fall with its "Indian summer." Churchill finally succeeded in convincing Cripps to postpone his decision to run but the Churchill of 1942 was no longer the Churchill of 1940 to early 1941.

In 1943 the situation worsened. Churchill believed that the best way to achieve victory was a landing in the Mediterranean and he thought he had convinced Roosevelt as well. But at the summit conference that took place in Tehran that year, Roosevelt and Stalin opposed Churchill. The landing would be realized in France, from England, across the Channel. This decision was a real slap in Churchill's face. One implication was that Russia would not be excluded from Europe, as Churchill hoped, but that it would join the Allies in the heart of Europe, in Germany. Also, the fact that Roosevelt and Stalin kept exchanging glances during the conference as if they were laughing at him – had not escaped Churchill's attention.

Churchill's condition began to decline. He became aged and spoke with a hoarse voice that could barely be heard. At the conference he warned of a future war with Russia for which these three leaders in Tehran would be responsible. "There might be a more bloody war," he said, "[but] I shall not be there."[20]

Returning from Tehran to England, Churchill became seriously ill from pneumonia during the trip and nearly died. When he arrived back in London at the end of 1943 he was psychologically in a shambles. This continued into 1944. Churchill began to have trouble concentrating and his speech was sometimes incoherent. Yet he suddenly decided to do something unacceptable; at the age of 70 he wanted to personally participate in the Allied invasion of France. Not surprisingly his decision caused an outcry and the king "threatened [to accompany him to the front] if Churchill insisted on going."[21]

Churchill's policy in 1944 consisted of a series of measures that didn't seem to lead anywhere. He visited the front in Italy, seeking a way to promote the landing from there, but of course in vain. Then he visited Stalin in Russia, trying to detach some countries from Communist domination, but again he was unsuccessful. In 1945 the final blow came. The war ended and on May 8, 1945, Churchill announced England's victory. This was the bitterest moment of his life as the end of this war meant according to his opinion, the start of a frightful World War III with Russia.

In the general elections that followed two months later his compatriots punished him in the worst manner; the Conservatives lost control of the government and Churchill was relegated to the opposition party, to inaction. To console himself during the next few years he wrote his Memoirs, the history of World War II, for which he later won the Nobel Prize. But in the summer of 1949, he suffered his first heart attack.

In the general elections of 1951 the Conservatives returned to power and Churchill again became prime minister. But his bad season couldn't be reversed, though his return to power could be considered as an upturn, in fact it wasn't. Churchill was now a shadow of his former self. At 77 he had trouble hearing and his memory often abandoned him, he sometimes even forgot his ministers' names. Instead of attending to the problems of the country he would read novels for hours. By the following year, disenchantment with his performance was spreading.

In June 1953, he suffered a second stroke. He became paralyzed on one side and was unable to speak. He was initially confined to a wheelchair and many times was seen crying. Later he managed to walk with the aid of a cane but couldn't stay on his feet for long.

In that disturbing condition, Churchill did something in 1954 that caused a stir in the government. Without informing anyone, he began corresponding with the leaders of the United States and Russia in order to set up a conference that would address the problem of the "Cold War" (a term he had coined). His cabinet members were appalled and requested his resignation. At first he refused but it was evident by now that he could not perform his duties properly. He was losing his mental faculties and also suffered from depression. When his closest associates again asked him to resign he finally gave in; on April 5, 1955, he submitted his resignation.

Churchill's resignation was not only a farewell to politics but also to life itself. Soon after his resignation, he became mentally deficient. He lived for another ten years in this sorry state. He was almost deaf, nor did he talk and sat for hours, silent and absentminded in front of the fireplace, looking but not seeing. In fact his life had ended a little after 1955.

Conclusion

Like other famous people, Churchill experienced a succession of seasons that alternated every 16-17 years, in 1875, 1892, 1908, 1924 and 1941. These dates extend the row of dates with Napoleon and Hugo. Combining the dates of all three individuals, we arrive at the following series shown in the accompanying graph – for a period of 181 years from 1776 to 1957.

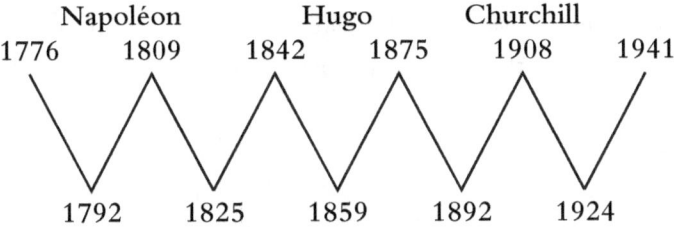

In Chapter 4 we saw a similar uninterrupted series of dates, every 16-17 years and also for a period of 181 years, from the time of Beethoven (1776) to 1957. We've found that there are two series of dates extending back 181 years – every 16-17 years, in the lives of the people whom we've seen so far; the one that starts with Beethoven and the other that starts with Napoléon I.

But there is a great difference between these two series; the dates are the same in both series, but the seasons are *reversed*. Where *good* seasons start from the dates of the one series, *bad* seasons start from the *same* dates of the other series and vice versa. I'll reproduce the graph from Chapter 4 so that you can see that reversal yourselves.

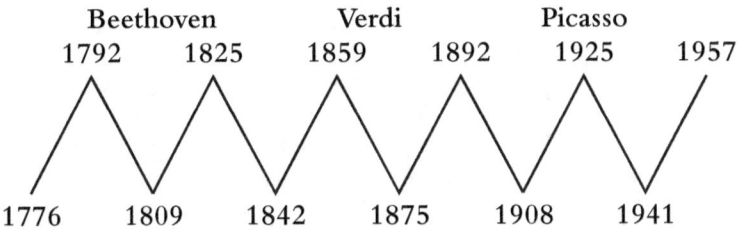

There are therefore, two opposite courses of seasons in the lives of the people whose we have explored. This observation is the second base of our discovery. That reversal of seasons is not a unique phenomenon, however, it is analogous to the climatic seasons on our earth. When there is winter in the Northern Hemisphere, there is summer in the Southern Hemisphere. And vice versa; when there is winter in Australia, South America and South Africa, there is summer in Europe, North America and Asia.

For convenience, we'll call the pattern that starts with Beethoven, the first course. We'll call the opposite pattern, which starts with Napoléon I, the second course.

Chapter 8

The Complete Picture

To extend and complete what we've seen so far we must now examine the good and bad seasons of some more people. At first we'll see their biographies *in brief;* later, we'll see them in detail in other chapters of this book. We start by seeing how the good and bad seasons alternated in the life of Mikhail Gorbachev, last president of the Soviet Union who was born 50 years after Picasso. His biography (that you'll see later in detail) shows that Gorbachev's seasonal alternations occurred in 1941, 1957, 1974 and 1990 – also every 16 -17 years. Adding Gorbachev's dates to those of Beethoven, Verdi and Picasso, we find a longer series of dates, extending to the year 1990, that is *to our time.*

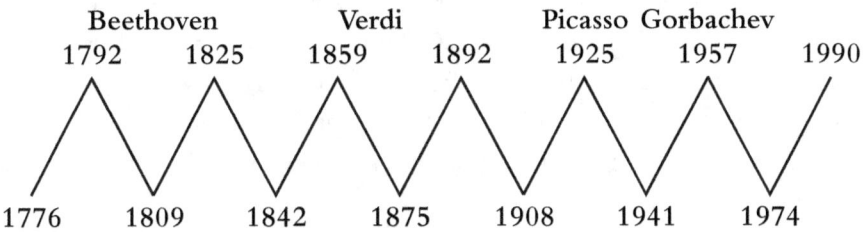

To further our discovery, we'll see now how the seasons alternated in the life of South Africa's national hero Nelson Mandela, who was born 44 years after Churchill. As with the other individuals profiled, Mandela's seasons have alternated every 16 – 17 years, in 1941, 1957, 1974 and 1990. Thus, Mandela's dates also extend the series of dates of Napoléon, Hugo and Churchill we have seen in previous chapters *to the year* 1990 that is to our time as the accompanying graph indicates.

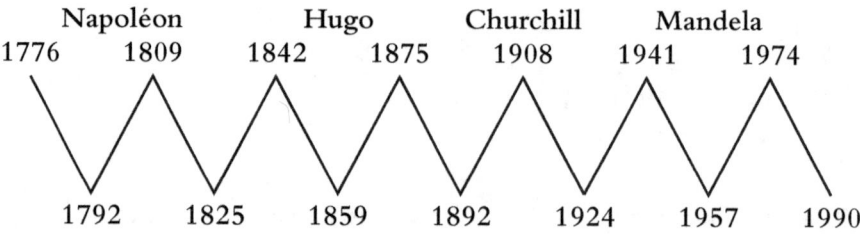

Since Napoléon, Hugo and Churchill belong to the *second* course of seasons, as we've seen, that means that the alternations of *seasons* every 16 -17 years from 1776 to our time (1990) are also valid in the second course of seasons.

To extend our discovery, we'll see now how the seasons alternated in the life of Christopher Columbus, who lived almost 500 years before our time. From his biography you'll see in detail that Columbus's good and bad seasons alternated at the dates 1479 and 1496, also every 16 -17 years (to be exact, every 16.5 years). If we extend these, Columbus's dates every 16 -17 years we will arrive at the date 1990. To perform the calculations, we add 16.5 years to 1479, the year Columbus's first good season began. That yields 1495.5. To this date, we again add 16.5 years and so on every 16.5 years. We arrive at the year 1990.

We find thus an uninterrupted row of dates every 16 -17 years from the age of Columbus (1479) to our times for more than 500 years as shown in the accompanying graph.

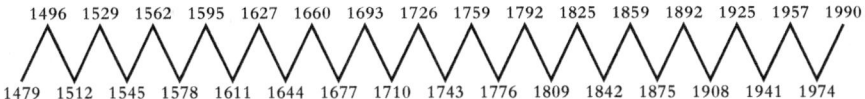

We'll again move back in time now and we will see how the seasons alternated in the life of famous King Henry VIII of England and what is further revealed from his alternations. Henry VIII's biography show the good and bad seasons in his life alternated every 16 -17 years in 1496, 1512, 1529 and 1545. If we extend Henry VIII's dates we arrive at the date 1990, the year in which the last alternation of seasons occurred in the life of Nelson Mandela.

But Mandela belongs to the *second* course of seasons, as we've seen. We find thus, that an uninterrupted row of dates every 16 -17 years for about 500 years also exists in the *second* course of seasons from the age of Henry VIII (1496) to our times, as shown in the accompanying graph;

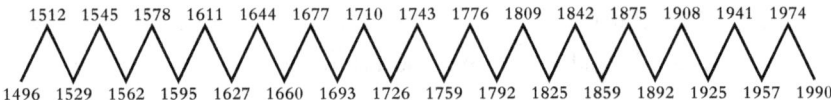

We haven't finished yet. To have a more complete picture of how the seasons of famous people alternate in life we must examine the seasons of some more people. We start by seeing how the seasons alternated in the life of ex-British Prime Minister Margaret Thatcher, a contemporary of Mikhail Gorbachev. Thatcher was born in 1925, Gorbachev in 1931.

Thatcher's biography reveals as you'll also see later that her seasons have alternated exactly as her contemporary Mikhail Gorbachev's; in 1941, 1957, 1974 and 1990 – every 16 -17 years. The conclusion is, therefore, that the described alternations of good and bad seasons are not happening only in the lives of famous men, *but also in the lives of famous women*. (Below we'll see the biographies of six more famous women; Queen Elizabeth I of England, Greek opera star Maria Callas, Hollywood actress Elizabeth Taylor, French theater actress Sarah Bernhardt, ex U.S. first Lady Jackie Kennedy Onassis and Josephine, Napoléon I's wife.

We continue by seeing what is revealed from the good and bad seasons in the life of Queen Elizabeth I of England. She was born 27 years after Columbus's death. Elizabeth I's biography reveals – as her biography cited later, shows that her life's seasons alternated in 1545, 1562, 1578 and 1595, every 16 -17 years, like all other individuals' we've seen. But if we extend her first turning point (1545) backward every 16 -17 years (to be exact, every 16.5 years), we arrive at the year 1496, the date of Columbus's final turning point, as we noted earlier. Elizabeth I's and Columbus's dates conform to the same cyclic pattern. That reveals that the uninterrupted row of dates every 16 -17 years stretches back for 500 years not only for men but also for women.

To complete our picture, we'll see now what is revealed from the seasons in the life of famous Greek ship owner Aristotle Onassis. As you'll see later in detail (in another chapter) the good and bad seasons in Onassis's life alternated on the same dates as Picasso, Churchill, Gorbachev, Mandela and Thatcher's as we've previously seen. Thus, Onassis's biography reveals that the alternating of seasons every 16 -17 years at certain dates happen not only in the lives of famous politicians, composers, writers, painters and other artists, as we've seen so far, but also in the lives of famous *businessmen*, like Onassis.

The Conclusion

The conclusion we've arrived at is based on the crucial facts that shape the good and bad seasons of the personalities profiled. All can be easily verified. For example, the facts that Napoléon I was proclaimed Emperor of France in 1804 or that he was defeated in Moscow in 1812 and in Waterloo in 1815, cannot be denied by anyone. Also, the fact that Winston Churchill was appointed prime minister of his country in 1940, or Beethoven became deaf at an early period of his life, cannot be refuted by anyone.

You will see in a chapter below why the conclusion we've arrived at cannot be mere coincidences. The shifts of seasons that happened in the year 1990, for example, in the lives of so many people profiled in the book, confirm that there is no coincidence. I cite in that chapter the examples of Margaret Thatcher, Mikhail Gorbachev, Nelson Mandela, Jimmy Carter, John Glenn, Elizabeth Taylor, Jackie Kennedy and the Dalai Lama all indicating their impressive shifts of seasons in that year, 1990.

To help convince you of the truth of my discovery I will explain how this arrived. As noted earlier, I started by examining biographies of famous men and women. For that purpose I followed this procedure, I started my research by *randomly* picking one of the biographies I had available in my home library, that of Beethoven. After finding that his life's seasons alternated the way my own life had, I picked another biography of a famous person who lived immediately after Beethoven's time – Verdi. The results were compelling. Then I picked another biography, Picasso's who lived immediately after Verdi. The results were again astonishing.

I followed this procedure in all the other biographies I studied. When the books on biographies I had in my library were exhausted, I ordered new ones from an international bookstore. The results derived from these biographies all confirmed my initial findings. I found that the alternations of good and bad seasons always occurred every 16 -17 years, at certain dates, as these were shown in this chapter.

The Seasons of Ordinary People

As I have mentioned earlier, after having arrived at the conclusions described so far, I pondered. But what about the rest of us, the ordinary people? Do their lives conform to the same cyclical 16 -17 year patterns? Of course, there is no reason to assume that the alternations of the seasons in the lives of the ordinary people are *different* from those of normal famous people.

To further confirm this, and since books on biographies of "normal" people do not exist or there are very few, I determined to research ordinary people's good and bad seasons. But the research could not include leading questions, such as drawing the subjects' attention to the specific years of 1990, 1974, 1957 and so on as their answers would be guided and the results would be unreliable.

I decided to follow another way; to discuss with friends and acquaintances' – mainly people who'd been my university classmates, how their good and bad seasons evolved. The results were again impressively confirming. My friends and relatives, all ordinary people, like me and most of you, confirmed the same alternation of the seasons that I described for famous people earlier in the book; every 16 -17 years, at the certain dates. In the next chapter, I will cite a characteristic example of such a discussion I had with a friend, regarding the alternations of his life's good and bad seasons.

My discovery is valid for all of us. It proves that your good and bad seasons will also alternate the same way as do the seasons of the famous people offered. Later I will explain how you can find your own good and bad seasons. In the meantime I will cite all the advantages deriving from this discovery.

Some readers may think that the fact a bad season will come for them that will last many years (up to 16 or 17) and they are not able to avoid their bad seasons as well, may cause unbearable disappointment; they would prefer to believe a bad season would not come at all, or at least it would last less.

This view is not correct. Ignorance, self-deceit and fear of the truth would not help you to see the real problems and solve these. On the contrary, knowing that a bad season will come at a certain time and how long this will last, is a great advantage. As noticed at the beginning of this book, this knowledge will help you to take crucial decisions regarding your career, marriage, family, relationships and all other life's issues. So, by the next Chapter, I explain in detail how you can benefit from our ability to foreseeing our lives' bad seasons, as well as the good ones and also how to successfully handle your bad seasons.

Chapter 9

The Advantages

The ability of foreseeing our life's good and bad seasons changes profoundly the way we all cope with our life today. Besides *being* a great advantage, it has also a lot of other advantages, all helping us to live a much better life. I begin with the benefits gained when we are in a *good season* of our life. If you find that you are in a good season of your life, you can benefit enormously from this knowledge.

First of all you can dare when you know you are in a good season, fate is with you. As we'll see in Christopher Columbus's biography, he succeeded in discovering the New World only because he was in a good season of his life, despite the fact that almost everybody and the Spanish royal council included, were skeptical and had rejected his idea.

Also, as we will see later in ex-British Prime Minister Margaret Thatcher's biography, though the majority of the British cabinet's members were against fighting the Falklands war, Thatcher disagreed and her good season helped her to succeed. Her risky action had ended in triumph as Argentina surrendered. Don't hesitate, therefore, to risk bold actions when you are in a good season of your life and take advantage of your good season before the opportunity passes.

Furthermore, when you are in a good season, you mustn't behave as if you assume that this season will never end. You have to take in time the necessary measures to face successfully the problems that may occur in the bad season that will follow. For example do not be a spendthrift; you have to save money for possible financial problems that will appear during the bad season. Also, you have to take care of your health, so that you can successfully face illnesses that may appear in your bad seasons. In short, you have to make provisions for the winter that will come, so that you can effectively diminish its chilliness. Take shelter for your bad season in time.

On the other hand, if you are a successful athlete or a singer or songstress, actor or actress and the likes and you see that a bad season is approaching, you had better retire before that bad season arrives. You'll lose when the bad season arrives and retiring is better than being defeated. Don't allow yourself to lose – retain your glory by retiring in time. Later, when a new good season arrives for you, you'll also realize success in another field of activity.

The Benefits of knowing Your Bad Seasons

There are many other advantages deriving from your ability to foresee your good and bad seasons. First of all, when you are in a *bad* season, you must not be seized by despair and pessimism, fearing that the bad season will never end. Instead you have to anticipate the arrival of the good season, knowing that this will surely come. Verdi, Picasso and many others often didn't even have enough money for food, as we've seen in their biographies. But later they became very rich. Also, Onassis arrived at bankruptcy at the age of 50, as we'll see in his biography, but later he became the world's wealthiest person.

If your problem affects your career in a bad season, wait to see it solved. Winston Churchill said when in one of his bad seasons; "I am done, I am finished," as we've seen in his biography. Later he became prime minister of his country. If, on the other hand, the difficulties are with your wife, husband, loved one, or children, you must be tolerant with all and don't despair, things will be cured later. The same outcome will also come in case you have divorced, for example, after a long or short period of happy marriage. When the woman Beethoven loved abandoned him he contemplated suicide, but later she came back, while lots of other women filled his life.

In addition, if you have health problems in your bad season, remember that they can be cured, or faced successfully. The doctors had said the famous French theater actress Sarah Bernhardt and the Dalai Lama of Tibet would die soon, as we'll see later, but both survived for many more years. Similarly, if your health problem is psychological, don't despair; it will pass. Picasso was given to bouts of anger during one of his bad seasons. He isolated himself in his house, refused to see anybody and didn't complete the paintings that he'd been commissioned to do. Later he became the famous Picasso.

Further, if you are a talented artist (painter, sculptor, writer and composer), but your works are rejected in your bad season, don't despair; you will be recognized at some time later. Picasso, great French sculptor Auguste Rodin (we'll see his biography later) and many others had seen their works rejected during their bad seasons, but later they were considered masterpieces. If you have difficulties with your studies in school or university in your bad season, don't worry; this will not have any influence in your future. Churchill failed his exams in school again and again and when Verdi applied to the Milan Conservatory the school rejected his application.

Despairing of a bad season will worsen your bad situation even more, or sometimes lead even to catastrophe.

Recall the case of Napoléon; if he knew in 1812 he was in a bad season of his life, it is unlikely he would have attacked Russia at that time, an action that lead to his humiliating defeat and marked the beginning of his end. For the same reason he would not have attacked the English and Germans in Waterloo, where he suffered total destruction that lead him to death.

Things may have thus taken another course for Napoleon and though his bad season couldn't have been avoided, it might have been less tragic. Perhaps he wouldn't have had the sad end he had or died at so early age. Who knows, a new good season of 16 -17 years may have started (he would be only 56 years old when that new good season would have started, in 1825). Napoléon's example shows with clarity that it is of great advantage knowing that you are in a bad season of your life.

Remember that a bad season is not necessarily a hell; there are many satisfactions within it. Verdi, for example, had a very happy event in the middle of his bad season from 1825 to 1842; this was his marriage to a wonderful woman, Margherita Barezzi in 1836. Beethoven had great successes with his concerts during the first years of his first bad season, though he began to have a hearing problem. Similarly, Onassis married in 1946 the daughter of the then greatest Greek ship owner Stavros Livanos, though he was in his bad season from 1941 to 1957. This phenomenon is also true with the seasons *in our earth*; there are sunny and warm days during winter, as there are cold and rainy days during summer.

Remember, when you are in a bad season, things might be *much worse* than they are. As we'll see later in Queen Elizabeth I of England's biography, when she was three she legally became a bastard, she was deprived of her title of princess and she didn't even have enough clothes to wear. But later, because her father King Henry VIII was preparing to invade France and his official successor, his son Edward then only seven years old, he decided, afraid of leaving the country in the hands of one child. He restored Elizabeth to the line of succession and thus she became a princess again and after some years, Queen of England. However, as queen, she also had a bad season. Parliament petitioned her to marry but she refused.

The rejection caused great difficulty in her relations with Parliament, a situation that continued for several years and worried her too much.

Things could have been *worse* for Elizabeth in this bad season; she would have been a bastard, poor insignificant, woman and not a queen.

I will cite also a similar example a friend has told me. To protect his privacy, I am not allowed to reveal his name. My friend was a high ranking officer in a large company, where he had a very successful career and was greatly esteemed by his superiors. But suddenly, the chairman of the company, one of the major shareholders was one day unbelievably rude to him, without any reason.* Soon, my friend learned that the chairman had decided to fire him because he had promised to put another person, the son of a politician, in my friend's position. The company's chief executive officer, who was to retire after one or two years objected and explained that he planned to propose my friend as his successor. After much hesitation, the chairman accepted, only to postpone his decision for a while.

Soon however, a large corporation started efforts to acquire the company by takeover and next year all was finished. The chairman and the chief executive officer were thus ousted and soon my friend followed because the new owners of the company said that he was, what an irony, "the chairman's man". A very bad season followed thus for my friend, a really tragic one, not only he hadn't become the company's next chief executive officer as this was planned, but also he couldn't find another job because he wasn't so young any more. His only means of survival was his very small pension. He lived thus, a quite miserable life.

At the same time he well knew, as he told me that things might be *much worse*; if he had been fired by the chairman of the company a year earlier, as according to law he would not be entitled to a pension.

---

* As my friend has confirmed, he had that year entered a bad season of his life, according to the theory explained in this book.

In any case, when you are in a bad season, remember that at the same moment millions of other people around the globe passing through a bad season at the same time. To prove to yourself, look around and examine the lives of people, your friends and relatives (famous or not). Remember that many people we think of being hugely happy and successful in their lives may suffer in this time. Recall for example, that when Giuseppe Verdi was in a bad season of his life, his beloved daughter Virginia died, then his second child, a son also died, while finally he lost his wife Margherita, whom he adored. Verdi's life became unbearable and grief stricken and so he fled Milan for his village Busseto, so as to find solace.

Or, recall the case of Pablo Picasso. When he was in a bad season of his life, his marriage to Olga Khokhlova ended definitively and she left, taking their 14-year-old son with her. "I am alone in the house," he wrote a friend, "and you can imagine what is waiting for me." He was at a complete loss; he was given to bouts of anger, isolated himself in his house and refused to see anybody. He didn't get any of the paintings done that he'd been commissioned to do. Instead he started writing surrealistic poems, without rules of grammar or form.

Also, recall the case of Winston Churchill. When he too, was in a bad season of his life, he caused, as first lord of the admiralty, the disaster at Gallipoli, in Balkan Turkey. The prime minister dismissed him and Churchill asked to return to the army. But all he was allowed to do there was to take part in procedures to rid the soldiers of lice. As a result the other officers treated him contemptuously and "members of Parliament and diplomats touring the front came to inspect the miraculous beast," a former minister in such a bad state, who was obliged to stand at attention before them. Finally, he left the army again and returned to England, idle and distraught.

Of course, there is also the case of Beethoven; when he was in a bad season of his life, he realized with terror, that he was almost totally deaf aged

24. He confided in a close friend; "I am extremely distressed, the most vital part of myself, my hearing has become impaired and is steadily worsening. And I do not know whether I will ever be cured. It is terrible." He composed his will, which said, among other things; "I want to end my life for so long I have never felt any real happiness, I live as if I am in exile, I feel I am a miserable creature."

Furthermore, don't forget that since there are two opposite courses of seasons, the people who belong to the other course of seasons, now are at their good season will experience a bad season later. Remember that the phenomenon of the alternations of our seasons is a *natural* one; so you must not worry for your bad destiny in a bad season, it is not your personal destiny and it is a universal one. At the same time, there is a kind of pleasure to be gained in remembering the prolonged unhappiness experienced by the wide range of famous, rich and powerful individuals we've already seen and we'll see later in this book.

Take heart, you haven't made any mistake to cause the arrival of this season and you couldn't have done anything to avoid it, the bad season would have inevitably arrived. In any case both seasons always come without any previous effort from our part. As you'll see, for example, again in Queen Elizabeth I's biography below, she became queen of England, though *third* in line to the throne. This is only because her half-brother, King Edward, died at the age of 16 and soon her half-sister, Queen Mary who had succeeded Edward, died 5 years after him, though she was only 42. Elizabeth had made no effort to achieve that outcome, on the contrary, she had remained in the shadow. Our seasons alternate without any action from our part and that means that we mustn't blame ourselves or feel guilty for the arrival of our bad seasons as we mustn't boast for our good seasons.

Finally, you mustn't stay *inactive* during your bad seasons. You have to make an effort if not to reverse but at least to ameliorate your bad situation.

These efforts may also help you achieve better results later when your good season will arrive. You mustn't become fatalists, awaiting simply the good season to come and the bad to pass. You need effort to succeed in life and without hard work you will lead a miserable life, even though some seasons may be less miserable than others. If Beethoven or Churchill, for example, had given up and accepted their bad luck as the last words in their respective lives (the former merely deaf and unable to compose and the latter as a washed up politician), they would of course have ruined their lives forever. Beethoven would never have become one of the greatest composers and Churchill never the "father of victory" in World War II.

Of course, people who are over 60 or 70 and who are in a bad season may think that there isn't enough time for a new good season to arrive. These people can find ways to ameliorate that fact. They can adjust their lives to the reality and pass their bad years as best they can, free from any unattainable expectations that only frustration would cause. They must also remember that a bad season isn't necessarily a hell and as explained earlier, things might be much worse in such a season.

Other Advantages

The understanding of how your seasons alternate can help you to take further advantage of it. For instance this ability can help you take advantage of other people's good seasons. You can for example, entrust an employee or colleague with the solution of a difficult problem, or a politician to govern your country, or even a coach of a football team if you know they are in one of their good seasons, thus operating from a position of strength. If the members of the French Parliament, for example, had known that Napoléon was to enter a bad season in 1809, they probably would not have named him the leader of their country *for life*. They might have avoided the destruction of France during Napoléon's bad season.

The ability to know how our seasons alternate in life can help to foresee the life evolution of the other people, of your friends and relatives, of famous people (artists, singers and songstresses, actors and actresses and the likes), or even of the politicians who govern you. Will for example, the prime minister of your country, or the president of a foreign power, win the next election? The answer depends, of course, on the season these people are at a given moment; if they are in a good season, they have many chances to win. But in case they are in a bad season, when the Election Day comes, they will probably lose. By the same way you can also predict how long a political leader will stay in power after his election, or for how long a famous singer, or even a football coach will continue their successful career.

Finally, the discovery we've seen in this book will radically change in the future the mentality and character of all people. People will become more philosophized, realists and peaceful, they will know that a good season doesn't last forever, as a bad season waits. It would be meaningless, being quarrelsome and aggressive. On the contrary, Man will become tolerant and merciful and have more understanding towards others. Superficiality and imprudence, even if they don't disappear completely, will drastically be reduced.

To help you take *further* advantage of our discovery, I cite now the biographies of the seven famous people previously profiled in brief in Chapter 8 – Gorbachev, Mandela, Columbus, King Henry VIII, Thatcher, Queen Elizabeth and Aristotle Onassis. In these biographies, you'll see how you can, first, avoid repeating mistakes these people made in their bad seasons and second, how you can take advantage of your good seasons in a similar way with these famous people's circumstances.

Furthermore, you'll also see how these people' lives were *radically* affected and influenced by the *alternations* of their good and bad seasons.

Chapter 10

Mikhail Gorbachev

Mikhail Gorbachev was born in Privolnoye, a small village near Stavropol, in 1931. That is 50 years after Picasso. The people in his village "lived in wretched poverty,"[1] as he says in his memoirs.* When he was six or seven years old (1937–1938), Gorbachev experienced the first real trauma of his life; his grandfather, with whom he was living was arrested and taken away by the police as an "enemy of the people." Neighbors "began shunning [their] house as if it were plague-stricken,"[2] and the boys from the neighborhood avoided him. This shock remained engraved in his memory for the rest of his life.

Three years later, in 1941, there was another shock. The Germans invaded Russia and his father left for the front. Town after town fell to the enemy and by fall the Germans were approaching Moscow.

---

* *I have based Gorbachev's biography on his* Memoirs *(New York, Doubleday, 1996).*

The Season of 16-17 Years from 1941 to 1957

At the end of 1941, the situation changed and a good season was initiated for the young Mikhail; Moscow thwarted the enemy attacks and next year, 1942, the Germans were driven back. In 1943 came the total defeat of the German troops at Stalingrad. When the war ended in 1945 Mikhail was again a happy young man. He returned to school and by 1946 he was operating a combine harvester with his father on the farm. His father treated him with respect and they became true friends.

In 1947 the Gorbachev family was "better off than the others,"[3] in their village and the next year they produced such a bumper crop that his father received the Order of Lenin and young Gorbachev the Order of the Red Banner of Labor. It was, as he says, "a lucky year."[4]

In 1950 the happy period for Gorbachev continued; he graduated from school with a silver medal and applied for admission to the Faculty of Law at the University of Moscow. To his great surprise, despite being a "worker and peasant," he was admitted as a top student. He left his village and went to Moscow, the Red Square, the Kremlin and the Bolshoi Theater.

At the Law Faculty he was exposed to a wide ranging curriculum; political history, economics, the history of philosophy, Latin and German and so on.

The university was "a temple of learning,"[5] as he says, revealing a whole new world to him. During his years at the university (1950–1955), other important things happened to him as well. In 1952 he joined the Communist Party. The same year he met Raisa Titorenko, a philosophy student and fell in love with her. The following year they were married, when he was 22 and she was 21.

After graduating from the university in 1955, Gorbachev returned to Stavropol where he joined the Communist Party's local youth organization (Komsomol) as deputy head of the propaganda department. He was soon promoted, without expecting it, to first secretary of the Komsomol's city committee for Stavropol.

The Bad Season of 16 -17 Years from 1957 to 1974

On January 6, 1957, a heavy burden was added to Gorbachev's life. His wife Raisa gave birth to their daughter Irina and soon their life became complicated. They "could not exist on one salary and Raisa had to go back to work"[6] despite having a really tough time, working and being a mother at the same time. They "lacked many things and led a frugal life… [they] were still wearing the clothes… [their] parents had bought for… [them in their] student days."[7] Conditions in Stavropol were miserable. The city lacked both a central water supply or sewage – sewage often poured into drainage ditches lining the streets.

Things were not much better in Gorbachev's career. As he says in his memoirs, the years from 1958 to 1961 were packed with bureaucratic routine. Innumerable instructions kept arriving from the Central Committee, as if without these directives "no grass would grow and no cow would calve."[8]

That situation prevailed until 1968. In 1962 Gorbachev was transferred from the Komsomol to Party work, at the agricultural department. He was spending days and often nights traveling around the district and visiting farms. In 1964 he found himself in the "eye of the storm"[9] of rivalry between two local Party organizations, while in 1966–1967 he was confronted with "scores of problems to worry about,"[10] as he says. Despite Gorbachev's efforts, he was unable to significantly improve the quality of life in Stavropol. He was so disappointed that he decided to leave the Party and turn to academic work.

He stayed however, the problems still remained unresolved and in 1969 a "period of stagnation" started, as he says, that lasted until 1974.

The Good Season of 16-17 Years from 1974 to 1990

The year 1974 marked the end of Gorbachev's bad season. That year the Great Stavropol Canal was almost completed. In 1976 Gorbachev proposed a plan to save the farms from droughts. Although his plan was met with great skepticism from his superiors, he flew to Moscow and succeeded in seeing General Secretary Brezhnev. There, Gorbachev's new good season enormously helped him and soon the big news arrived, Brezhnev telephoned him and said "Go ahead."[11] He had won. In 1977, they had "a bumper crop" [12] as a result of Gorbachev's plan, while in 1978 there was an unheard of yield. Gorbachev's fame had started to spread.

At the end of 1978 a crucial moment arrived. Without expecting it, Gorbachev was unanimously elected Secretary of the Soviet Union's "all powerful" Central Committee. He left Stavropol for Moscow. "Colleagues, ministers and acquaintances surrounded… [him] to congratulate… [him],"[13] while a limousine was placed at his disposal and bodyguards escorted him everywhere. He was 47 years old.

From then on, Gorbachev's march to power would continue uninterrupted. In 1979 he was elected a candidate member of the Politburo, a decision making government board consisting mainly of ministers and other high-ranking party officials and in 1980 he was elected a full member of the Politburo. In 1982, when General Secretary Andropov became seriously ill, Gorbachev chaired the Politburo meetings and he continued doing so during 1983 as well as 1984 when the new General Secretary Chernenko also became ill.

In 1985, the culmination of his good season came; Gorbachev was elected General Secretary of the Soviet Union. A new era thus began that would radically transform the picture of world politics. Early the next year at the Party Congress, Gorbachev called for radical economic reform in his country and in October of the same year he met President Ronald Reagan to discuss extensive arms cuts.

In 1987, Gorbachev proposed political reforms in the Soviet Union (including multi-candidate elections) and the Supreme Soviet adopted his proposal to give more independence to business enterprises. In 1988 he emphasized the need for *glasnost* (transparency) in the work of Party organizations and proposed a new presidential system and a new parliament. He also argued for *perestroika* (restructuring of the system). Simultaneously, in addressing the United Nations in New York, he called for a new world order and renounced the use of force.

The transformations continued. In 1989, the first free elections were held in the USSR and a new parliament, the Congress of People's Deputies was convened. Gorbachev was elected chairman of the Congress. In the summer of the same year Gorbachev astonished the world by declaring that Warsaw Pact nations were free to choose their own path. The Berlin Wall came down by the end of the year. For his efforts to improve East-West relations, Gorbachev was later honored with the Nobel Peace Prize.

In 1990 Gorbachev proposed that the Soviet Communist Party abandon its leading role in the USSR's political and economic life and the proposal was accepted by Congress. Thus the Party's monopolization of power for more than 70 years ended. At the same time, the Congress elected Gorbachev as the first Soviet president.

But somewhere in 1990, Gorbachev's good season came to an end.

The Bad Season from 1990 onwards

In the middle of 1990, alarming signs of the breakup of the Soviet Union suddenly appeared. In July 1990 Ukraine declared its sovereignty. In August Armenia, Turkmenistan and Tajikistan followed and in October Boris Yeltsin's Russia declared its laws sovereign over the laws of the Soviet Union. In 1991, the situation worsened; Estonia, Latvia, Belorussia, Moldavia, Georgia, Azerbaijan and other republics declared their independence. Yeltsin ordered the Communist Party of the Soviet Union to suspend its activities in the territory of the Russian Federation.

Gorbachev's bad season that had just begun didn't allow him to reverse the situation. By the end of 1991, the Soviet Union no longer existed. Under these circumstances he appeared to have only one alternative. He resigned as President of the Soviet Union on August 24, 1991 and advised the Central Committee to dissolve. In his address to the Soviet citizens on December 25, 1991, Gorbachev said; "Given the current situation… I am ceasing my activities as president of the USSR…. Events have taken a different course. A trend toward dismembering the country and the disintegration of the state has prevailed, which I cannot accept."[14]

This bad season for Gorbachev continued uninterrupted. His attempt to be elected president of Russia in 1996, failed. In 1999 he lost his beloved wife Raisa, his life's companion for more than 46 years. To survive, he delivered speeches all over the world.

Conclusion

Gorbachev's biography shows that his seasonal alternations occurred at the dates we've seen in brief in Chapter 8; in 1941, 1957, 1974 and 1990, every 16 -17 years. But his biography also shows how Gorbachev's life was radically influenced, by the alternations of his good and bad seasons.

You can benefit from his case. Recall, for example, that in 1966–1967 Gorbachev was so disappointed that he had decided to leave the Communist Party and turn to academic work. But finally he stayed and in 1985 he was elected General Secretary of the Soviet Union. Of course, if he had then left the Party, he wouldn't have become the leader of his country. Don't act forcedly in your bad seasons; wait for the good season that will come and who knows, it may lead you to unprecedented heights.

Chapter 11

Nelson Mandela

We continue seeing how the alternations of good and bad seasons influenced the lives of famous people by exploring now the life of Nelson Mandela.

Nelson Mandela was born in 1918 in a village near Umtata in the black South African territory of Transkei.* As a boy, from 1924 on after the age of a six, he lived a fulfilling life. He was loved deeply by his mother and thrived within his extended family of cousins, stepmothers and half brothers and sisters. His father, a hereditary chief, had four wives. "I had four mothers who were very supportive and regarded me as their son,"[1] he recalled. He also vividly recalled the richness of his life as a child in the country where there were hills and streams to explore and pools to swim in.

His father was a political leader and the young Mandela commanded respect in the community. His family was privileged and at the age of 9, in 1927, he was exposed to even greater privilege. That year his father died and his mother took him to the Regent of Tembu, who had been his father's friend. It was here that Mandela lived his most constructive years, 14 years in total, from 1927 to 1941 and acquired a kind of kingship which influenced

---

* *All the facts and details in this Mandela's biography derive from Anthony Sampson's* Mandela, *Alfred A. Knopf, New York, September 1999.*

all his life. There, "he saw himself as a member of the royal family,"[2] and experienced a much grander lifestyle than before.

At the age of 16, in 1934, the Regent sent Mandela to Clarkebury, the largest educational center of Tembu land, to board at the great Methodist Institution there, where distinguished British missionaries were teaching. There, Mandela's eyes were opened to the value of scientific knowledge and he entered a much wider world. In 1936, he transferred to a bigger Methodist Institution at Healdtown and in 1939 he went on to the University of Fort Hare, where he was seen by his teachers and other students as a prince ready to become the leader of his people.

Mandela bloomed at university. He not only took advantage of its academic offerings but he also learned to dance, among other things and made many friends. During his second year, 1940–1941 he was elected to the student council.

The Season of 16 -17 Years from 1941 to 1957

The majority of the students refused to vote in the elections for the council because they wanted to improve the food. Thus, Mandela resigned from the council. The president of the university warned him that he would be expelled, but he insisted and was in fact expelled. He then went home to the Regent. Who became angry and demanded that Mandela go back to the university. He refused and so the Regent brought things to a head. He tried to arrange a marriage for Mandela but he wasn't interested and decided to run away to find his fortune in Johannesburg. This meant the end of Mandela's good season.

Suddenly his expectations were dashed. "All my beautiful dreams crumbled and the prize that was so near my grasp vanished like snow in the summer sun," [3] he said later. It was April 1941 and he was 23 years old. To make matters worse, Johannesburg was not what Mandela expected. An increasing African migration to the city in the last five years had produced disorderly hut-towns near the city and had caused the Afrikaners to seek a kind of segregation, the *apartheid*.

Mandela first looked for work in the gold mines but as soon as it became known that he had left his home, he was fired. He managed to get a job at a black owned real estate agency and a law firm. "It was the most difficult time in my life,"[4] he wrote later. For the next five years he wore a decayed suit, which the lawyer had given him. He lived in a slum with no electricity or indoor plumbing. He was very poor and had to walk miles every day to go to the office.

Mandela always wanted to become a lawyer and so in early in 1943 he enrolled at the University of Witwatersrand for a law degree. He spent six years there but it was often a painful experience. He encountered a great deal of racism, for example, on the part of white students who moved away when he sat down near them. In the same year (1943) Mandela met a young black woman, Evelyn Mase and in 1944 they married, he was 26, she was 22. In 1945, Evelyn gave birth to a son and in 1946 to a daughter. This was a difficult period; Mandela was forced to help his wife by bathing the babies and preparing the meals, while at the same time he was attending at the university and working at the law office.

At the same time he became a member of the African National Congress (ANC), the blacks' political union and in 1952 he and four other members of the ANC wrote a letter to the government and asked for the annulment of some laws they considered unjust. The season was a bad one for Mandela, that letter had a negative result and soon had his first imprisonment, he stayed in jail for two nights. In July 1952 he experienced a worst treatment; he was sentenced to nine months imprisonment (which was suspended for two years), while at the end of 1952 the situation worsened; he was prohibited "for six months from attending any meeting or from talking to more than one person at a time and was forbidden to leave Johannesburg without permission."[5]

In 1953 he received another ban, again restricting him to Johannesburg for two years and after that ban expired in 1955, he received a new one for another five years. "I found myself treated like a criminal,"[6] he said later. At home Mandela also faced severe problems. His wife Evelyn disapproved of his political activity and did not want to hear anything about politics. Finally, in 1956, their marriage fell apart. Evelyn left, even taking the curtains with her.

But the final blow came at the end of 1956; in December of that year Mandela and another 155 leaders were charged with high treason. The preliminary hearings got underway in January 1957.

The New Good Season of 16 -17 Years from 1957 to 1974

At that same year 1957 a year after Evelyn's departure Mandela met, a beautiful young woman from Transkei, Winnie Madikizela, who was awed by his political acumen. A new good season started thus for Mandela. They got married a year later – he was 40, she was 24 and his image now "acquired a new dimension; not just the lawyer and the revolutionary but the lover with the adoring partner," [7] his biographer Anthony Sampson says. They were in deep love and while Mandela was on trial for treason, their affair seemed like "a wartime romance."[8]

The trial started in February 1959 and in August 1960 Mandela testified with a speech that revealed a thoughtful politician; it was the most powerful speech he had made until then. In March 1961 the court announced the victory; a verdict of not guilty. Mandela and the other accused celebrated the verdict with a spontaneous, great outburst of joy.

Soon after his release, Mandela went underground as the chief ANC leader and became more famous. Seeking help in liberating black South Africans, he traveled in 1961 and 1962 throughout South Africa and visited Tanzania, the nations of West Africa, Egypt, Tunis, Morocco, Ethiopia, Britain and other countries. When he returned home in August 1962, he did what he had already planned, he let himself be arrested for leaving the country without a passport. As his biographer Anthony Sampson says, "he seemed… to be *courting* [his} arrest."[9]

In the trial that followed, he played an almost theatrical role, the court was his theater. "The leader of a new type emerged in South Africa," a local newspaper wrote; "the leader who would neither surrender… nor flee the country."[10] During the trial he did not dispute the facts and he was sentenced to five years imprisonment. From prison, Mandela "established him [self] as the lost leader who had defied the system, [and though] hunted and underground… [he was] yet in the midst of his people," [11] Anthony Sampson says.

Though he waited to be free in five years, scores of documents incriminating him were found by the police in 1963 and a new trial opened. Mandela and the other accused now faced the death penalty. However, he was jubilant and confident, his morale was high and he had decided to accept responsibility, despite his lawyers' warnings. He was prepared to face even death if that was necessary. When in 1964, the court sentenced him and the other accused to life in prison instead of the death penalty, as had been expected, Mandela actually smiled; he had achieved what he had pursued.

Mandela "went to jail with all the glory of a lost leader, in an aura of martyrdom."[12] Many of his friends were with him. Soon, with Mandela as their leader, the prisoners began to exert pressure on their guards until they gained control over them. Conditions in the prison gradually improved and by 1967 there was even hot water for them to use. The prisoners' recreation included outdoor games such as rugby and cricket and Mandela's favorite form of relaxation was tending the small garden he had planted in the courtyard.

His wife Winnie, visited him whenever she could and he was particularly satisfied that she was, as he said, "a woman who is loyal to me, who supports and who comes to visit me, who writes to me." [13] Mandela was optimistic, insisting he was never depressed because he knew his cause would triumph. Though for almost all people, life in prison is not a good season, for Mandela it was; he believed his goals to free his people would be realized only if he remained imprisoned and for that reason he was happy, though he wasn't free.

All the prisoners believed they would serve ten years at the most from 1964 to 1974. But 1974 came and no light of release loomed ahead. Mandela's optimism faltered and this good season for him ended here.

The New Bad Season of 16-17 Years from 1974 to 1990

By 1975 the majority of the prisoners started challenging Mandela's leadership. Some of the new prisoners regarded him as a "sellout" because he had reached agreements with the guards. "The year 1975 started off badly and was disastrous from beginning to end," [14] Mandela told his wife. In 1977 Winnie was banished to a small, bare house in a desolate Afrikaner town where she would stay for the next seven years. She was forbidden to meet with more than one person at a time and she had lost almost everything else. Mandela felt guilty and in that period he was tortured by the thought what would happen to his wife and children.

By 1980, Mandela, now 62 looked frail, sometimes spoke haltingly and often seemed lost in thought. The conditions in the prison remained grim and the monastic lifestyle caused much psychological strain. Mandela worried that his children would never forgive him for his absence. In 1982 the situation worsened; Mandela was moved to a new prison, a colossal building for thousands of criminals. The government wanted to separate him from the other political prisoners so he was transferred to that castle. There were six prisoners in each cell; the cell was dreary and the amenities were worse than before.

In 1985 Mandela had prostate surgery. After the operation he was taken to an isolated section of the prison, in a damp, uncomfortable cell on the ground floor where the prisoners who were ordinary criminals shouted racist insults at him. For the first time in his years in jail Mandela felt alone and had lost all hope of being released. In 1986 he wrote to Winnie;"There is not a living soul in South Africa today… who knows when we will be released."[15]

The following year Mandela was invited by the minister of justice to help negotiate the future of South Africa's black population. This turned out to be an ordeal for Mandela. He was alone in encountering the government; he had been cut off from his colleagues. "One false move could destroy his leadership," [16] Anthony Sampson says. Between 1987 and 1990 there were twelve more torturous meetings between the government and Mandela, whilst Mandela was still in jail.

At the same time Mandela's health was not good; he coughed, was sweating and vomiting and had trouble standing up. In 1988 the doctors said he was suffering from tuberculosis. By 1987, he also faced severe problems with his wife; she had involved herself in outbreaks of violence and murder. In July 1988 Winnie's opponents set fire to her house. Mandela learned of it in jail and was mortified. In December 1988 moreover, Winnie's supporters stabbed and killed a 14-year-old boy, accusing him of being an informer. Winnie witnessed the assault. Mandela learned about it early in 1989 and was enormously worried.

In 1989 and early 1990, Mandela was faced with a diplomacy of intrigue; the government insisted on the abandonment of majority rule, which meant that the black population of the country could not in fact govern. Mandela would not accept that provision and thus he would remain in jail. By November 1989, Mandela was the only black leader still in prison. "His eyes looked so dead," [17] a friend said.

The Season from 1990 onwards

In February 1990 the big moment arrived. The government announced that the political prisoners, Mandela included, would be freed. Mandela was released on February 11, 1990. At last he had won. As he walked out the prison gate he received a hero's welcome from the thousands of well-wishers crowding around the prison. Soon Mandela started negotiations with the government to peacefully transfer the power to the blacks and a conference for that purpose was held in September 1991.

The next year Mandela "began a new happy life ;"[18] he announced he would divorce Winnie because he could not ignore her infidelity and other misdeeds. Early in 1994, he started campaigning for the general election. Projecting a superb politician's charm and skill he won the election easily. On May 10, 1994, he was inaugurated president of South Africa.

Mandela "occupied the presidency as if he had been born to it;"[19] he "seemed more like a [philosopher] king than a politician."[20] In 1995 he acquired a new love; he was enchanted by Graça Machel, the widow of the former president of Mozambique. By 1997 she became his consort. In 1998 they were married; he was 80 and she was 53. "Late in my life I am blooming like a flower," [21] he said. This feeling continued for many years.

Conclusion

From Mandela's biography we confirmed that his seasonal alternations occurred at the dates we've seen in brief in Chapter 8; 1941, 1957, 1974 and 1990 every 16 -17 years. But his biography also shows how Mandela's life was radically influenced by the alternations of his good and bad seasons. Recall, for example, that in 1985, when Mandela was in a bad season of his life, he lost all hope of being released from jail he wrote to his wife that "there is not a living soul in South Africa today who knows when we will be released." But after five years, in1990, when his good season started, he triumphantly walked out the prison gate and in 1994 he was inaugurated president of South Africa. Don't despair therefore, during your bad seasons; the good season will come with certainty in the future.

Chapter 12

Christopher Columbus

Continuing, we explore the life of Christopher Columbus and how he was affected by the runs of good and bad seasons.

Columbus was born in Genoa, Italy, in 1451.* We know almost nothing about his childhood and early youth years until 1479. We do not know whether those years were good or bad for him. We only know that at the age of 9, in 1460, he went to sea. Later, in 1473, at the age of 22, we find him as a sailor on a ship near Sardinia. In 1476, the ship on which Columbus was serving sank during a naval battle off Lagos, Nigeria. Wounded, he came close to drowning but managed to swim to the shore. After being rescued he was sent to Portugal and from there he went to sea again. In 1477 his employer sent him to the then unknown north; perhaps to Iceland or Greenland.

---

* *I have based all Columbus's biography of this chapter on Cesare Giardini's* Columbus, *published in Greek by Fytrakis Publications, Great Men of All Seasons series, Athens, 1965. There are also Columbus's biographies in English, a) Gianni Granzotto's* Christopher Columbus, The Dream and the Obsession, A Biography, *Olympic Marketing Corporation, 1985, or b) Salvador de Madariaga's* Christopher Columbus, *Greenwood Publishing, 1979.*

The Season from 1479 onwards

From 1479 we have lots of facts on Columbus's life. These facts show that a good season began for him, in fact, a triumphant season. He would discover the New World, win widespread admiration and become a symbol of courage and virtue.

From the beginning of this season, Columbus (about 28 -30 years old) began to think of becoming a sea captain. A revolutionary goal, almost inconceivable in that period, occurred to him; to try to reach India by sailing westward across the Atlantic, not by the eastern route through which was the accepted route.

Columbus became obsessed with the idea and the only thing that distracted him were the practical problems involved in its realization. To carry out the plan he needed official assistance. His first step was to apply to King Alfonso V of Portugal in 1481. However, the royal council was skeptical and rejected Columbus's proposal. The visionary was persistent, however and turned next to the Spanish court for help. Sometime between 1482 and 1484, he left Portugal for Spain. Initially he stopped at a monastery near the borders which had well educated monks; one was applying himself to astronomy. When Columbus explained his plans for India he found unexpected support.

The monks introduced Columbus to a duke in Seville who was also a ship owner. The duke was impressed by Columbus's plans and he solicited the help of others on Columbus's behalf. Seville had a large Italian population, including a banker and other wealthy individuals. With their help, the duke managed in 1485 to assemble three or four caravels for Columbus, enough for the long trip.

State assistance was also needed for such an enterprise. The duke sought the help of Spain's Queen Isabella, who expressed interest and asked that Columbus come to Cordoba to meet her. Filled with enthusiasm, he arrived in Cordoba in 1486 and was received by both Queen Isabella and King Ferdinand. To the king, Columbus's idea was not attractive, but the queen was fascinated.

However, the queen was then embroiled in the Granada war which had started three years earlier, so she could not give immediate attention to Columbus's case. The great visionary wasn't disappointed, he realized he had to wait. The same situation also happened in 1487, when the king informed Columbus that he was willing to help. Filled again with enthusiasm, he rushed to the royal court at Cordoba but there they continued to talk only about the Granada war.

In 1491, Queen Isabella again invited Columbus to the royal court. An advisory committee she had formed had given a favorable assessment of the great enterprise. So the dream began. Only the terms and conditions remained to be finalized. Columbus asked for "one-tenth of the profits of the land he would discover as well as one-tenth of the gold, precious stones and other goods he would bring back."[1] He also demanded the title "Admiral of the Ocean,"[2] as well as the position of "governor and viceroy of all the countries he would discover."[3]

The royal court at first reacted negatively to those demands but Columbus was unyielding and threatened to abandon the project. As his season was a good one, when he walked out a messenger was quickly sent to ask him to return. Finally, his terms were accepted and the agreement was signed on April 17, 1492. Everything was in place for the great adventure.

On August 3, 1492, the adventure started. Columbus set out from the Spanish port of Palos with a fleet of three caravels and an 87-man crew. After a stop in the Canary Islands he sailed toward an unknown world. While many of the sailors were terrified of what lay ahead, Columbus was jubilant. "Thanks God," he wrote in the ship's log, "the air here is sweet and fragrant and it is a *great pleasure* breathing it."[4]

On October 11, 1492, after about two months at sea, Columbus arrived at the first island he would discover in the New World. It was San Salvador (as he named it) in the Bahamas. When he found a suitable place for the ships to anchor a crowd of curious and frightened natives ran to the shore to see the ships, "sea monsters with the big white wings,"[5] which had suddenly appeared out of nowhere. When the sailors set foot on land, they "knelt down, kissed the earth and thanked God."[6]

During the next three months, Columbus explored almost all the other islands in that area, including Cuba and Haiti. At the end of December he headed back to Europe. He stopped first at the Azores on February 15, 1493 and then returned to the port of Palos, Spain, from which he had sailed. He had realized his dream.

News of Columbus's return, after a seven-month absence in uncharted waters, immediately spread throughout Spain. The delighted king and queen welcomed him with a triumphal reception in Barcelona. Huge crowds, nobility and commoners alike, greeted him. He was feted like royalty and crowned with a special crown. Six natives that Columbus had brought back with him, "live trophies"[7] of his success, were baptized Christians before the crowd.

In September 1493, Columbus, now 42, set sail on his second voyage to the New World. This time it was a much bigger undertaking; 17 ships, 1,200 men and provisions for six months. After 40 days, he reached the islands again. He stayed there for more than two years, until March 1496. He explored other islands; Puerto Rico, Jamaica and Santa Cruz. In June 1496 he returned to Spain.

The Bad Season from 1496 onwards

At the second half of 1496 Columbus's psychological state suddenly changed dramatically. Immediately after his return to Spain, he discarded his admiral's uniform and "adopted a Franciscan monk's frock which he never took off again."[8] And shortly after he returned to Spain, he was charged in a Spanish court with serious offences that he had committed. According to his accusers, that during his second voyage to the New World he'd tried to challenge the king's authority on the new lands.

Columbus was eventually acquitted but his reputation had been tarnished. The trouble had been his failure to bring back the gold he'd promised to Isabella and Ferdinand. It could have meant the end of his voyages but the queen and king agreed to support him on a third expedition. He sailed in January 1498, with eight ships. After two months he arrived at Trinidad. But he suffered from arthritis and eye problems. When he reached the island of Hispaniola (today Haiti and Dominican Republic) in August of the same year, he found that the Spanish colonists he'd left behind during his previous visit had revolted.

Columbus did his best to quell the revolt but Isabella and Ferdinand sent an independent governor to investigate the situation. Based on the depositions of some of the rebels, the governor accused Columbus of being culpable and sent him back to Spain, bound in chains. Columbus's humiliation had been completed. When he reached Spain in October 1500 he never got over the humiliation of appearing before the people, in his Franciscan monk's frock and in shackles. He expressed a desire to be buried in his chains. His reputation had sunk to such depths he felt that, "no one – no matter how worthless, hesitated to deride"[9] him.

After his arrival in Spain, Columbus was transferred to a monastery in Seville, still in chains, to await his fate. Six weeks later the chains were removed and he was brought to the royal palace of Alhambra in Granada. The king and the queen received him in a friendly manner and they promised "justice would be done."⁽¹⁰⁾ But that promise was not fulfilled.

The worst blow for Columbus came next year (1501). After his meeting with the king and queen he again withdrew to a monastery and started examining the results of his explorations. He suddenly realized the terrible mistake he had made; the islands he had explored *were not India* as he had thought, but some other part of the world. The disappointment was unbearable.

To find out what happened, he decided to make another voyage to try to find a passage to India. He again applied to the king and the queen who immediately agreed to his request, either because they believed in him, or, as his biographers suggest, "Because they wanted to get rid of him forever."⁽¹¹⁾ On May 9, 1502, Columbus set sail again. This time with four small ships on his fourth expedition to the New World.

Columbus wasn't in position to reverse his bad season; the fourth trip was ill fated. When he reached Hispaniola on June 29, 1502, a terrible hurricane struck. The governor of the island did not permit him to land. For the next three months Columbus explored the islands and the coast of Central America in the midst of terrible storms, always looking for a passage to India. His ships were badly damaged; "the sails were tattered and anchors, masts, rigging, boats and provisions had mostly been lost."⁽¹²⁾

When Columbus arrived in Panama late 1502, his bad season prevented him from seeing that the passage he was seeking was there. What separated him from the Pacific Ocean was a strip of land "only 40 miles wide."⁽¹³⁾ Disappointed, the great navigator returned to Jamaica in June 1503. But his ships couldn't hold out any longer; only 2 of the original 4 were left and he was forced to abandon them. He was now essentially shipwrecked.

Ill and exhausted, Columbus waited for help. His men mutinied and the natives repeatedly attacked them. Finally Columbus made his way to

Hispaniola; from there he sailed in September 1504 for Spain. He "would never see the lands he discovered again."[14]

Columbus arrived in Spain in November of 1504. It was a sad return; nobody was there to greet him. A few days later he lost his main support, when Queen Isabella died. Alone and seriously ill he could not even go to the queen's funeral – Columbus again retreated to a monastery. He felt old, tired and above all, embittered. On May 20, 1506, the greatest navigator of all seasons died at the age of 55, in obscurity.

Conclusion

From Columbus's biography we confirmed that his good and bad seasons alternated at the dates we've seen briefly in Chapter 8; 1479 and 1496, every 16 -17 years.

But his biography also shows how you can take strength from his case. Recall, for example, how the good season of Columbus's life helped him to succeed in discovering the New World, despite the fact that almost everybody, the Spanish royal council included, were skeptical and had rejected his idea. Columbus's example confirms, as noted earlier, you too can dare when you know you are in a good season of your life – fate is with you.

On the contrary, when you are in a bad season, you have to act carefully. Remember how Columbus's bad season destroyed him during his fourth trip. Of course he didn't know he was in a bad season. His bad season prevented him from seeing that the passage to India he was seeking was in front of him in Panama. When he returned to Spain disappointed and shipwrecked, ill and exhausted, his glory had been lost forever. Columbus's example shows that you have to be very careful when you know you are in a bad season of your life.

Chapter 13

King Henry VIII of England

Henry VIII was born in London in 1491; his father was King Henry VII and his mother was Elizabeth of York. Little is known about his early childhood. From the few facts available we know that from 1496 on – after Henry was 5, the season was good for him.* As a young boy Henry attracted much attention and was an active participant in the court festivities. In 1502 he became heir apparent and was named Duke of Cornwall. In 1503 at the age of 12 he became Prince of Wales. The same year he was betrothed to Princess Katherine of Aragon. Six years his senior, she was the widow of Henry's brother Arthur, who had died the previous year.

But Henry's greatest moment of this season came in 1509. After his father's death, Henry became King of England, at age 18. At the same time he inherited a vast fortune from his father. He married Katherine of Aragon – after a papal dispensation permitted him to marry his brother's widow.

---

* My source for all Henry VIII's biography in this chapter is Alison Weir's Henry VIII, The King and His Court, *Balantine Books, New York, November 2002.*

Of course Henry was extremely happy. In a letter to the king of Spain – Katherine's father – he wrote; "If I were still free, I would choose her for a wife before all others."[1] And Katherine loved him. "Our time is spent in continuous festival,"[2] she wrote her father. Between 1510–1512, Henry was so busy enjoying his life that he relied exclusively on his ministers, whom he had inherited from his father to govern the country. An expert dancer he preferred taking part in court festivities to taking part in politics; hunting interested him more than the problems of his government.

The Season of 16 -17 Years from 1512 to 1529

In 1512 a bad season got underway for Henry. He decided to embark on an expedition to conquer Aquitaine in France. But much to his disappointment this was an unsuccessful operation; after only four months the demoralized English army returned home having achieved nothing. The next year Henry decided to personally lead his army against France. But though he took the towns of Thérouanne and Tournai, in fact he accomplished very little. As his biographer Alison Weir points out; he conquered "two minor towns of little significance"[3] at a cost of nearly $2 million, which was equivalent to $600 million at today's rates.

In the meantime, Henry begun to be frustrated with his wife because she hadn't yet borne a son to succeed him. In 1515 the situation worsened; she gave birth to a boy, but he survived only a few days. Though they had been married for four years, Henry still did not have a male heir. In 1516 Henry's disappointment deepened; the queen bore a girl, Princess Mary, not a son. (Princess Mary later became Queen of England, as we'll see in another chapter.). From then on, Henry and Katherine grew apart.

In the spring of 1517 another source of concern was added; an "epidemic of the sweating sickness"[4] broke out in London. Fearful, Henry fled London to escape the epidemic, moving from house to house in the country where no one was allowed to come near him. That situation lasted throughout 1518. In November of that year Henry had another disappointment. The Queen had another child, but it was again a daughter and she died within a few days.

In 1520 another failure was added; Henry had always hoped for harmonious relations between England and France. So in May 1520, he left for France to meet King Francis I to negotiate a peace treaty. But the old rivalry resurfaced when Henry challenged Francis to a wrestling match. To Henry's unbearable chagrin he was thrown by Francis. As a result, Henry left and the treaty never materialized.

From now on the situation worsened even more for Henry. Between 1521 and 1525 he became more and more preoccupied with the problem of his succession. He had started to realize that Queen Katherine "would never bear him a son."[5] And "he had begun to see his lack of sons as a judgment on him for offending God,"[6] because he had married his brother's widow.

Henry's main need was to marry a woman who could give him a successor. All other matters came next. He found that woman in 1526. She was Anne Boleyn who had just returned to England after serving as a maid of honor at the French court. She was 25, he was 35. However, she would cause Henry much trouble in the following years. Henry was passionately in love with her. In a letter to her he wrote; "My heart shall be dedicated to you alone.... [I am] your loyal and most ensured servant."[7] But to Henry's great disappointment Anne refused to become involved with him until he divorced his wife. That meant he had to ask the Pope to annul his marriage, something he realized the Pope would be extremely reluctant to do.

Henry became increasingly anxious, a situation that worsened when the sweating sickness broke out in London again in 1528. Terrified, this time Henry fled to an isolated tower. Fearing that "the plague might be a sign of divine displeasure,"[8] he attended mass almost every day, took communion and confessed and visited holy sites for the improvement of his soul.

In October 1528 the final blow came. The Pope sent a cardinal to London to discuss the annulment of Henry's marriage. But his bad season was against him and soon it became clear that the Pope was not prepared to take that step. On July 23, 1529 and after several months of discussions the cardinal referred the case to Rome without reaching a decision. Henry thus couldn't marry Anne Boleyn and worried that the son he hoped she would produce as his heir would never arrive.

The Good Season of 16 -17 Years from 1529 to 1545

In 1529 Henry finally found a solution to his marriage problem. In October of that year, he accused English Cardinal Wolsey of illegal interference in the public affairs and stripped him of his post. The next year he appointed another cardinal to replace Wolsey; Thomas Cromwell. Early in 1531 Cromwell and all of the clergy recognized Henry as Supreme Head of the Church of England. Henry had now attained the power that allowed him to do whatever he wanted. In July 1531 he took the decisive step; he ordered the Queen to move to other quarters. Anne Boleyn was installed in the Queen's lodgings and from now on she was constantly at Henry's side, acting as a queen.

In 1532 Henry broke with the Pope, while at the same year, a majority of the universities declared in his favor, finding that his marriage was null and void. So in November 1532 Henry "secretly married Anne."[9] In May 1533 the English Archbishop "pronounced the King's union with [Queen] Katherine null and void, [and]… declared that Henry's marriage to Anne Boleyn was valid and lawful."[10] According to Henry's desire, Anne's coronation, which took place at the end of that month, outrivaled the splendor of "any of those of her predecessors."[11]

In September 1533 Anne gave birth to a girl, Princess Elizabeth, who would later become Queen of England as we'll see in another chapter.

Though Henry was disappointed that he still didn't have a son, he took up with other maids of honor in his court, believing that one of them could produce the male heir he longed for. One of these women was 27 years old Jane Seymour. He decided to marry her. Early in 1536 he said that, "he had been seduced by witchcraft into… [marrying Anne] and for this reason [he] considered… [the marriage] null."[12]

In May 1536 he took the final steps to get what he wanted. Anne was accused of seducing various members of the King's government – "including her own brother."[13] After a short trial she was sentenced to death and "despite… [her] protestations of innocence,"[14] she was executed on May 19, 1536, at the age of 35. During Anne's trial Henry showed "extravagant joy,"[15] dining in the company of ladies until after midnight and being accompanied by his musicians and other entertainers. One day after Anne's execution, Henry and Jane were formally betrothed and ten days later they were married.

One of Henry's other passions was acquiring property. He owned "more houses and property than any other English monarch."[16] His property included 70 residences and 85 hunting parks and forests, including the two now famous parks, Hyde Park and Regent Park. Most of his properties came via the dissolution of the monasteries that he ordered in the year Anne was executed; 1536. He "took possession of monastic lands… [that represented] one-fifth of… [England's] landed wealth."[17] At the same time, the monasteries' "vast revenues… were diverted into… [Henry's] treasury… [thus financing the] acquisition of new property"[18] for him. "Wagonloads of jewels removed from crucifixes, relics, [and] shrines,"[19] even found their way into the royal treasury.

In October 1537 the exciting news arrived for Henry. Queen Jane gave birth to the long awaited son. He was Prince Edward, later King of England, as we'll see below in Queen Elizabeth I's biography. Henry was ecstatic – though 12 days later Jane died of puerperal fever.

After Jane's death Henry was ready to marry another woman. She was Anne of Cleves, daughter of the Duke of Cleves in Düsseldorf, Germany. This time Henry wasn't motivated by the desire for a son, since he already had an heir. Instead he thought it was wise to form an alliance with the German states. After negotiations that lasted almost two years, Anne of Cleves arrived in London late in 1539 and in January 1540 Henry married her. But soon he changed mind. "She has nothing fair and has very evil smells about her,"[20] Henry complained. So Anne never achieved true carnal copulation since Henry "avoided consummating the marriage so that it could be annulled"[21] later. After six months Henry accomplished what he wanted. In July 1540, the marriage was proclaimed invalid, "on the grounds of the King's lack of consent to it."[22]

In the meantime Henry had begun having other women in his life. Governing his country had almost no interest to him. One of these women was Katherine Howard, niece of the Duke of Norfolk. She was 15 and Henry was 49. In the same month that his marriage to Anne of Cleves was proclaimed invalid Henry married Katherine Howard. He also became displeased with Katherine and the next year (1541), he sought pleasure elsewhere. In February 1542, one year and a half after her marriage, Katherine's end came. She was accused of withholding information on her past from the King, was sentenced to death and was executed at age 17. Within a week of Katherine's execution, Henry was hosting banquets for his councilors and nobles and for a number of ladies. ★★

★★ *Executions were another passion of Henry's, which he accomplished very well. He ordered executions not only to rid himself from wives who he tired of, but also for retaining his reigning power. According to one of his early biographers, Henry executed 70,000 people, his cardinal Thomas Cromwell included, though that number may be exaggerated. The fact, however, that he had executed two of his six wives (Anne Boleyn and Katherine Howard), later gave him the title of the "bluebeard", the legendary French knight with a blue beard, who had killed six of his seven wives. Their skeletons were later found by his seventh wife in a locked room of his tower.*

In February 1543 he began to show an interest in another woman, Katherine Parr, a well-educated woman about 30. Five months later she became Henry's sixth and last wife. The next year (1544), Henry experienced the culmination of this season. Imbued with a new zest for life, he led an invasion of France. Riding at the head of his army he first captured Boulogne-sur-Mer, Montreuil followed. He had at last defeated the French. On September 30, 1544, Henry returned to England in triumph.

The Season After 1545

In March 1545, Henry became seriously ill and was feverish for several days. He was depressed and said he felt much better in France. The malady had attacked his leg; racked with pain, he was confined to a chair much of the time. In the meantime, the war with France continued, but it was frustrating. In July 1545, French ships harassed the south coast of England and there Henry experienced a terrible blow, the Mary Rose, his best ship sank and more than 600 men drowned. Henry replaced his general, Norfolk, with Surrey, but in vain. In 1546, Surrey lost St. Etienne, outside Boulonge. And if that wasn't enough, Henry suddenly found that the war had left England financially crippled; his treasury was nearly bankrupt.

In 1546 Henry was ill again and his legs caused him great pain. He had two invalid chairs made for himself and could not go up or down stairs. He was in low spirits and spent his time in privacy. He was losing his grasp on affairs and struggled to maintain his control over the warring factions in his government. In December 1546, he asked his will to be read to him. His face was ashen.

On January 1, 1547, Henry was feverish again; it was obvious he was dying. Three days later, he summoned the Queen to his bedside and on January 27, he saw his confessor and received Holy Communion. The next day, the wealthiest king of England, who had married six wives and had executed thousands of people, died at the age of 55.

Conclusion

From Henry VIII's biography we confirm good and bad seasons that alternated every 16 -17 years, in 1496, 1512, 1529 and 1545. Since Henry VIII belongs to the second course of seasons, we also confirmed that an uninterrupted row of dates every 16 -17 years for about 500 years exists in the second course of seasons – from the age of Henry VIII (1496) to recent times.

But Henry VIII's biography also shows how you can derive knowledge from his case. As you may recall, when he was at the end of a bad season, he became totally disappointed because he wasn't allowed to marry Anne Boleyn. But when he entered his good season, he found a spectacular solution to his problem that permitted him not only to marry the woman he loved, but also to marry in the following years 4 more women. His example shows, if you are in a bad season, you mustn't be seized by despair and pessimism. Instead you have to anticipate spectacular solutions, the arrival of the good season that you know will come at a certain time.

Chapter 14

Margaret Thatcher

We will now see how the life of Margaret Thatcher was deeply affected by the runs of her good and bad seasons.

Margaret Roberts Thatcher was born in 1925. The few facts available regarding her early years suggest that her childhood was a bad season compared to what followed. Her family's small apartment was furnished with used furniture and lacked conveniences like hot running water. On Sundays the family went to church four times; at 10.00a.m., 11;00a.m., 2.30p.m. and 6.00p.m. Margaret began to dread Sundays so she finally got the nerve to ask her father "why they couldn't just go to church once or twice [like everyone else] instead of all day."[1] Her father was silent for a while and then gave a reply that worried her very much; "Margaret… never do things… just because other people do them."[2] ★

★ *I have taken all facts and details for Thatcher's biography in this chapter from Libby Hughes's* Madam Prime Minister; A Biography of Margaret Thatcher *(An Authors Guild Backinprint. com Edition, Lincoln, NE, 2000).*

The Season from 1941 onwards

In 1941 Thatcher decided to go to Oxford University and so she applied in 1942. She took the entrance exams for the chemistry school and some weeks later received a telegram from the university offering her a place and a scholarship. It was a major victory for her; her joy was indescribable.

In October 1943 Thatcher arrived at Oxford as a chemistry student. She was not only caught up in her studies but also became active in campus politics, joining the university's Conservative Association (OUCA) which had 1,750 members. She also found time for a couple of boyfriends and learned ballroom dancing. Chemistry didn't seem to interest her. Her spare time was increasingly devoted to politics and before long she was elected president of OUCA.

That was the start of her political career. She met the politicians who visited Oxford and was increasingly in the political spotlight. When a friend asked whether she was interested in becoming a Member of Parliament she could not conceal her desire, but she replied; "Yes, but I don't know whether it's possible."[3] In the 1945 general election, Thatcher worked on the campaign of a Conservative candidate and "succeeded in stirring the enthusiasm of the crowds."[4]

In 1946 she received a Bachelor of Science and a Master of Arts degree from Oxford but she commented to a friend; "I should have read law. That's what I need for politics."[5] First, however, she had to find a job to support herself. She was able to get a position with a plastics factory, though this was not her real interest. Her life revolved around her political activities. She joined the local Conservative group as well as the Oxford Graduate Association.

In 1948 the big opportunity arrived when the Graduate Association chose Thatcher to represent it at the annual Conservative Party conference.

There, an old friend from Oxford encouraged Thatcher to submit her name as a candidate in the next national election. She made a formal application and when she spoke before the selection committee everybody was amazed. She was selected unanimously to run for Parliament as the Conservative candidate. It was February 28, 1949.

A young man, Dennis Thatcher, had also been invited to attend the conference. He was from a moderately wealthy family with a socially respectable background. That evening Margaret began a relationship with the man who would become her husband. Within a month, Thatcher began organizing political fundraisers and campaigning against the Labor candidate. Even though Thatcher lost, the failure didn't discourage her. The same feeling also existed in October 1951 when another general election was called. Thatcher again decided to be a candidate, but she lost. As she stood before the voters, "Dennis jumped onto the platform and announced"[6] their impending marriage. They were married in December 1951.

For the time being, Thatcher "put aside her desire for a parliamentary seat and concentrated on becoming a lawyer"[7], a barrister specializing in tax law. In 1953, she took the first exam and passed, she already was pregnant. A year later, she passed the final examination. In the meantime, she had given birth to twins, Mark and Carol. Eventually she looked for a firm in which to practice law and found one where she remained from 1954 to 1961. At the same time she joined the Society of Conservative Lawyers where she triumphed, she became the first woman member of its executive committee and she stayed at that position from 1955 to 1957.

The Bad Season from 1957 onwards

Though very successful as a lawyer, Thatcher was not satisfied during the year 1957–1958. Her dream of becoming a Member of Parliament was unfulfilled. When a seat became available in 1959, she applied for it and was chosen to run. In October 1959 she was elected. It was not a happy period in her life. Her first two years in Parliament (1960–1961) involved more paperwork and other drudgery than she'd expected. Though Prime Minister Harold Macmillan appointed her secretary to the minister of pensions in 1961, she was dissatisfied as she didn't agree with Macmillan's economic policies.

The unhappy period worsened. In July 1963 Macmillan resigned and Alec Douglas-Home became prime minister. The next year, Douglas-Home called a general election. Although Thatcher was reelected with a small majority, the Conservative Party lost the election. Thatcher and her party withdrew to the opposition until 1970. The bad times continued. In the general election of 1970, the Conservatives returned to power and Thatcher was elected again. But though the new Prime Minister, Ted Heath, appointed her secretary of state for education, serious problems began to emerge for her.

Thatcher demanded that "children should not be allowed to drop out of school before the age of 16."[8] This decision angered large segments of the public. When she quipped before an audience of 5,000 women that, "if you want something said, ask a man, if you want something done, ask a woman"[9] she became unpopular even with the members of her party.

That wasn't all. Thatcher's bad season caused more mistakes. Her next step as minister of education in 1970 antagonized so many people that it nearly ended her political career; she cut the free milk from schools for children age's seven to eleven. As her biographer Libby Hughes says, "The country went into uproar, the press called her a milk snatcher and cartoonists made endless fun of her in their drawings."[10] It was such a bad time for Thatcher, her husband asked her why she didn't "chuck it all in."[11]

In February 1974 came the final blow, the Conservatives called an election but they lost; the Labor Party returned to power. Thatcher was reelected but she was now in the opposition. She gave up her lavish facilities and went back to a small office.

The Good Season from 1974 onwards

In the spring of 1974 the situation changed for Thatcher. The Conservative Party was in a deep political crisis, the members disliked Prime Minister Heath. Someone asked Thatcher whether she wanted to succeed him. She laughed and said; "I don't see it happening in my lifetime."[12] Fortunately a new good season had entered her life. When she later put her name forward as the leader of the Conservative Party, the miracle happened after the final election in February 1975. Thatcher was elected the leader of the opposition.

A new era began for her. She started traveling abroad to solidify her knowledge of foreign affairs. She went to the United States to meet President Jimmy Carter, as well as to Hong Kong, China and Japan. The Russian news agency TASS gave her a name that would stick to her; Iron Lady. "That's the greatest compliment they could ever have paid me,"[13] she said.

The decisive moment came on March 30, 1979. The British people had been angry with the Labor government all winter because of repeated workers' strikes (lorries were not delivering oil, petrol stations had no gas, "trains stopped running, unheated schools closed"[14]. Thatcher asked for a vote of no confidence against the Labor government and after a seven-hour debate in the House of Commons, the great victory arrived; the government lost. Thatcher was excited; "A night like this," she said, "comes once in a lifetime."[15]

A new election was scheduled for May 3, 1979. During the campaign, Thatcher was tireless. Though the press predicted a Labor victory, in the end

Thatcher and her party prevailed. Thatcher had become the prime minister of Great Britain. As her biographer Libby Hughes also says, Thatcher's "eyes filled with tears.... This would be a historic night to remember."[16] Outside her new residence at Ten Downing Street, "a cheering crowd and the news media were waiting for her."[17]

Thatcher's first priority was the restoration of the British economy. The following summer she made large cuts in the budget to decrease the trade deficit. In 1980 she went to the United Nations and spoke in many international summits. At the Conservative Party's annual conference in 1981, "party members gave [her]... a six-minute standing ovation."[18]

In April 1982, the historical moment arrived. Thatcher faced with courage and grace the great challenge of the Falklands war. On March 31, 1982, Argentinean ships had set out to attack the islands. They would get there in 48 hours. The British cabinet was in an uproar. The majority of the members were against fighting but Thatcher disagreed; "Gentlemen, we shall have to fight,"[19] she said. Her good season helped her to succeed; the war cabinet then agreed to send two aircraft carriers and other ships to defend the islands.

Meanwhile, the Argentinean ships landed on the main island and seized control of its population – mainly British citizens. When a British submarine sank an Argentinean cruiser, an enemy plane sank a British ship. But the British prevailed and on June 14, 1982, Argentina surrendered. Thatcher's good season had again won. When she heard the news, she said, "it was the most marvelous release I have ever had."[20] The people also rejoiced.

For her conduct of the war, Thatcher won the respect of international leaders and became the hero of her party. In January 1983 she went to the Falklands. The local people responded with an outpouring of affection. If becoming a prime minister was a great event for Thatcher, the Falklands adventure elevated her even more; to the triumph. In May 1983, Thatcher called a general election the following month. She was triumphantly elected to a second term.

In March 1987 Thatcher was invited to visit Moscow to meet with the Soviet Union's new leader, Mikhail Gorbachev. The visit reinforced "the public's faith in Thatcher's abilities as a world leader."[21] She had fulfilled almost all her campaign promises; more Britons now had their own homes, Britain was "again becoming a prosperous and powerful nation."[22] So she set a new election date, June 11, 1987, when she won an unprecedented third term. It seemed that she would "stay in power for years to come."[23] In 1989, she had in the budget a surplus of $20 billion and was planning to make "her philosophies a way of life for Britain."[24]

The Bad Season from 1990 onwards

But in November 1990 the end of Thatcher's political life came. The Conservative party's members disagreed with her tax policy and so she was forced to resign. It was the bitterest moment of her life. At first she hoped she would return. But she didn't appreciate that as she entered a bad season the situation worsened; Thatcher lost the magic influence she exercised over the British people and so she remained far removed from politics. Her grandchildren became her only joy. When they visited England, she'd take them "to the public gallery of the House of Commons… to show them where their grandmother once presided,"[25] Libby Hughes says.

Thatcher's bad season continued into the next years. She lost her beloved husband, her son was accused of serious criminal actions and she was completely removed from the political scene.

Conclusion

Thatcher's biography confirms that also her seasons have alternated as we've seen them in brief in Chapter 8; in 1941, 1957, 1974 and 1990, every 16 -17 years, exactly as her contemporary Mikhail Gorbachev's. Once again you can benefit from her examples. Recall how her decision as minister of education (when she was in a bad season of her life, a fact she didn't know of course), to cut the free-milk from schools for children ages seven to eleven, seemed to mark the end of her political career. Her example shows that as noted earlier, you have to act very carefully when you know you are in your bad seasons.

Conversely, when in a good season, don't hesitate to risk bold actions. I cite, for example; the case of the Falklands war. Though the majority of the British cabinet's members were against fighting, Thatcher disagreed and her good season helped her to succeed; Argentina surrendered. Her risky action had ended to triumph.

Chapter 15

Queen Elizabeth I of England

Queen Elizabeth was born in 1533 at Greenwich Palace, London. Her father was King Henry VIII; her mother was Anne Boleyn, Henry's second wife. Soon after her birth, Elizabeth was sent far from London to Hatfield. Her parents rarely visited her. When Elizabeth was three her mother was accused of adultery by Henry VIII and was executed, while her marriage to the king was annulled. As a result, Elizabeth legally became a bastard. She was deprived of her title of princess and Henry VIII paid no attention to her upbringing. She didn't even have enough clothes to wear and suffered from headaches and other maladies. That situation lasted until 1544 when Elizabeth was 11. But the next year a good season, began for her.*

---

* *My source for all facts and details in Elizabeth I's biography in this chapter is Susan Doran's* Queen Elizabeth I, *New York University Press, 2003.*

The Good Season of 16 -17 Years from 1545 to 1562

Elizabeth had a half-sister, Mary, whose mother was Henry VIII's first wife, Katherine of Aragon; she also had a half-brother, Edward from the King's third marriage, to Jane Seymour. In 1544 Henry VIII was preparing to invade France but his official successor was his son Edward, then only seven years old. Afraid of leaving the country in the hands of one child, the King "decided to restore his two daughters to the line of succession."[1] Elizabeth thus became a princess again, by parliamentary statute and was now third in line to succeed the king, after Edward and Mary.

This change hadn't at first any immediate effect on Elizabeth's life. The favorable impact only began appearing by the next year (1545). In 1545 and 1546 she was living in the countryside but made frequent and extensive visits to court. When her father died early in 1547, that fact didn't cause her any concern; she knew her father had executed her mother. After her father's death she inherited an annual income of $6,000, while at the same time she was invited to live with her stepmother, Queen Katherine Parr, Henry VIII's widow and sixth wife, at her residence in Chelsea.

It was there that Elizabeth had her first love interest. After Edward ascended the throne, at the age 10, the widow Katherine Parr secretly married Lord Thomas Seymour. But Seymour immediately started showing an interest in the young princess, who "blushed hearing Seymour's name and smiled if he were praised in her presence."[2] However, it was too soon for her to have serious feelings of love.

In May 1548 Queen Katherine noticed what was happening and sent Elizabeth to Cheshunt, in October 1549 Elizabeth returned to court. Queen Katherine died in August 1548. By 1550, Elizabeth had her own house in London though she was invited many times to lodge at the palace. She also became a great landowner after her father's will was settled. Her household consisted of 120 people and, "when she rode into London in March 1552 to visit her brother, she was accompanied by a retinue of some 200 horsemen."[3]

In the spring of 1553 she moved ahead in the line of succession. King Edward became seriously ill and died four months later at the age of 16. Elizabeth's half sister Mary became Queen of England, according to the terms of Henry VIII's will and Elizabeth became first in line to succeed her.

Early in 1554 a rebellion burst out. English courtiers conspired to overthrow Mary and place Elizabeth on the throne, which of course would have advanced Elizabeth's interests, though she was unaware of the plot. However, the conspirators failed and were captured. Believing that Elizabeth knew of the plot, Mary ordered her arrest and imprisonment. But the season was a good one for Elizabeth. Not having any evidence against her, Mary soon released Elizabeth and only put her under house arrest far from London. This situation had the unintended effect of making Elizabeth popular. "Throughout her journey [to her new residence], men and women flocked to see her… [offering] cake and wafers… while church bells were rung to celebrate her freedom."[4]

Elizabeth stayed far from London for only about a year. In April 1555, Mary was forced to bring her back because she feared that in case she died, Mary Stuart (Mary, Queen of Scots), would claim the throne, since she was the granddaughter of Henry VIII's sister Margaret. Elizabeth, should be ready to ascend the throne if necessary.

In London, Elizabeth returned to the life of the court. She had her own household, was free to travel and resumed her studies. Extremely well educated, she was taught by a series of tutors. Though in 1556 her household became "the center of another plot against Mary"[5] which failed. Elizabeth wasn't arrested. Mary was in poor health and again wanted Elizabeth at liberty to block Mary Stuart's claim to the throne.

2 years later Elizabeth reached the height of her good fortune, though at her half-sister's expense. Mary's health worsened and late in 1558 she died. Thus Elizabeth became the new Queen of England at the age of 25.

Her coronation took place on January 15, 1559. The child who had been proclaimed a bastard 22 years earlier and had been deprived of the title of princess was now at the top of her country's hierarchy.

The following 3 years (1559–1561) were very satisfying for Elizabeth. In 1559 she negotiated a peace treaty with France regarding the occupation of Calais, a treaty that, under the circumstances, was the best possible solution. The following year she negotiated another treaty with France by which it was agreed that the claimant to the English throne, Mary Stuart of Scotland (who was married to King Francis II of France), "would neither bear the title nor quarter the arms of England."[6]

In 1562, however, this good season for Elizabeth would end.

The Bad Season of 16 -17 Years from 1562 to 1578

In October 1562 Elizabeth fell seriously ill with smallpox. She feared she would die and lacking a successor, appointed John Dudley, Duke of Northumberland, as "Protector of England" – though nobody knew what this title meant.** Luckily however, she recovered, but the illness would soon bring her lots of worries. In the same month (October 1562), Elizabeth learned a bitter lesson. She ordered that a campaign be mounted against France but the project wasn't well conceived and the result failure. In July 1563, "the remnants of the English army surrendered and returned home.... Calais was irretrievably lost"[7] for England.

The same year (1563), the situation worsened. Because of Elizabeth's recent illness, Parliament "petitioned the queen to marry or, if not… to lay down the succession in a parliamentary statute."[8] But Elizabeth only wanted

---

** *During the previous two years, Elizabeth contemplated marrying John Dudley, but in the summer of 1561 she changed her mind.*

to marry a man she could trust. The fact that her father had ordered the execution of her mother may have made her weary toward any potential husband. Also, she didn't want to name a successor fearing that she might be assassinated by that person. So, she rejected Parliament's petition.

The rejection caused great difficulty in her relations with Parliament, a situation that continued for several years. In 1566 Parliament submitted the petition again but Elizabeth rejected all marriage proposals, including one from the Archduke Charles of Austria, the son of the Holy Roman Emperor.

As if the pressure to marry wasn't enough cause for concern, a new threatening element emerged. Queen Mary Stuart of Scotland was forced by the Scottish lords to abdicate and in 1567 she fled to northern England. Elizabeth originally offered refuge but since Mary was "the strongest contender"[9] for the English throne, Elizabeth decided to hold her prisoner. Their rivalry was not only political. As a Catholic, Mary posed a major religious threat to Protestant England under Elizabeth.

In 1569, that threat was realized. A rebellion against Elizabeth was discovered – the "Northern Rebellion"[10] led by the Catholic earls of Northumberland and Westmorland who wanted to put Mary on the throne. The rebellion was suppressed but in January 1570 a new rising occurred. Though this also failed, Elizabeth was badly shaken. It was the first time in her reign that she seriously feared for her throne.

In 1571 another plot was uncovered. The plan was for "Elizabeth to be assassinated and for a small Spanish army to invade England."[11] As a result of this plan the relations between England and Spain deteriorated. In the next few years (1572–1576), England was in a state of siege by a combined Franco-Spanish offensive. It is not surprising, therefore, that in 1577 Elizabeth was troubled with a leg ulcer and suffered from terrible toothaches.

But this bad season ended in the middle of 1578.

The New Good Season of 16-17 Years from 1578 to 1595

In the summer of 1578 Elizabeth finally decided to get married. She was 45. Her choice was Francis, Duke of Anjou, brother of France's King Henry III. Francis was more than 20 years her junior and Elizabeth believed she could trust him. In August 1579 Anjou arrived in London to court the Queen. Though Elizabeth's council of ministers was divided over the marriage because Anjou was French; seven members of the council were opposed, while five were in favor Elizabeth announced in 1581 that she would marry Anjou.

A strong protestation immediately broke out and she retreated. After all, she wasn't enthusiastic about getting married, viewing marriage as a duty. After renouncing her intended marriage, Elizabeth became extremely popular among her subjects. For the next few years (1582–1585), she walked carelessly in public, travelled in open carriages and barges and when underway ate and drank without fear of being poisoned. In 1586, an opportunity arose for Elizabeth to get rid of the threat posed by Mary Stuart, forever. From Mary's secret correspondence a plot to assassinate Elizabeth was uncovered. Elizabeth was outraged. She ordered a trial and the court sentenced Mary to death. On February 8, 1587, Mary was executed.

The next year, the greatest moment in Elizabeth's reign arrived. Spain's King Philip II decided to invade England. In July 1588, a Spanish "Armada of 125 vessels"[12] was in the Channel, off Calais, where it anchored. But there, "English fire ships loaded with explosives were released and drifted"[13] by the currents towards the Spanish fleet. Panic ensued. The Spanish Armada dispersed and "driven by strong winds northwards… [were] forced to return to Spain by circumnavigating the British Isles."[14] On the journey home, about 40 vessels were shipwrecked and about 15,000 Spanish seamen were drowned.

The defeat of the Spanish Armada brilliantly enhanced Elizabeth's reputation. As her biographer Susan Doran says, "sermons, ballads, pamphlets and commemorative medals celebrated the victory,"[15] all demonstrating Elizabeth's courage and success as a leader in war. That triumph dominated her life for the next five or six years (1589–1595). Her happiness was palpable and could be seen in the stylish clothes and fabulous jewelry that she began to favor.

The Bad Season After 1595

In 1595 a rebellion erupted in Ireland against England but Elizabeth's coffers did not contain enough money to handle this new situation. England was in a bad economic recession. On the other hand, Elizabeth's "generals and naval commanders frequently disobeyed her or deliberately misconstrued her instructions."[16] As a result, she was under stress, made more difficult by the fact that she was no longer young (she was 62). She increasingly withdrew to her chamber and "accusations of [her] indecisiveness"[17] began to be heard.

Among her accusers was the second earl of Essex, who showed great disrespect for her. "In the midst of an argument in council [in July 1598]… Essex quarreled with Elizabeth and turned his back on her…. She… gave him a cuff on the ear… Essex laid his hand upon his sword and had to be restrained by another councilor."[18]

Finally, Elizabeth agreed in 1598 to quell the rebellion in Ireland and she sent an army of 17,000 men under the command of Essex but her decision would soon cost her a lot. Essex didn't achieve anything; on the contrary, he negotiated a truce and returned to London in September 1599, despite Elizabeth's instructions to the contrary. Outraged, she put Essex on trial in 1600. He was found guilty and was "suspended from all his offices."[19] In a state of despair, he decided to plan a coup and in February 1601 "he marched with about 200 armed men through the streets of London."[20]

Though Essex failed and Elizabeth ordered his execution, she sunk, after his death into a state of melancholy. She knew that the rebels who had followed Essex were, as her biographer Susan Doran notes, "Representative of a wider group of soldiers, gentlemen and aristocrats who were disaffected and disillusioned with Elizabeth's rule."[21]

The final blow on Elizabeth came in March 1603. At first she suffered from insomnia, and then she had problems with her throat. Soon after she had a stroke and couldn't speak. On March 24, England's warrior queen died at the age of 70.

Conclusion

Elizabeth I's biography confirms that also her life's seasons alternated the way we've seen in brief in Chapter 8, in 1545, 1562, 1578 and 1595, every 16 -17 years, showing thus Elizabeth I's and Columbus's dates conform to the same cyclic pattern. That also confirms that the uninterrupted row of dates every 16 -17 years stretches back for 500 years not only for men, like Columbus but also for women.

But Elizabeth I's biography also shows how her life was radically affected by the alternations of her good and bad seasons. When she was in a good season of her life, she became queen, though she hadn't made any effort to achieve that outcome. Elizabeth I's example shows that you have to be patient in your bad seasons; luck will decide how far you will go in a good season of your life and how low in a bad one.

Chapter 16

Aristotle Onassis

The few facts available suggest Onassis's childhood was difficult. Born in 1906 in the Greek town of Smyrna (later occupied by Turkey), he lost his mother when he was still a baby. His father remarried a year and a half later. His relationship with his stepmother was extremely bad where they were in a state of continuous warfare, "he regarded… [her] as a usurper,"[1] and refused to obey her. At one point, the situation with his stepmother became so bad that the young boy was sent to a friendly neighbor's house to stay for a while. In addition, his relationship with his father was not much better. A wealthy wholesale merchant in Smyrna, he was a strict father who was feared by his son.*

As a result of these problems, Onassis was mostly brought up by his grandmother. He also did poorly in school, which he entered at the age of seven in 1913. He did not like studying and constantly skipped class. He was disruptive and annoyed his classmates. As a result he was expelled from all the schools he attended. His desperate father then wrote to one

---

   * *All the facts and details in Onassis's biography in this chapter derive from N. Fraser, P. Jacobson, M. Ottaway, L. Chester's* Aristotle Onassis, *Lippincott Co., New York, 1977.*

of Aristo's teachers that he was contemplating "suicide because of... [that boy]."[2] Under those circumstances it was not surprising that Onassis never finished his studies. When he took the final exams required for a high school diploma in 1922 he failed and he never tried again.

The same year, the situation became even more difficult for him; the Turks invaded Onassis's town of Smyrna after defeating the Greek Army. Young Onassis then 16 was caught up, as he would often recall later, in the disaster that followed. The Turkish Army swept the town from one side to the other for many days, killing, looting and burning. Men and women were taken forcibly out of their homes and "killed in the streets."[3] Churches filled with refugees were covered with oil and set on fire, while people trying to come out "were bayoneted on the church steps."[4] When the mayhem ended five days later, about 120,000 Greeks had been lost. Smyrna was entirely destroyed.

Onassis's father gathered his family inside their home when the Turks entered the town and closed the doors and windows. Terrified, they watched the destruction through cracks in the walls. Their only source of income, the shop in the town, had been destroyed. On the fifth day, the Turks entered the house and arrested the father, leaving young Onassis as the only male there. The next day, Onassis took on the responsibility of rescuing his family. He went out into the chaotic streets of Smyrna and there by chance he met the American vice-consul. With his intervention, the Onassis family was transferred on a small boat to the nearby Greek island of Lesbos. But Onassis stayed behind to rescue his imprisoned father.

He soon managed to visit his father in prison where he found him ill and distraught. When Onassis was leaving the prison the Turks arrested him but he managed to escape. Terrified he ran to the vice-consul's office. The next day he was on his way to Lesbos, disguised as a sailor on an American warship. Three weeks later the Onassis family arrived at the Greek port of Piraeus as war refugees in a miserable condition.

Onassis's father was later released and joined them. The family's uprooting was, for young Onassis, an oppressive experience. Throughout the next year (1923) he had "a feeling of futility"[5], as he said later and spent his days in Athens lonely and withdrawn. He didn't have any contact with his former classmates who'd also come to Greece and he was not willing to get involved in any way in the business, tobacco trading that his father had started under difficult circumstances.

In desperation, he decided to immigrate to the United States but he could not obtain a visa so as a second choice he decided on Argentina. His father was vehemently opposed to this, so much so that he refused to give him the money for the tickets. Onassis was forced to ask some of his friends for a loan. He obtained an insignificant amount and with it embarked on a risky venture. In August 1923, he departed from the Greek port of Piraeus, arriving a month later in Buenos Aires. He was only 17, clutching a torn suitcase. He was penniless.

His first priority of course was to find a job. He soon realized that wouldn't be easy. To keep himself alive he washed dishes in restaurants and hauled bricks on construction sites. Finally, in March 1924 he found a job at the Telephone Company of Buenos Aires as an electrician. Since he wasn't making enough money, he worked the night shift so that he could do another job during the day. This was not the Argentina Onassis had dreamed of.

The Good Season of 16-17 Years from 1925 to 1941

In 1925, Onassis's fate changed.** As soon as he found a decent job, his next step was to work out a deal with his father so that he could start selling Greek tobacco in Argentina. Early in 1925 he began corresponding with his father and soon they'd reconciled. Before long, he convinced his father to send him samples of high-quality Greek tobacco. With the samples in hand Onassis started visiting the cigarette manufacturers of Argentina to try to sell them tobacco. He quickly received his first order for $10,000. Since the quality of the tobacco was excellent, a second order followed soon, for $50,000. The orders came faster and faster. Onassis couldn't even find time to sleep. By May 1925 he had managed to put $25,000 in the bank, not bad for someone who had recently been penniless.

The same month he quit his telephone company job and started a business of his own. He began manufacturing his own cigarettes in the small room he was living in. That business was very successful and soon Onassis started living the high life. He frequented music halls and clubs and formed friendships with wealthy young men. Early in 1926, he moved out of the small room he had been living in and took a hotel suite in the most distinguished part of Buenos Aires. He also bought a car and took French and English lessons.

Although the season was still "springtime", there were some rain showers. In the summer of 1929, the Greek government increased the import duties from countries with which it did not have commercial agreements, by 1,000 percent. Argentina was among those countries and Onassis feared that Argentina would retaliate by increasing the import duties for the Greek products, making the trade of Greek tobacco impossible. He decided

---

** Note that since the seasons alternate every 16 to 17 years, it is not easy to distinguish whether a certain season starts, for example in 1924, or in 1925. For Onassis, this season seems to start in 1925, while for Churchill; the same season seems to start in 1924. The same phenomenon may happen in some other biographies' seasons as well.

to return to Greece the same year (1929) to persuade the authorities to exempt Argentina from the increased duties. After a stormy discussion with the Greek prime minister, Onassis then only 23 finally won the battle. The spring shower had passed.

Onassis's visit to Greece had another benefit, not only was he reunited with his family, but the reunion had a touch of triumph. He was the successful son who had come back, the son who was sending money to the widows in the family for the educational expenses of their children. The reconciliation with his father, was now complete. Returning to Argentina later in 1929, Onassis made his first foray into a field of activity that would eventually bring him staggering wealth, shipping. He bought a dilapidated 7,000 ton ship that was 25 years old.

But the money still came from the tobacco trade. Between 1930 and 1931 he expanded the business to Cuba and Brazil. A year later, a new source of profits was added; the Greek government acknowledged his commercial potentials and appointed him the country's consul in Buenos Aires, at the age of 26. In that position Onassis could now obtain foreign currency at official rates and resell it in the free market at huge profits. That position gave him two more advantages, he was able to acquire Argentinean citizenship and he made many important contacts in the international shipping world.

In the fall of 1932, Onassis assembled all of his savings (around $600,000) and sailed to London, the maritime world's capital, to buy ships. Because of the economic crash of 1929–1932, ships' prices had declined precipitously. A "10 year-old freighter which had cost $1 million to build in 1920"[6] could now be obtained for $20,000. Onassis didn't take long to find what he was looking for – a fleet of 10 such ships was for sale in Saint Lawrence in Canada. In the winter of the same year he was in Saint Lawrence and after brief negotiations, he bought 6 of those ships in 1933 for $20,000 each. Onassis's career as a ship owner had begun.

The next year a new and important element was added to his life. During a trip from Buenos Aires to Genoa, he met Ingse Dedichen, the daughter of one of Norway's biggest ship owners and a love affair developed between them that would last for more than 10 years. After they met, Onassis abandoned Argentina and settled in Norway, to be with Ingse. Over the next two years the doors of that country's ship owners and upper classes opened to him.

In 1937, Onassis entered a new field of business activity, that of tankers. He ordered his first tanker of 15,000 tons from the Swedish shipyards, it was about 3,000 tons bigger than any other tanker at that time and valued at $800,000. He was prudent enough to lease the ship, in advance, for one year to the oil company of U.S. tycoon J. Paul Getty. In 1938 the Swedish flag flew over the tanker.

The following year World War II broke out. Onassis was not anxious at all, he didn't know that a bad season was to start soon for him. On the contrary he predicted the hostilities would end soon. To avoid any trouble he left Europe in June 1940 and settled in New York in a luxurious apartment on Park Avenue. Within a few days, Ingse followed.

The New Bad Season of 16 -17 Years from 1941 to 1957

Soon after the declaration of war, Onassis realized that things were not as simple as he thought. Most of his fleet, particularly the tankers, were immobilized in hostile countries. Only the aged small ships he had bought in 1932 in Canada were available. His revenues were declining dramatically. To help the situation he resumed the tobacco trade, based in New York this time. To this he added olive oil. But the profits were limited.

For the first time Onassis started living a tedious unsatisfying life. He rented an old house in New York and his relationship with Dedichen began to sour. As she said later, Onassis told her at the time that, "the years were passing him by"[7] and he had not lived his life. He had given all his attention to business; he lamented and had neglected everything else. As a result he now lived a dissolute life, carrying on with various women. Many were Hollywood's young and marginal actresses with whom he became acquainted during his business trips to California. He also pursued a wealthy heiress in San Francisco, but in what was a humiliating experience for him she rejected his marriage proposal.

Whenever he came back from California he would see Dedichen, but their relationship was in serious trouble, especially after he beat and kicked her. Onassis, Dedichen says, had begun drinking heavily. That situation lasted for three more years (1942–1944). Finally, after repeated quarrels and abuse, Ingse decided to leave him.

With the end of the war (in 1945–1946), things got even worse for Onassis. During the war, all Greek ship owners had put their ships at the disposal of the military in the fight against Hitler's Germany, for the transporting of equipment and materials *and they had lost all of them*. The only exception was Onassis, who had not made any ships available. That ultimately proved to be a great disadvantage to him.

In 1946 the U.S. government had the biggest commercial fleet in the world. They were the Liberty ships which had been built by the thousands to meet the needs of the war and now were immobilized in various ports around the country. To get rid of them, the U.S. government decided to give them to the Allied countries' ship owners who had lost their own ships during the war. This transfer was made under very favorable terms. While each ship had cost about $1,500,000 to build, the price was fixed at $550,000 per piece, with a down payment of $125,000 and the remainder to be paid in seven years. The sole condition was a guarantee by each country's government for the payment of the installments. A hundred of these ships were given to Greece and went to those ship owners who had lost their ships in the war. Having lost none of his ships, Onassis got none of the Liberty ships, though he had asked for 13.

The other Greek ship owners thus now had the most competitive fleet in the world. The Liberty ships were in excellent condition and for the most part were modern. Onassis, on the other hand, remained with an antiquated fleet. The game, it was evident, would be unequal. Onassis would not be able to overcome the competition, so, he made desperate attempts to obtain Liberty ships from the Greek government. But seemingly because of his bad season his attempts failed.

Then Onassis made another attempt to acquire ships. In 1946 but this one would soon land him into an American prison. The U.S. government was offering many tankers of 16,500 tons each, again under favorable terms but only American citizens could buy them. Onassis submitted a petition to buy 20 of these, but of course he was rejected. He then created phony companies ostensibly run by American citizens and so acquired the tankers but that illegal act would later prove costly.

In 1946 Onassis married Tina Livanos; the daughter of the great Greek ship owner, Stavros Livanos she was 17 and he was 40. If he hoped that with this marriage he would profit financially from the connection with his wealthy father-in-law but that did not happen.

Onassis's business problems persisted in 1947. The U.S. government again offered to Greek ship owners seven tankers of 16,500 tons each, like those offered to American citizens the previous year, under equally favorable terms. Onassis immediately asked to buy all seven tankers. But, for the same reason as before, the Greek government would not acquiesce.

Then he did something unprecedented for that time. He borrowed money from American banks and bought tankers and also he borrowed the dizzying amount of $40 million from the Metropolitan Life Insurance Company of New York to build new ships. These acts astonished the shipping world, since buying or building ships with borrowed money was considered too risky for maritime transportation and indeed, the above loans later drove Onassis to the threshold of bankruptcy.

It was 1948 and with the $40 million loan in hand, Onassis went to Germany to negotiate the terms under which his ships would be built. But he became indecisive and was unable to complete the deal. On the contrary, next year he decided to take up a line of work quite different from shipping, hunting and killing whales, a pursuit that would soon make him notorious. For that purpose, he assembled a fleet of 17 ships and hired Norwegian and German whale gunners. That act provoked protest from the Norwegian Whaling Association.

In 1950, Onassis finally decided to proceed with the construction of his ships in Germany, using the borrowed money. This was a huge, complicated order that gave him many sleepless nights. It involved 16 ships of 20,000 tons each and two ships of 45,000 tons each, a total of more than 400,000 tons. At the same time, Onassis's business troubles worsened. The American government started investigating the illegalities involved in his 1946 purchase of the tankers only U.S. citizens were permitted to buy.

Onassis anxiously tried to avoid the consequences. In August of 1950, with the Korean War underway, he sent a cable to the U.S. Department of the Navy, setting "five [of his] newly built supertankers"[8] at the department's disposal in case of need. Of course, his offer was rejected with a polite pro-forma letter. The investigation continued. More troubled now, in October 1950, he sent another cable offering not only his ships but also his own services as a sailor. This offer, too, was rejected.

In 1951, Onassis added to his notoriety. Not satisfied with the results of his whaling enterprises, he decided to continue hunting the whales well after the season was over, flouting international regulations. The season had ended on March 9 and he continued for two more months, until May 10. The news spread and a general outcry arose, damaging his reputation.

The same situation prevailed in 1952. In 1953 the U.S. government decided to institute legal proceedings against him for the issues with the tankers. Onassis sent another cable offering his ships but without any results. In fact, the government took severe measures against him; each time an Onassis ship arrived in a U.S. port, a customs official "would inform its master by letter that the ship [as well as its profits] was under seizure."[9]

The same year, Onassis bought the majority of shares in the Casino of Monte Carlo which belonged to the Principality of Monaco – a purchase he made without previously informing the Principality's Prince Rainier. While Onassis expected huge profits from that investment, the profits were disappointing. In 1954, Onassis suffered a major blow; the U.S. government ordered his arrest.

As soon as he learned the news he sent a cable to the Department of Justice and placed himself at the disposal of the attorney general. The next day, gloomy and "accompanied by his legal entourage"[10] and several newsmen, he presented himself at the attorney general's office where he assumed he would arrange some kind of settlement there. Unable to reverse his bad season, the opposite he had hoped for happened. After having been fingerprinted and photographed from all angles he was put in jail in the company of a group of Puerto Rican terrorists. Later he was released on bail but was not a free man. Most important, he had been profoundly humiliated. After negotiations lasting another two years the case was closed. Onassis would deposit a fine of $7 million.

In 1954 a second humiliating experience awaited him. He wasn't satisfied with the results of his whale hunting in Norway so he decided to hunt off the coast of Peru. The Peruvian government sent two warships to prevent him from doing so. But he persisted so five of his ships with 400 German sailors were arrested and escorted to the nearest port. The remaining ships, chased by Peruvian planes, took refuge in Panama. Soon after, a Peruvian court fined Onassis about $3 million. The fine was paid by the insurance companies but Onassis's name and fame had been badly wounded.

The same year Onassis did something else that drove him to the brink of destruction. After a series of negotiations that lasted many months and after having bribed some of the highest officials, he concluded an agreement with the king of Saudi Arabia that would give him the exclusive rights to use his tankers to transport that country's huge oil output. As soon as the agreement became known, a storm of protest broke out against him. This was not only from the big U.S. oil companies, which had had the exclusive right to produce the Saudi Arabian oil, but also from the government of the United States itself.

The oil companies submitted an official protest to Saudi Arabia and simultaneously made clear to Onassis that each time his ships would arrive in that country's ports to load crude oil, they would not let him have it. U.S. Secretary of State, John Foster Dulles, warned the Saudi Arabians that if they insisted on upholding the agreement with Onassis the American oil companies would stop oil production in that country. In the face of that reaction the king of Saudi Arabia was forced to cancel the agreement. For Onassis, that was yet another serious blow and it was to soon have even worse consequences.

In 1955 the Norwegian Whaling Association issued a report indicating that for a number of years, Onassis had systematically violated the whaling regulations by hunting off season and killing very young whales, pregnant females, or whales belonging to a protected category. The damage he had caused, the report said, was incalculable. Because of the general disapproval the report created, Onassis was forced to abandon whaling in 1955 for good.

The most devastating blow came that year as a result of his questionable agreement with Saudi Arabia. The U.S. oil companies decided, out of revenge, to discontinue any cooperation with him. Each time a charter contract for any of his ships expired they would not renew it, giving it instead to other ship owners. At the end of 1955, half of Onassis's tanker fleet was idle. His main source of income was drying up at tremendous speed.

That situation continued into 1956 as well. More and more of his ships were becoming idle and those ships were mortgaged with the huge loans he had borrowed to build them. But Onassis no longer had sufficient income to repay the loans. In despair, he went around to the American banks to which he was indebted asking them to take over the management of his ships. That was, "the worst time of my life,"[11] he said. The international shipping community expected him to announce bankruptcy at any moment.

The Second Good Season of 16-17 Years from 1957 to 1974

The bankruptcy never happened. In October 1956 the Suez Canal closed to shipping because of the crisis between Egypt and Israel. As a result, ships had to circumnavigate Africa, adding considerable time to each trip. Too few ships were available to meet the demand and freight costs skyrocketed to unprecedented heights. The only ship owner who had ships available was Onassis. Because of the boycott the American oil companies had imposed on him, he had a huge number of ships standing idle in various ports. The results were predictable, his ships were chartered by desperate merchants, the boycott ended and the acrimonious relations with the oil companies were forgotten.

Instead of destruction, triumph arrived. Onassis's new good season had started. He began to realize dizzying profits. In 1957 he earned $70 million, while ten years earlier, he had been head over heels in debt with the $40 million loan he had taken out. The profits were huge. Onassis didn't know what to do with all this money. His first act was to repay all the loans he owed. His second act was to commission the building of new ships, among them a 100,000-ton tanker, the biggest in the world at that time. His third act was to give a resplendent reception in Monte Carlo to celebrate his improved fortunes. That same year he transferred his business activities to Greece where he established Olympic Airways and became the first private individual in the world to own a national airline.

From 1958 on Onassis became an international celebrity. He invited many international personalities to cruise the seas on his yacht *Christina*, the most luxurious yacht in the world. Originally a 2,200-ton frigate in the Canadian Navy, Onassis had transformed it into a floating palace. Celebrities that would be seen relaxing on the yacht included Hollywood's famous actors and actresses like Marlene Dietrich, Greta Garbo, Ava Gardner and others. Even aged ex-Prime Minister Winston Churchill, in a wheelchair, was hospitably received. Every time the *Christina* arrived in port with Churchill aboard, ambassadors, other distinguished visitors, even prime ministers and kings, paid their respects.

In 1959 Onassis got to know Maria Callas, at that time the most famous Greek opera singer (we will see Callas's biography below). The bond between them piqued intense global interest for many years with scores of reporters and photographers following the couple closely, "from one end of Europe to the other."[12] Because of that bond, Callas separated from her Italian husband – Giovanni Meneghini. Later that year Onassis divorced his wife, Tina Livanos.

Onassis's busy social and business life continued through 1962 causing a great deal of interest all over the world. In 1963, he impressed international society even more by buying a whole Greek island, Skorpios, which he converted into a fabulous summer resort. In the summer of that year, gossip mongers had a field day, the wife of the president of the United States,

The Seasons of our Lives

Jacqueline Kennedy, cruised the Greek islands aboard the yacht Christina as Onassis's guest. In November of that year, President Kennedy was assassinated.

In 1964, Onassis began to increase his fleet at a tremendous pace. He arranged for ships of 50,000–60,000 tons to be built while the next year he acquired a newly built 100,000 ton tanker. In 1966 he commissioned the building of huge tankers of 175,000–200,000 tons each. The size of his fleet now amounted to *4 million tons*, while in 1950, when he had taken out huge loans, he had only 400,000 tons.

In 1967 Onassis realized staggering new profits. The Suez Canal closed again to shipping because of a renewed conflict between Egypt and Israel and freight charges rose to unprecedented heights. Onassis ordered the building of six super tankers in 1968, so that the tonnage of his tankers alone amounted to 2,500,000 tons. The same year, Onassis's rise to social prominence culminated in his marriage to Jackie Kennedy, in a fabulous wedding ceremony on his privately owned island. That was the social event of the year; Onassis was now known all over the world. (Later we'll also see Jackie Kennedy's biography). That triumph, success and world admiration would continue for the next four years. By 1973, however, Onassis's brilliant season would end abruptly. What followed was a tragic season, the last of Onassis's life.

The Bad Season from 1973 onward ✱✱✱

In January 1973, Onassis's son Alexander was killed in a plane crash at the Athens airport. He was 19. At first it appeared that Onassis showed that he overcame that event. Immediately after his son's funeral and burial on the island of Skorpios, he started expanding his fleet. At the time the fleet consisted of more than 100 ships, among them 15 supertankers of 200,000 tons each. Onassis commissioned six more tankers to be built, two of them of 400,000 tons each, the biggest tankers in the world.

From 1974, things deteriorated with Onassis's marriage to Jackie. In a visit to Acapulco, where Jackie had spent her honeymoon with John Kennedy. She asked him to buy her a house there. He understood that the reason was sentimental and refused. During the quarrel that followed, Jackie said she now expected nothing from him.

The worst blow though was to Onassis's health, perhaps aggravated because of his son's death. In 1974 he began to suffer from myasthenia gravis, an incurable disease affecting the eyes and other parts of the body. He couldn't hold his eyelids open and had to hold them up with tape. He also had a hard time swallowing food and slurred his words when speaking. Not surprisingly, he was full of complaints; about his life, about himself, his marriage, about everything.

Next year, in 1975 it was the last in Onassis's life. Olympic Airways, his Greek airlines company, suddenly found itself in a precarious financial situation. Onassis asked the Greek government to lend him money to resolve the situation, but the government refused. On the contrary, he was informed that the government intended to nationalize the airline.

✱✱✱ *For Onassis, this season seems to start in 1973, not in 1974. The seasons alternate every 16 to 17 years and as noted earlier, it is not easy to distinguish exactly when a certain season starts.*

"Against his doctors' orders,"[13] he left the hospital in New York, where he was undergoing treatment and returned to Athens in an effort to reverse the nationalization but in vain. On January 15, 1975, he was forced to accept his company's takeover.

A few days later, Onassis became seriously ill from pneumonia. In an awful condition he entered a hospital in Paris where he was operated on to no avail. On March 15, 1975, the wealthiest man in the world died at the age of 69. Only his daughter Christina was at his bedside.

Conclusion

Onassis's biography shows how his life was deeply influenced by the alternations of his good and bad seasons. As you may recall, when in a bad period in 1956, almost all his ships were idle, because of the boycott of the U.S. oil companies. Those ships were mortgaged with huge loans he had borrowed to build them. All expected him to announce bankruptcy.

In October 1956, because the Suez Canal closed to shipping freight costs skyrocketed to unprecedented heights. The only ship owner who had ships available was Onassis and so he began to realize dizzying profits. In next few years he became the wealthiest person on earth. His example, once again confirms; don't despair in your bad seasons as the good season, perhaps a fantastic one will surely come later.

Chapter 17

John Glenn

To further convince you of our discovery and for you to take advantage from it, the following chapters will reveal important revelations. You will see, for example, how the phenomenon of the alternations of our seasons is *universal*, happening all over the world and in all human races. We start by seeing in this chapter how the good and bad seasons alternated in the life of America's national hero, astronaut John Glenn. Born in 1921 he is of the same era as Margaret Thatcher (born in 1925) and Nelson Mandela (born in 1918).

As he himself says in his memoirs, a boy could not have had a more idyllic early childhood than me [1]. In those years he lived in a big house and "never doubted even once that… [he] was loved."[2] Even during the Great Depression of 1929, he was eight years old and did not suffer much. His family "grew almost everything in… [their] gardens,"[3] so they had enough to eat. His father sold cars, making them better off than many in their town, New Concord, Ohio.★

At the end of the Depression in 1934, his father's new jobs resulted in "another step toward… [their] financial recovery."[4] By the age of 14, Glenn

---

★ *All the facts and details in Glenn's biography derive from his autobiography* A Memoir, *Bantam Books, New York, and Nov. 1999.*

was earning big money working for his father. In 1937 he got his driver's license and his father let him use an old car. In the summer of 1939 he also had a wonderful time. With three other friends, he took a trip from New Concord to New York where the World's Fair with the theme "The World of Tomorrow" had opened.

The highest moment in this good season came in 1941. Glenn had dreamed of becoming a pilot since the age of eight, when he had the opportunity to fly in a plane with his father but the cost of flight training seemed prohibitive; he had abandoned the idea. But early in 1941, when he was 20, he saw a notice that the U.S. Department of Commerce was offering free training for pilots. The era that would shape the rest of Glenn's life had started.

This notice, however, signaled the end of this idyllic season for Glenn.

The Season from 1941 on

When Glenn told his parents that he was entering flight training, they strenuously objected. World War II was escalating in Europe and the application he signed for the free training said that if necessary he would be trained for military purposes. He was not unaware of the risks; as he says in his book, "the war news from Europe dampened… [his] enthusiasm."[5]

Glenn's enrolment to the army didn't take too much time. He entered flight school only a few days before the Japanese bombed Pearl Harbor in December 1941. The war in the Pacific had started. Glenn then signed up for the Army Air Corps, saying goodbye to his parents, to his girlfriend Annie Castor (later his wife) and to his boyhood. In the next two years, he was first trained as a military pilot and then the war started for him, he was sent to the remote Midway and Marshall Islands in the Pacific, fighting the Japanese there, not having any fresh vegetables or meat available for months. He wrote letters to Annie (whom he had married in the meantime, when he returned home for a few days on leave) almost every day, describing the horrors of war.

After the war ended in 1945 Glenn continued to serve in the army and went with the marines to China. Deployed there in 1946–1947 he found China so different from anything he was accustomed to that he longed for home and Annie. He also experienced weariness and futility, as he says in his book. In 1948, he was in the Pacific again, on Guam, facing the same situation. In the meantime, Annie had had two children (in 1945 and 1947); they knew their father from photographs only.

Though Glenn spent the years 1949 to 1952 at home, he wasn't happy; serving in the army in assignments he didn't like. In 1953 he was ordered to the Korean War, where his plane was hit twice by the communists and he miraculously survived. Between 1954 and 1956, Glenn was assigned another extremely risky job back in the United States as a test pilot. On this assignment he came near death at least three times.

Early in 1957 Glenn was transferred to a bureau in Washington, D.C. Of course he wasn't happy that place was for a bureaucrat. When early in the same year, he fantasized about crossing the United States in a plane at supersonic speed for the first time, he had a great disappointment; the navy and Pentagon couldn't be persuaded, his bad season prevailed.

The Good Season from 1957 onwards

In July 1957 the navy and the Pentagon suddenly came around and Glenn realized his dream. He crossed the country by plane, from California to New York, at supersonic speed, in 3 hours and 23 minutes. When he landed, he was greeted by reporters and television crews while a military band marked the event. The next day, *The New York Times* ran a profile of him and Annie. A brilliant season had thus begun for Glenn.

The next year Glenn took another step forward, he decided he would become an astronaut, in order to go into space. Early in 1959 he volunteered for that purpose. He passed his exams successfully and during the following two years (1960–1961), was trained for the great experience, along with six other elite astronauts, waiting for the final go ahead. In February 1962 the big event happened; Glenn became the first American to orbit the earth. After a spectacular trip of three orbits that lasted 4 hours and 56 minutes he returned to earth when his capsule landed in the cold waters of the Atlantic.

He had no idea of the tumultuous welcome that awaited him. Vice President Johnson accompanied him back to Cape Canaveral with thousands of people lining the parade route. President Kennedy presented Glenn with NASA's Distinguished Service Medal and the whole country watched the events on the television sets. Glenn's good season had helped make him an American hero.

In 1963 Glenn entered politics and he developed a growing friendship with Senator Bobby Kennedy and his wife Ethel. They discussed a Kennedy proposal for Glenn to run for the Senate. The following year Glenn announced his decision to pursue the nomination for the seat of the Ohio Senate. Because of an accident, he withdrew after a month. He would try later and would succeed.

The same year Glenn became financially independent, he was appointed vice president of the Royal Crown Cola Co., at a salary of $50,000, which compared favorably with the $15,000 he had earned in the marines. He retired from the marines in 1965 while in 1966 he increased his financial independence through a joint venture in four Holiday Inn franchises. He spent the next seven years (1967–1973) in a climate of financial abundance. In 1974, his political ambitions were finally realized. He decided to seek the nomination for the Ohio seat in the U.S. Senate and triumphantly won the general election. Glenn had thus arrived – he had become a U.S. senator.

The New Bad Season of 16-17 Years from 1975 to 1990

However, as soon as he took the oath of office in the Senate in January 1975, Glenn felt as if he was imprisoned and tortured there, like "Daniel praying in the lions' den,"[6] he says in his book. The next year Glenn had his first great disappointment, he was mentioned as a possible vice president for Jimmy Carter but after a "dull" speech he gave at the convention, Carter picked Walter Mondale.

In 1979 he had another similar disappointment. He'd prepared a speech to give in the Senate on the occasion for the verification of the SALT II treaty. But when he sent the speech, in advance to President Carter, the president phoned him and expressed strong disapproval. "No president before or since had ever talked to me that way,"[7] he says in his memoirs.

The disappointments and Glenn's bad season continued. In 1982 he decided to seek the Democratic presidential nomination for 1984 announcing his candidacy in April 1983. Mondale was his opponent. But he did poorly in the primaries and withdrew from the race in March 1984. His campaign "was almost $3 million in debt"[8] when he withdrew. When in 1988, Glenn's name appeared once more as a potential vice president, Michael Dukakis, who was the nominee for president, chose Lloyd Bentsen.

In 1989 came the culmination of this season's problems for Glenn, where press reports questioned his integrity. They accused him of having been involved in the savings and loan industry's crisis that occured that year. The Senate Ethics Committee initiated investigations and sent him a letter calling him to give his replies to the charges. He fought the case "with every fiber of... [his] being,"[9] he says in his book, but he felt that was at the *lowest point* of his life. The episode "cost him $ 520,000 in legal fees and great personal anguish."[10]

The Season from 1990 onwards

In the summer of 1990, however, the counsel of the Senate's Ethics Committee's recommended that Glenn "be eliminated from the investigation."[11] In February 1991, the committee decided that the charges against Glenn "failed to produce a single finding."[12] Glenn was at deeply relieved. In 1992 he was reelected to the Senate by a sound margin; he was the only senator from Ohio to serve 4 consecutive terms.

In 1995 a good era began. "What would happen if somebody older went [into space]?"[13] Glenn wondered, and why shouldn't that person be him? So at the end of 1995 he mentioned his interest to NASA's director Dan Goldin. "You're serious about this?"[14] Goldin asked. "Serious as I can be,"[15] Glenn replied. He was then 74. But he was in a good season. In February 1997 Glenn announced his decision to retire from the Senate; he wanted "to serve… [his] country in other ways,"[16] he said. "When I leave the Senate, it will not be an end, but a new beginning,"[17] he added.

In January 1998 he learned from Goldin that he had been accepted to go into space again. The idea of "an ancient guy like… [him] going into space was exhilarating,"[18] he says in his autobiography. People stopped and wished him good luck, while in Houston "a forest of red-white-and-blue banners with… [his] picture on them, proclaimed the road 'John Glenn Parkway.'"[19]

On October 29, 1998, the great day arrived. Cape Canaveral "hadn't seen reporters and photographers in such numbers since the Apollo moon launch days,"[20]. The crowds on the beaches and along the waterways were huge. He "couldn't have been happier,"[21] Glenn said.

After a trip of 134 orbits and 3.6 million miles, the *Discovery* and its crew returned to earth. A great parade followed in New York City, then a tour of Europe and Japan early in 1999. The flight had received international recognition and this good season continued for Glenn through the next years.

Conclusion

Glenn's biography confirms the same patterns we've seen in other chapters; his seasons alternated in 1941, 1957, 1975 and 1990, every 16 -17 years, exactly as Gorbachev, Thatcher and Mandela. But though Glenn was of a high profile, he cannot be considered as great as Napoléon or Beethoven. Thus Glenn's biography also reveals that the alternations of seasons every 16 -17 years at certain dates happen not only in the lives of great people but also in the lives of the very important people, like Glenn.

Chapter 18

Elizabeth Taylor

We further confirm and extend our discovery. We'll see how the good and bad seasons alternated in the life of the famous American film actress Elizabeth Taylor, a contemporary of Mikhail Gorbachev. Taylor was born in 1932, Gorbachev in 1931. From her biography we'll also see a new revelation. Elizabeth Taylor was born in London to American parents who soon returned home. Since we do not have many details on her early years we do not know whether she was happy or not at that age and therefore whether she was in a good or bad season. She apparently had a normal childhood, attending school and playing with friends. But we do know that in 1941 a really good season, a spectacular one, started for her.*

---

* *My source for Taylor's biography in this chapter is Larissa Branin's* Liz, the Pictorial Biography of Elizabeth Taylor, *Courage Books, New York, 2000.*

The Good Season from 1941 onwards

Thanks to her mother's connections, little Taylor signed in 1941, at age nine, a contract with Universal Movies. Her career as an actress had begun. Although the next year she was dismissed because she was talentless, as the studio executive said. Her career soon continued. In 1943, Metro Goldwyin-Mayer, the most important movie studio, signed Elizabeth up with a one-year contract for a role in the upcoming movie *Lassie Come Home*. The movie became a box-office hit.

Elizabeth's successes would continue into the next years. In 1944 she played an impressive role in *Jane Eyre*, as well as a small part in *The White Cliffs of Dover*. In 1945 her passionate performance in *National Velvet* brought her a new contract and a salary of $1,200 per month, thus becoming her family's major breadwinner. Acknowledging her success, *Life* magazine featured her in a cover story on her thirteenth birthday in 1945.

In 1946 Taylor starred in *The Courage of Lassie* and in 1947 it was the Broadway hit *Life with Father*, as well as *Cynthia* where she had her first kiss on the screen. In *Cynthia*, she performed a very touching role and the film had enormous success. As a result, the studio now treated her "like a beautiful princess, kept behind protected walls."[1]

The successes continued. In 1948 she starred in the films *A Date with Judy* and *Julia Misbehaves*, while in 1949 there were the *Little Women* and *The Conspirator*. In 1950 there were two more films; *The Big Hangover* and *Father of the Bride*, which became an immediate box-office hit. The same year, Taylor announced her engagement to hotel heir Conrad "Nicky" Hilton, "America's most eligible bachelor."[2] They got married on May 6 of that year. She was 18 and he was 23.

Taylor soon became disillusioned with her marriage, after only seven months and asked for a divorce. She was unperturbed by that fact and continued to play starring roles. In 1951, she appeared in *A Place in the Sun* with Montgomery Clift and the film met with much critical acclaim. After her divorce, she starred in *Love Is Better Than Ever* (1952) where she had a love affair with Stanley Donen, the director of the film. Soon after Taylor starred in London this time, in the extravagant film *Ivanhoe* (1952), where she fell in love with Michael Wilding, the British star of cinema. Wilding was married, but after his divorce early in 1952 he and Taylor married. A year later she had her first child.

In 1954 Taylor appeared in other major productions including *Beau Brummel* and *Elephant Walk*. But by 1955, when her second son was born, her marriage to Wilding began to deteriorate. He was out of work and his nonchalance about it disturbed Taylor. It was at this time when she met the famous producer and showman Mike Todd, 49 years old, who soon proposed marriage. Dazzled, she separated from Wilding and married Todd, early in 1957. Soon after her marriage, she began living a much more lavish lifestyle. Todd wined and dined her with champagne and caviar, showered her with diamonds and furs and made his Rolls-Royce and private plane available.

The Bad Season from 1958 onwards

On a blustery night in March 1958, Mike Todd's plane was engulfed in fog over New Mexico and fell to the ground, killing everyone aboard. The man who had enthralled Taylor was forever gone after only a year of marriage. After having learned the terrible news Elizabeth became hysterical and in her nightgown, ran down the stairs heading to the front door where she collapsed.

From now on Taylor's private life would be in ruins. Immediately after Todd's funeral, his best friend, singer Eddie Fisher, was sent by his wife, actress Debbie Reynolds to comfort Taylor. Soon, however, "their counseling sessions turned into something more,"[3] her biographer Larissa Branin says.

By the next year Fisher admitted publicly that he and Taylor had become lovers and after the Fisher-Reynolds divorce, they "conducted their affair openly and defiantly."[4]

Those circumstances inevitably caused public animosity and even death menaces. Everywhere "Taylor and Fisher went, they were heckled by crowds and various organizations upholding decency. Even the Pope... [deemed] Taylor a lascivious, immoral adulterer,"[5] a fact that would nearly ruin her career. Though the couple got married in 1959, the event had destroyed Taylor's chances of obtaining an Oscar for her role in *Cat on a Hot Tin Roof* or in *Suddenly Last Summer*.

Further, Taylor was not happy in this period of her life. While still a newlywed, she confided that "her marriage to Fisher was clearly a mistake and... [though] she had tried to keep Mike's memory alive through Fisher,"[6] she had his ghost only. In the meantime she had another reason for dissatisfaction, Fisher's career began to deteriorate, he became more and more restless and spent his time drinking heavily and lost lots of money while he played cards.

That was the state of affairs when Taylor, while filming *Cleopatra* in Rome in 1962, met famous Welsh actor Richard Burton. Burton played the role of Marc Antony in the film and a love affair was kindled between them. Both, however, were married. "La Scandale" was soon known worldwide. Once again, Taylor "was condemned as a wanton woman, a shameless home wrecker."[7]

After their divorce from their respective spouses, she and Burton married in 1964, their marriage marked the beginning of a tumultuous period in Taylor's life. A year before her marriage to Burton, she had signed a million dollar contract to perform in *Cleopatra*, receiving 10 percent of the film's gross sales. As a result, in 1965 she had gained about $7 million. So, when she and Burton got together, she was "living like a queen." [8] That lifestyle escalated after their marriage. Both actors commanded huge salaries and had "a fleet of Rolls-Royces, a yacht adorned with original… [works by famous artists] and later, their own jet."[9]

But the season was still a bad one for Taylor. The couple's lifestyle isolated them from the outside world and caused them boredom and heavy drinking. At the same time, Taylor had serious health problems "chronic back pain, sciatica, a partial hysterectomy"[10], that caused a severe dependence on pain killing drugs and hard drinking. Soon she became an addict, a situation that lasted until 1984. All this put pressure on her marriage. Burton tried many times to turn things around, but in vain, the bad season couldn't be reversed.

Also, in her career Taylor was not as happy as before. Though she won the Academy Award for best actress in 1966 for her role in *Who's Afraid of Virginia Woolf*, critics said that that role "marked the peak of her career, for none of her future roles would match it."[11] And when the film *X, Y and Zee* was released in 1972, critics said it was her worst performance.

Later in 1972 a tragedy came that destroyed Taylor and Burton's relationship. Burton's brother died and Burton began drinking heavily. Severe quarrels with Taylor followed and finally Burton committed adultery. As a result, they separated in 1973. The next year (1974) they were reunited but Burton "was still succumbing to the charms of other women."[12] So, Taylor walked out, though she loved Burton very much and their divorce followed soon after.

Fortunately this bad season of Taylor's life, which lasted 16 -17 years, was at an end. A new season would begin for Taylor, a good one again, during which she would live a dignified and quiet life, would be cured of her drug and alcohol addiction and through a lucrative perfume business, recouped the money she had lost since her multimillion dollar days.

The Good Season from 1975 onwards

In 1975, Taylor lived a happy year, she remarried Burton. But since nothing had changed in Burton's behavior, Taylor decided to free herself forever from the problems Burton caused her and so the couple received the final divorce decree in 1976. From now on, Taylor would pursue happiness through a quiet life. After her divorce from Burton, she met John Warner, a handsome and wealthy politician from Virginia, who was elected a U.S. senator several years later. He soon became her seventh husband. Taylor told reporters that "all she wanted to do was to live her life on [her husband's] farm"[13] in Virginia. So the next two years she did exactly that.

Later, Taylor decided to put some fun into her life. In 1979 she appeared in the scene of the nightclub *Studio 54* in New York, where she "presided over the trendy scene… and spent many dizzying nights under the disco ball."[14] In 1980, she decided to return to her career. This time it was in the theater, in the Broadway production of *The Little Foxes*. The play was an immediate hit. But because her husband, now a senator had objectioned, Taylor decided at the end of 1981 to separate.

3 years later in 1984 Taylor entered a clinic in California and emerged from it, completely cured of the drug and alcohol addiction and "stronger, both physically and mentally,"[15] her biographer Larissa Branin notes. Taylor's good season had caused a miracle.

In 1985 Taylor became involved with another sphere of activity that soon brought her great satisfaction – she joined the fight against AIDS. At first she spearheaded a crusade to educate the public about the disease and to help raise money for research. For that purpose she became one of the cofounders of the American Foundation for AIDS Research. At the same time, she was the first person to testify before Congress to solicit for funds for the National Institutes of Health. Taylor's efforts were enormously successful; her support and personal appearances reaped millions of dollars for AIDS research. She had now become a humanitarian and felt happy.

Over the next three years (1988–1990), Taylor would continue her successful AIDS work, "helping to raise millions for the cause, while [at the same time] keeping up a rigorous schedule to promote her lucrative fragrance enterprise."[17]

But this good season would end in 1990.

The Bad Season from 1990 on

In 1991 Taylor entered another marriage; she married a construction worker, Larry Fortensky, her eighth husband but the marriage caused her many troubles. First, many suggested that her marriage was not proper to her status nor, to her age; she was 59, he was 39. Then, Taylor faced serious health's problems and in 1995 her hip joints were replaced. The prolonged convalescence that followed created irretrievable damaged to her relation with Fortensky and in 1996 the couple divorced. Taylor's "lawyers battled with Fortensky over his exorbitant monetary requests."[18]

In the meantime Taylor appeared in mediocre made-for-television movies that many said were not "worthy of an Academy Award-winning actress."[19] In 1997 her bad season continued; the health's problems worsened. She suffered a seizure caused by a brain tumor. She faced a dangerous surgical procedure and was terrified she'd die. During the operation a tumor the size of a golf ball was removed from her brain, leaving a scar from the ear to the top of the head.

The calamities did not stop. After "several falls and many broken bones", [20] in 1998–1999, Taylor remained in bed for almost a year. At that age (Taylor was 74 in 2006) health was for her the main factor shaping her season. The indications were not favorable, her health problems hadn't finished.

Conclusion

Taylor's seasons reflect the same 16–17 year cyclical pattern, with the turning points occurring in 1941, 1958, 1975 and 1990, exactly as Gorbachev, Thatcher, Mandela and Glenn. However, both Glenn and Taylor can be considered as important people but not great people like Napoléon or Beethoven were. That fact reveals that the alternations of seasons are not only happening in the lives of important men but also in the lives of important *women*. The same is true for both courses of seasons. Taylor belongs to the first course, while Glenn belongs to the second.

Chapter 19

Maria Callas

Callas was born 1923 in New York City to Greek immigrant parents (her father's name was George Kalogeropoulos, later changed to Callas). From the few facts available regarding her early years, it appears that the first 16 -17 years of her life were good years.* In her early childhood, one of her joys was to listen to the phonograph records her parents played. She had a very good voice and a phenomenal ear for a young child. She sang selections from the records, like *La Paloma* and others.

At the age of ten, in 1933, she sang Gounod's "Ave Maria" and Bizet's Habanera from *Carmen* at a school performance. At her middle school graduation two years later she sang Ambroise Thomas's "Je Suis Titania" from *Mignon*. The same year she sang in one of America's very popular talent contest radio programs, coming second and won a watch and $50, a large sum in that time.

At the end of the school term early in 1937, Callas's mother, believing that her daughter needed education in music which she could have only in Greece, took her together with her sister, despite her father's objections, back to Greece.

---

* *I have based all Callas's biography on Anne Edwards's* Maria Callas, *St. Martin's Griffin, New York, 2003.*

On the ship, Callas sang the Habanera again and the captain gave her a doll as a gift which she kept for years, decorating the headboard of her bed.

Later that same year in Greece, Callas sang "La Paloma" at a tavern and the customers gave her an ovation, asking for more. When she finished a young tenor congratulated her; he was with the Athens Opera and proved to be of great assistance. He introduced her to Madame Trivella, a teacher at the National Conservatory of Greece. When Madame Trivella heard Callas sing the Habanera, she was astonished. She immediately accepted Callas as her pupil and soon Callas won a scholarship at the Greek National Conservatory.

Thrilled, she sat down to work, not even taking time for meals and the next year she was invited to see Verdi's *La Traviata* at the Lyric Theater of Athens. She "was transfixed. She now knew... [at the age of 15] that opera was to be her world,"[1] her biographer Anne Edwards says. The same year, Callas sang at a concert in Athens. When she finished the applause was overwhelming as it was when she sang her first role in opera, in Mascagni's *Cavalleria Rusticana* in 1939. The audience rose from their seats and cheered her. The following year Callas became a member of the chorus of the Greek Opera, at a salary of $15 a month, at age 17.

The Season from 1941 onwards

Early in 1941 Callas developed a slight tremor in her voice. Her alarmed teacher kept her off the stage for a year. She was extremely unhappy. In the meantime, the worst had happened – Hitler's army had invaded Greece in April 1941. Food was scarce; the Germans destroyed everything. The winter was severe and there was no wood for the fireplace. Callas was distraught; "The occupation of Athens was the most painful period in my life,"[2] she said later.

In 1942 Callas's life worsened, when the Germans permitted public performances, Callas sang *Tosca* at the Athens Opera but she returned home miserable, convinced that her performance had been ruinous. When in 1943 Callas made the faulty step to give a concert for the occupation army, the board of the Athens Conservatory decided that the concert was unpatriotic and discontinued her scholarship. She could not attend classes any more and cried bitterly but in vain.

At the same time Callas became enormously fat. Despite the food shortage, she was eating huge quantities of nuts and dried figs. The next year, the situation worsened. The Germans left Athens after their defeat. But then Communist Party's guerrillas seized the city of Athens in an effort to install their own government. Callas and her mother and sister were imprisoned in their apartment and they had no food or water.

When that situation ended in 1945, Callas decided to realize her long awaited dream; to return to America, to be reunited with her father and to sing at the Metropolitan Opera House. Over her mother's strong objections, she sailed back to New York in September 1945, alone. Not being able to reverse her bad season, things were not as anticipated. She first called a Greek tenor with the Metropolitan Opera whom she knew from Athens before the war but he refused to see her. She also tried to see opera agents and managers in New York, but to no avail.

After six months of rejections, she managed to be heard by a famous tenor, but he told her coolly that she needed further training. When at last, Callas was asked in 1946 to sing at the Met, she made a terrible mistake; she didn't like the role offered her – Leonore in Beethoven's *Fidelio* – and to the manager's great surprise, she refused it. She thus ruined any chance she had of making a name for herself in the United States anytime soon. Not long after that she was asked to audition at the San Francisco Opera but it didn't go well. The manager "treated her like a schoolgirl,"[3] saying that she should lose weight because she was too heavy and that she had to get her career started in Italy first.

The opportunity to build her career in Italy came unexpectedly the following year. She was asked to sing at the Arena di Verona during the 1947 summer festival there. Though successful, her role did not produce enough excitement to make the opera companies want to ask for her services. To her great disappointment, "no agent or opera company in Italy displayed even the slightest interest in her,"[4] Callas's biographer Anne Edwards says. Only an Italian businessman named Battista Meneghini, who was a supporter of the opera and knew many important artists and conductors in Italy, recognizing Callas's talent offered to become her agent. She gratefully accepted but his first effort to take her to an audition at Milan's La Scala failed; there was no audition.

Later, Meneghini succeeded in arranging for Callas to sing at La Fenice, the old opera house in Venice, in late December 1947 and early January 1948. She sang *Tristan and Isolde*, but the acclaim she had hoped for didn't come. Only some minor opera houses in Trieste, Udine, Genoa and Rome sent her offers. On Meneghini's advice, she accepted them, but reluctantly. When she came back to Verona in the summer of 1948, she was dispirited. Her problem with her weight had worsened (she stole food and hid it under her bed) and nights filled with anxiety began to torture her.

Another cause for concern was Callas's belief that Meneghini was indispensable to her life and that she had to marry him but he had not proposed though. She sang *I Puritani* in Venice with great success early in 1949 and "there was now a growing demand for her services, [while] articles about her… appeared in newspapers all over Europe and the States"[5]. Nevertheless she was again deeply depressed, gaining even more weight.

Finally, Callas became Meneghini's wife in April 1949; she was 26 and he was 56. But the bad season continued, the happiness she expected did not come. First, there were Meneghini's brothers who were hostile toward her because she was not of an aristocratic origin. When she was to leave on a tour of South America the day after her wedding, Meneghini said he wouldn't accompany her. She became hysterical and warned the tour would be cancelled, but finally she went alone, a "bride of 24 hours,"[6] her biographer Anne Edwards notes. In Buenos Aires she sang *Turandot* but the critics emphasized the unpleasant intonation of her voice. Not surprisingly, her earnings from the South America tour were modest.

In 1950 Callas was at last invited to sing at La Scala, three performances of *Aïda*. However, she wasn't satisfied. La Scala's production of *Aïda* wasn't suitable for her. Finally, her performance in *Aïda* was a failure. Callas was depressed; her "disastrous engagement at La Scala… had seriously injured her self-esteem"[7] and reputation. That same year Callas had a very successful tour in Mexico, where she sang *Norma, Aïda, Tosca* and *Il Trovatore*. But when she returned to Verona, disappointment awaited her, she found that the money with which Meneghini had bought a new car was not his but from her earnings. That fact was to raise serious doubts in Callas's mind about Meneghini's faithfulness for years to come.

In 1951 she realized that Meneghini was not as good at handling her contracts as she'd assumed despite her success in many Italian cities including Rome, Venice, Naples, Palermo and others. She also hated having to stay in various hotels around the country while she was performing. For these reasons, her weight increased more and there was restlessness in her voice and a sharp tongue.

When Meneghini arranged a series of performances in Mexico City during the hot summer months of 1951, she said that was a stupidity; the heat when she sang *Aïda* "was so intense that… she suffered from heat exhaustion… her legs and ankles had swollen painfully, [and] she spent two days in bed."[8] Later in Rio de Janeiro she had to cancel her performance in *Aïda* because she was still too ill. Her other performances in Brazil, furthermore, were frustrating. Though in *Norma* she had great success, in *Tosca* many members of the audience shouted against her. When she finished the concert manager nearly refused to pay her, saying that her performances were awful.

The unpleasant situation continued into the next two years. Though in late 1951 and early 1952 she sang *I Vespri Siciliani* and *Norma* at La Scala with great success and at the end of 1952 she sang *Norma* again, at London's Covent Garden, also with great success but she still was not happy. When she was home in Verona trying to relax the animosity with her husband's brothers was extreme. They were disrespectful. Callas began to hate her own home and became hostile towards her husband.

In 1953 she went on a strict diet and lost 68 pounds (30 kilos). But because of this diet, a new eating problem arose next year, the opposite of her previous weight problem. She couldn't eat sufficiently and her weight was only 117 pounds (53 kilos). However, she sang 17 operas in 1953 in many Italian cities. But when she was back home in Verona she "still suffered the worst insults and indignation"[9] from her husband's brothers. She swore to leave Verona and never to come back and she never did.

In 1954, the situation worsened. Callas sang *Norma*, *La Traviata* and *Lucia di Lammermoor* with great success at Chicago's Opera House. But she wasn't happy; she felt terribly alone. Her situation became worse when she fell in love with the famous Italian film and stage director Luchino Visconti. Though Visconti was a known homosexual her bad season prevented her to see that fact. When she sang *La Traviata* at La Scala under the direction of Visconti in 1955, the audience became delirious, yet Callas had eyes only for Visconti. Naturally, however, he wasn't available.

In 1955 Callas had a second tour at Chicago's Opera House. Though she was again a big hit she was still unhappy; she "was becoming less and less patient with… [Meneghini, since] her sexual appetite [was] unsatisfied."[10] At the same time another worry was added, her mother wanted to exert influence on her daughter, a fact that Maria refused to accept.

Their relationship was never good but worsened during the last years. Her mother gave interviews to various newspapers, blaming her daughter and describing her as a monster.

The next year Callas, at last sang at the Met in New York; *Norma, Tosca* and *Lucia*. Though she received applause and many encores her appearance was less successful than she had anticipated. At the same time, *Time* magazine published a cover story quoting Callas's mother as saying that when she asked her daughter for money, she replied "Jump in the river and drown yourself."[11] The story was also broadcast on radio and television causing Callas enormous worries and difficulties.

Early in 1957 Callas was feeling more alone than ever. Her mother had betrayed her, she didn't trust her husband and she was extremely bitter with Visconti. But this bad season in Callas's life ended in the middle of 1957.

The New Season from 1957 onwards

In April and May 1957 Callas sang Donizetti's *Anna Bolena (Anne Boleyn)* at La Scala under the direction of Visconti. But now her feelings for him had suddenly changed where she became less tolerant of his homosexuality and she was no longer bewitched by his genius. Her love for him had thus evaporated. At last she was free. Her role in Anna Bolena was an unprecedented triumph. The audience went mad, "the applause… rose in a tremendous crescendo… [and] continued for 24 minutes, a La Scala record."[12] The crowd outside the theater was so big so that the police came to contain it.

On September 3 1957, the crucial moment arrived; Elsa Maxwell, the famous American gossip columnist and socialite, arranged a party in Venice in Callas's honor. Among the guests were Greek tycoon Aristotle Onassis and his wife. When they met he took Callas's hand and kissed it. Later, they had a short dance. "His touch seemed somehow magnetized and it set up an alarm in me,"[13] Callas said later. That was the start of a new life for her, a life she had always wanted but never achieved a life full of love.

Simultaneously her career continued on its meteoric ascent. In 1958 Callas sang brilliantly at the Metropolitan Opera, at La Scala and at London's Covent Garden where Queen Elizabeth was present. Onassis who was in London at that time, sent her a magnificent bouquet of roses. When at the end of the same year she sang, also with great success at L' Opéra de Paris in front of the president of France, Onassis attended the gala, though he disliked opera. At the dinner reception that followed he again took Callas's hand and kissed it. The touch was "so pleasing,"[14] she said later.

In June 1959 Onassis and his wife Tina invited the Meneghinis to a party they would give in Maria's honor in London. In the meantime Onassis had sent to Callas a superb chinchilla coat as a gift. She wore it immediately despite the warm weather. When they had a tango at the party (she said she loved that kind of dance), Onassis ordered the orchestra to continue with tangos. A month later the Meneghinis were invited to a cruise on Onassis's yacht, the *Christina*. By the end of the first week, Callas spent little time with Meneghini and she "was seen going in and out of Onassis's apartments… late at night and leaving the next morning."[15] After the cruise was over Onassis arranged a suite for her at the Hôtel de Paris in Monte Carlo.

She was now extreamly happy. "For the first time I understand what it means to be a woman. My singing, my career… come after Ari,"[16] Callas told her maid and confidante. Toward the end of 1959 Callas ended her unhappy marriage, a court decreed her separation from Meneghini since divorce is not permitted in Italy. At the same time Tina Onassis filed for divorce in New York.

That idyllic situation continued into 1960 and 1961. Callas had greatly curtailed her singing engagements so that she could stay with Onassis. When in 1960 Onassis organized one more tour on the *Christina* with

Callas; she was, as she admitted, "madly happy."[17] That summer she sang *Norma* in Greece at the ancient theater of Epidaurus. When she finished the audience wept. A few days later she was honored with the Medal of Merit by the Greek government. When in 1961 she again sang *Medea* in Epidaurus, again it was an amazing performance. The crowd shouted; "Greece's Queen of Opera!"[18]

In 1962, she and Onassis spent most of their time together in Monte Carlo and Paris, where he had bought a flat for her. Her passion for Onassis was undiminished. He was equally devoted to her, his gifts to her were extravagant and the bills for the furnishings she ordered for her apartment weren't questioned. So, when Onassis told Callas in 1963 that he was going to arrange a cruise on the *Christina* with President Kennedy's wife Jackie as a guest, a cruise on which Callas could not be present – she had no objections. She knew that the president's friendship was crucial to Onassis and that her presence as his mistress on the same cruise as the first lady of the United States would be problematic.

In late 1963 Callas found that she was pregnant, at the age of 40. But the only thing that interested her was her love with Onassis. The child had not any meaning for her. So, early in 1964 she had an abortion. On her return from the hospital a magnificent necklace was delivered to her apartment from Onassis. The summer of 1964 was "the most intimate time [Onassis and Callas had shared]… since the early days of their relationship"[19], on Skorpios, Onassis's private Greek island.

The next year Callas's successes continued undiminished, she sang *Tosca* at the Opéra de Paris and soon after at the Metropolitan Opera. There it was an unprecedented success. The cheers lasted for almost 6 minutes and the critics said that was the most superb *Tosca* New York had ever seen. After that, she sang *Tosca* again before the Queen at London's Covent Garden, with equally great success. The good times continued through 1967.

Then in 1968, Onassis told Callas that he was going to marry President Kennedy's widow, Jackie. Not because he loved Jackie, he said he loved only Maria but because he *needed* her for his business in America. He always would love Callas, he added. Callas knew very well how much Onassis loved her. So she did believe him. Onassis was true to his word. Soon after his marriage to Jackie in March 1969 he went back to Maria. Again, they were lovers as we'll see later in Jackie's biography.

Their lasting love continued for several years, until late 1973. When Onassis's son Alexander was killed in a plane crash at the Athens airport in January 1973 he went to Callas for consolation. In the meantime Callas successfully continued to sing in various places around the world. When at the end of 1973, Onassis stopped seeing or calling her she wasn't disturbed; she soon found another love, Italian tenor Giuseppe di Stefano, who made her very happy. He planned to abandon his wife and to propose to Callas, he had told her.

The Season After 1974

In the fall of 1974 di Stefano's wife appeared suddenly and forced her husband to break off his relationship with Callas. Callas was distraught. She took an overdose of sleeping pills and the next morning a friend found her in coma. A doctor came and Callas recovered over the next few days.

A worse blow came at the end of 1974. Onassis was admitted to a hospital in Paris, he suffered from incurable myasthenia gravis. Early in 1975 he was operated on. Callas was distressed. She wanted to go see him, but his wife Jackie had given orders to the hospital staff not to permit it. Callas stayed in her apartment waiting to hear news about Onassis.

When Jackie left for New York a few days later, Onassis's daughter Christina and his sister Artemis called Callas and told her she could come to see him. When she arrived, they left her alone with Onassis. He "appeared to be unconscious,... [but] there was a moment when he opened one eye and seemed to recognize her."[20] "It's me," she said, "Maria, your canary."[21] Five days later, Onassis died. Callas was inconsolable, she was a widow. She shut herself up in her apartment, became moody and depressed and kept the TV set on day and night because of her loneliness and fear of the dark. Onassis's photo rested on her piano.

The above situation lasted throughout 1976 and for the first nine months of 1977. In September 1977, Callas called her sister in Athens and told her, "[since] Aristo died, I want to die, too."[22] A few days later Callas's maid found her unconscious in the bathroom. The doctor who was called pronounced she was dead, from a heart attack. She was only 54. Onassis's "canary" had followed him as quickly as she could.

Conclusion

Callas's biography confirms that the good and bad seasons in her life alternated in 1941, 1957 and 1974, every 16 -17 years. These dates are exactly the same but opposite to those of Thatcher, since Thatcher belongs to the first course of seasons while Callas to the second, as we've seen earlier. That also confirms that the seasons of women's lives alternate at the same 16 or 17 year intervals, regardless of whether the women conform to the *first or second* course of seasons.

Chapter 20

Jacqueline Kennedy Onassis

A new revelation and a further confirmation of our discovery derive from the alternations of good and bad seasons in the life of ex U.S. first Lady Jackie Kennedy Onassis. A contemporary of Elizabeth Taylor (she was born in 1929, Taylor in 1932), Jackie Kennedy Onassis was born as Jacqueline Bouvier, on Long Island New York. The 1929 stock market crash had severely hurt the fortunes of her father, John Bouvier, giving her "a sense of insecurity and fear of poverty."[1] ★

When she was 7 or 8 her family started to crumble. Her parents quarreled frequently over her father's pursuit of other women and they separated. The other kids needled Jackie and she was "like a motherless kitten,"[2] her biographer Sarah Bradford says. In 1940 the humiliation went public; the news of the separation of her parents became known in the local press with details of her father's womanizing. That fact caused Jackie deep insecurity and shyness toward the world.

★ *All facts and details for Jackie's biography derive from Sarah Bradford's America's Queen*, The Life of Jacqueline Kennedy Onassis, *Penguin Books, New York, 2001.*

The Good Season from 1941 onwards

From 1941 on things would change, a good season was about to begin for her. In 1941, at the age of 12, she had her first big success winning a prize for horsemanship at a horse show. In 1942 things became even better, her mother married a rich man, heir to an oil company and with two luxurious houses. Jackie embraced her new family with love, experiencing a stability she had never known before.

In 1944 she enrolled in a school for wealthy girls where she soon became an outstanding pupil. In 1946 she won first prize in literature and when she left the school in 1947, she was "a bright, confident, imaginative 17-year-old"[3] girl, looking forward to unlimited possibilities. The same year she entered a prestigious college for women, Vassar. In 1948, Jackie was dubbed as "Queen Debutante of the Year," a fact that immediately "put her almost on the level of a Hollywood star."[4]

The good season continued into the next years. Between 1949 and 1951 she traveled to Europe visiting England, Switzerland, Italy and France where she plunged into the cultural scene. In 1952, a lifelong dream came true for her when she was hired as a columnist at the *Washington Times* where she soon established herself. The same year was monumental.

Jackie met the man who was to have the most profound influence on her life; Congressman John F. Kennedy, "America's most eligible bachelor"[5] and one of the richest members of Congress. Soon Kennedy proposed to her and in September 1953 they were married; he was 36 and she was 24. It was the happiest day of Jackie's life.

The couple spent their honeymoon in Acapulco. Deeply in love with her husband she wrote him a poem. For the next three years (1954–1956), Jackie lived a life full of grandeur and satisfaction. The parties given by Kennedy's fabulously rich friends were endless. In 1957, she had one more joy, her first child, her daughter Caroline was born, something she had eagerly anticipated.

But 1957 was the last year in this good season of Jackie Kennedy's life.

The Bad Season from 1957 onward

The first clouds in Jackie's life began appearing immediately within 1957. Soon after her daughter's birth Jackie started to decorate and redecorate her home but her husband objected. He was furious. "What's the point of spending all this money?"[6] he demanded. It was her first clash with him. The turn in Jackie's own life had started. When he campaigned in 1958 for re-election to the Senate, she accompanied him with, "a phony show of enthusiasm," [7] Sarah Bradford, Jackie's biographer, notes.

The next year, Kennedy announced his candidacy for the presidency but Jackie was unhappy. The previous year her husband was so tired while he was campaigning that they barely spoke. What would happen if he was elected president? So, while Kennedy and his friends were celebrating their victory in the 1960 West Virginia primary, Jackie was so miserable that she disappeared from the scene and "went out to the car and sat by herself."[8]

The same situation persisted when Kennedy gave his speech accepting the Democratic nomination for president. While all the Kennedy family members were present, Jackie was not. She watched the speech on television at home, feeling that she "was all alone in the country,"[9] as she said later. When Kennedy was elected president in November 1960, Jackie again was not happy. When she heard the news, she "put on a raincoat and a headscarf and headed for the beach for a solitary walk as the other members of the family were dressing for a victory photograph."[10]

Jackie became first lady after the inauguration in January 1961 but she soon found herself "buried behind a façade of suspicion, mistrust and… [a sense of] imprisonment."[11] Most devastating was the fact that she became aware of her husband's many "other women", among them Hollywood star Marilyn Monroe, a fact that started to terrify her. As if all that was not enough she became increasingly aware that her husband's health was not good at that time. He had Addison's disease and his back pain was so severe that he needed cortisone for relief and had to rely on crutches to be able to walk. As she said later, she and her husband were at that time "emotionally, twin icebergs."[12]

In the next year (1962) Jackie decided to go away. She traveled to India and Pakistan, then to Rome and London. The press was increasingly critical of Jackie's Italian vacation and of her nightclubbing activities; "Doesn't she have enough respect for her husband to be a good wife?"[13] they asked. The news about Kennedy's "other women" were not known publicly at that time.

The following year was even more devastating for Jackie, a year of tragedy. First, she was pregnant, but the baby was premature and was stillborn. Withdrawal and depression followed. In November of the same year, the end came. On November 22 1963, while campaigning in Dallas, Texas, together with Jackie, the president was assassinated. At 34 Jackie was a widow.

The first year of mourning (1964) was a year of emotional turmoil. The now ex-first lady was disturbed and couldn't sleep at night and she felt her life was over. At the same time, she began to worry about money; the $50,000 annual appropriation she was receiving from the government was not enough, especially with the kind of life she had become accustomed to in the White House. She drank too much and sometimes wanted to commit suicide. She lived in an atmosphere of profound anxiety and grief, describing herself as a "living wound."[14]

Another cause of concern was her desire to find another husband, a desire that started to surface in 1965. This goal was not soon fulfilled. In the year after her husband's death, Jackie had worked with a successful architect, Jack Warnecke on the design for Kennedy's grave. In 1966 they contemplated marriage but he was not rich, had no private plane or yacht and so Kennedy's brother Robert objected. Jackie "had to return to the stratosphere of the superrich,"[15] so said her biographer Sarah Bradford.

Such a super rich person appeared in 1967; the Greek tycoon Aristotle Onassis. Jackie had first met Onassis in 1955 aboard his yacht *Christina*, where she and her husband had been invited for cocktails. The second time was in 1963 when Jackie was despondent over the loss of her baby. Onassis invited her for a cruise on the *Christina*. Jackie was impressed by his charm, so, on the day of her husband's funeral in 1963, Onassis, invited by Jackie, was a guest at the White House.

Ever since, Jackie and Onassis had kept in touch by phone and in the summer of 1967, Onassis invited her for a vacation on Skorpios, his private island in Greece. There, she agreed to marry him and they married the next year. She was 39 and he was 62. However, her bad season couldn't be reversed. Jackie's marriage immediately was greeted by worldwide hostility. Everyone felt that Jackie was betraying John Kennedy's memory. Also the Vatican accused her as "a sinner, who would be banned from taking the sacraments,"[16] because Onassis was a member of the Greek Orthodox Church while Jackie was a Catholic.

The marriage was not a happy one for Jackie. Soon after the wedding, Onassis went back to Maria Callas and they continued their love affair. Jackie learned about it and was furious. The next year (1969) was boring and more disturbing for her, she remained alone and sad on the island of Skorpios when Onassis flew off on business. She would burst into tears saying she felt she would never again be really happy.★★

★★ *Jackie's daughter Caroline (born in 1957) and son John (born in 1960), though they had not any objection to their mother's marriage (they were then at the age of 11 and 8 respectively), never stayed in Skorpios, except on the day of the wedding ceremony.*

In 1970 the situation worsened. Onassis and Callas were photographed in Paris dining together at the famous restaurant Maxim and the nightclub Régine. Jackie could not pretend she didn't know her husband met Callas on a regular basis and the marriage started to degenerate. Though she did everything she could to please him, Onassis "was constantly complaining… yelling and screaming at her,"[17] and humiliated her publicly by calling her "stupid" and so on in front of their friends.

The situation continued into 1971. In 1972 Onassis presented Jackie with a legal document stating that she relinquished any rights to his estate. Jackie signed it. Two months later Onassis started gathering evidence against Jackie to ask for a divorce. Soon, she found out about it and was unnerved. In 1973, the crucial moment came; Onassis's beloved son Alexander was killed in an airplane accident at the Athens airport (as we've seen earlier) and next year (1974) Onassis's health began to deteriorate. He was diagnosed as suffering from the incurable disease myasthenia gravis.

But the approaching end of Onassis's life also meant the end of Jackie's bad season from 1957 to 1974.

The New Good Season from 1974 onwards

In the first year of this season (1974) Jackie ceased worrying about what would happen to her marriage or to her husband Onassis. When he died in Paris in March 1975, Jackie wasn't there at the moment of his death; she was in New York at a party her daughter was giving. At the funeral, "she appeared fierce, icy, remote, uncaring."[18] Nor did she weep.

Fortunately for her Onassis's death gave her the means to become, at last, financially and personally independent. After his death negotiations started between Jackie and Onassis's daughter Christina for a financial settlement regarding Onassis's estate. Though Jackie had signed the document stating that she relinquished any rights to Onassis's estate the season was a good one for Jackie. Christina's lawyers informed her that the document wasn't valid according to Greek law. So, in May 1975, a settlement was reached under which Jackie received the huge sum of $20 million. Also, under a second settlement in 1977, it was agreed that Jackie would receive an additional lifetime income of $150,000 per year. Jackie's life had entirely changed.

With all that money in hand Jackie moved back to New York. It was here that she could come into her own as an individual. During the two years after Onassis died (1976–1977), her life changed drastically. She revived her old dream of being a writer by taking a job in 1977 as a journalist. In 1978 she took "two major steps toward independence and self-fulfillment."[19] First, she bought a magnificent house in Hyannisport, Massachusetts. She fulfilled her dream of a literary career, becoming an editor with one of the most prestigious publishing houses in New York.

There Jackie "revealed a side of her that… [no one had] been aware existed."[20] Within four years of joining the company she had become what a colleague describes as an "incredibly positive life force"[21]. Being a status symbol, she also attracted many big-name authors to the publishing house. Meanwhile, a new satisfying element was added to her life; the presence of Maurice Tempelsman, a partner in one of the biggest diamond firms in the United States. Almost the same age as Jackie, Tempelsman left his wife in 1982 and moved into Jackie's apartment. He loved her deeply and was very protective of her.

For the next five years, "Jackie felt free to lead an independent life, to travel, to see old friends and to make new ones"[22] and to return to her beloved horsemanship. In 1988 she became a grandmother at age 59 when her daughter Caroline gave birth to her first child. Jackie had now also become the head of the family as everyone turned to her for advice, a situation that lasted into 1989.

But in 1990 this good season would end for Jackie.

The Season from 1990 onward

After becoming a grandmother Jackie began to drastically change. She altered her look from that of "sexy opulence… to… [a] more ladylike restraint"[23], especially after Caroline gave birth to two more children. In 1993 she began to experience bouts of ill health, soon diagnosed as cancer. A painful swelling in her groin was diagnosed first and then it was found that her brain had been affected. She began experiencing mental confusion so in March 1994, she drew up a will.

In April 1994 she collapsed and was taken to a hospital; the cancer had invaded her liver. The next month she died at the age of 64. The woman, who was wife of two of the most famous men of 20th century, had left this world.

Conclusion

In Jackie Kennedy Onassis's biography we've seen that the shifting patterns in her life match those of other individuals whose lives we've explored in that they lasted 16 -17 years and in that they alternated on the same dates of; 1941, 1957, 1974 and 1990 as happens in the lives of Gorbachev, Thatcher, Glenn and Taylor. But as Jackie was not a great politician, composer, writer, painter or artist, her biography confirms that the alternation of life's seasons also applies to people who are known less for their own achievements than for the relationships and events they were caught up in.

Chapter 21

The Dalai Lama of Tibet

We'll now see how the seasons alternated in the stormy life of the Fourteenth Dalai Lama of Tibet. Born in 1935, the Dalai Lama is a contemporary of Gorbachev (born in 1931) and Elizabeth Taylor (born in 1932).

The Fourteenth Dalai Lama was born in a small rural village 9,000 feet above sea level in northeastern Tibet. His name was Lhamo Thondup. When about 3, a delegation was sent by the government as he was deemed to be the reincarnation of the previous religious leader of Tibet. The 13th Dalai Lama who had died 3 years earlier. Thus, the little boy was taken from his family and was put in a monastery. It was an "unhappy period of my life,"[1] he says in his autobiography, "I was a small child detached from my parents".*

When he was transferred to the capital, the Holy City of Lhasa, in 1939, he confessed he suffered from various restrictions put on him. For example, he was not allowed to eat eggs and pork. He remembers how scared he was of his teacher, even of "the sound of... [his] footsteps, at which... [his] heart missed a beat."[2] That situation prevailed also in 1940 until he was officially installed as the spiritual leader of Tibet.

---

* *I have based my information on the Dalai Lama on his autobiography* Freedom in Exile, the Autobiography of the Dalai Lama, *Harper Perennial, New York, 1990.*

The Good Season from 1941 onwards

But in the following year (1941), a new season began for him. This was not only a good season but perhaps the best of his life. As a young boy he began to enjoy life. He had many toys, among them; a pair of beautiful singing birds and a magnificent gold watch. "[3] He also had a telescope on the roof of the palace, with which he had a magnificent view of Lhasa.

Another passion at that time, especially from about the age of 15 on, were the three cars his predecessor had imported into Tibet. Once he even managed to drive one of them around the garden.

In 1950 a massive event occurred when; Communist China's troops invaded northern Tibet. The people demanded that the young Dalai Lama receive complete power and be enthroned immediately, 2 years before his majority. Thus, in November 1950, the enthronement ceremony was held and so the 15-year-old became the Dalai Lama and the leader of a country of 6 million people. Throughout 1951 to 1953 a kind of truce with the Chinese prevailed. In 1954 the big event came, at the age of 19, the Dalai Lama was officially invited to visit China. He was not only excited at the prospect of seeing the outside world and that great country, but also thought he could help improve Tibetan-Chinese relations. "The prospect of the adventure that lay ahead was thrilling,"[5] he says in his autobiography.

When they arrived in Beijing, a retinue of 500 people, including his family and many high officials were greeted at the railway station by the Chinese prime minister himself, Chou Enlai. The next day, he officially met Chairman Mao Tsetung. They had about twelve meetings and Mao treated him exceptionally; he "always made… [the young Dalai Lama] sit next to him and on one occasion he even served… [him] food."[6] Most important, however, was the fact that during those meetings Mao assured the Dalai Lama that his desire was to establish a constructive relationship between China and Tibet, whose nature would be directed by the Tibetan people only. Buoyed by those promises the Dalai Lama left Communist China in the spring of 1955. When he returned to Lhasa he had every reason to be happy and optimistic.

Early the next year, another invitation came that this time made him feel ecstatic, he was invited to visit India. For Tibetans, India is the Holy Land and the young Dalai Lama had always wanted to make a pilgrimage there. "It was the place that… [he] most wanted to visit,"[7] he says. In November 1956, filled with joy, he left Lhasa for India. When he arrived in the capital New Delhi, the Indian Prime Minister Pandit Nehru was there at the airport to greet him and there was even more ceremony and pageantry than he'd encountered in China before.

The general atmosphere in India made the Dalai Lama, now 21, feel that a sincere friendship could be developed between India and Tibet. That would decidedly help Tibet's case with the Chinese, who, despite Mao's assurances, had not shown in the meantime any sign of peaceful cooperation. With this optimism the Dalai Lama left India in the spring of 1957 and returned to Lhasa, believing that he would offer the Chinese one more opportunity, to would keep their promises as Nehru had advised him.

But 1957 was the last year in this good season of the Dalai Lama's life.

The Bad Season from 1957 onwards

Soon after his return to Lhasa in the spring of 1957, the Dalai Lama's optimism about his country's peaceful cooperation with the Chinese began weakening dramatically. Widespread fighting had started in the eastern part of the country between the Tibetans and the Chinese and the situation seemed out of control. "Whole areas were laid waste by artillery barrages,… while thousands of people… had fled to Lhasa…. Disaster was [thus] in the offing."[8] The Dalai Lama was powerless and knew that Tibet would become a subject state of Communist China.

The situation had worsened even more by the summer of 1958 and early in 1959 a terrible crisis emerged. The general commanding the Chinese troops in Tibet invited the Dalai Lama to attend festivities to be held at the Chinese military headquarters. The Dalai Lama felt he was obliged to accept the invitation. The news spread like wildfire, with catastrophic results. Thousands of people gathered outside the palace and warned him not to go to the Chinese headquarters. Though he assured them he wouldn't go they refused to leave the palace.

As soon as the Chinese general learned of the Dalai Lama's decision, he became furious and accused him of arranging opposition against China because he permitted the crowd to stay outside the palace. The Dalai Lama realized after that that the Chinese intended to use arms to scatter the people. It was "a horrifying moment,"[9] he says, should he try to escape, or should he stay? Finally he decided that leaving was the only way; if he was no longer in the palace the people would have no reason to stay. His bad season couldn't offer any other solution.

Thus the ordeal began that led the Dalai Lama out of his country. The trip to India, the Dalai Lama's country of exile, lasted three weeks. Escorted by his mother and a party of about a hundred people he crossed the high mountain passes, one of them 16,000 feet high, in the midst of blizzards. Physically exhausted and mentally distraught from the ordeal the Dalai Lama and his party crossed the Indian border and then were escorted to the nearest town. The long period of self-exile had started.

The beautiful days of his good season had gone forever; the days when he was "accompanied by a retinue of servants,… was surrounded by government ministers and advisors clad in sumptuous silk robes, men drawn from the most aristocratic families in the land,… [as well as by] brilliant scholars and… religious adepts,… and was escorted by a procession of hundreds of people"[10] every time he left the palace.

Soon the Dalai Lama learned the bad news; the Chinese had crushed the rebellion of his countrymen in Lhasa. Even worse was the fact that when he met Nehru a few days later, Nehru denied help to Tibet; he didn't want to destroy the amicable relations between India and China. With that the Dalai Lama "experienced a profound feeling of disappointment,"[11] according to his autobiography.

In June 1959 another calamity came. The Indian government officially announced that it did not recognize the government the Dalai Lama had established in that country. Soon after the Dalai Lama was transferred to a new place, in a small house at a remote location near the border with Tibet, at Dharamsala, a 24-hours trip from New Delhi, the capital. It was obvious that they wanted to hide him away, incommunicado, hoping he "would disappear from the view of the outside world,"[12] he says.

Soon great difficulties appeared with the Tibetan refugees who had left their country and went to India. The majority of the refugees were settled by the Indian government in various locations but the problems were insurmountable. Hundreds had died from the heat, in part because they had to work as laborers on road building projects. The Dalai Lama was heartbroken at their condition but could do nothing to help. And "one of the greatest difficulties... [he] faced... was lack of money,"[13] he says. The Indian government gave him an allowance of about a dollar a day, which was theoretically enough to pay for his food and clothing.

That situation continued for the years 1960 to 1967. In 1968, the "winter" had already entered the Dalai Lama's life for good, he fell seriously ill of jaundice. His skin turned yellow, he was exhausted and the illness caused permanent liver damage, so that the doctors said that he wouldn't live for long. He became so depressed that in 1973 he had, as he says, "a strong desire to undertake a 3-year retreat"[14] to withdraw himself from the active life, and he did that. He was only 38.

But in the next year (1974), this bad season finally ended.

The New Good Season from 1974 onwards

The Dalai Lama's retreat for rest and meditation that started in 1973 gave him the rest he so much needed. At the same time, he completely recovered from the jaundice. In 1976 a hopeful turning point arrived, Chinese Chairman Mao Tsetung died in September. The Dalai Lama says that the day after Mao's death, he saw "the most beautiful rainbow he had ever seen.... [He] was certain that it must be a good omen... [of] the dramatic pace of change [that would soon follow in China]."[15]

Indeed, the next year, that change appeared in full bloom. The Chinese government announced that they would welcome the Dalai Lama to return to Tibet. At the same time, the Chinese announced that they would permit a restoration in Tibet, of the Tibetan customs, the national dress included. That announcement promising new freedoms came as a surprise and brought the Dalai Lama enormous joy. Soon after that, to his great joy, Chinese authorities allowed foreigner's access to Tibet and permitted Tibetans to visit their relatives living in exile in India and vice versa.

In November 1978 another joy came; many prisoners in Lhasa, members of the Dalai Lama's administration, were publicly freed. In February 1979, the Dalai Lama was informed that Deng Xiaoping, the new Chinese prime-minister, wished to start direct communications with him. The Dalai Lama asked that first a fact-finding mission be permitted to visit Lhasa to ascertain the real situation there. The Chinese agreed to this request and in August 1979 a delegation of five members of the Dalai Lama's government in exile, his brother included, left New Delhi for Tibet via Beijing.

The welcome they received in Lhasa "was ecstatic...they were greeted by an immense crowd... and the streets... [were packed] with thousands and thousands of well-wishers,"[16] the Dalai Lama says. The same happened with two other delegations sent in May 1980. So, in April 1982, the Dalai Lama decided to send a team of negotiators to Beijing to discuss the future of his country. There, the Chinese declared that they wanted very much the return of the Dalai Lama to Tibet. They assured him that he would "enjoy the same political status and living conditions as he had before [his exile]."[17]

Soon, however, it became clear that he must not return to Tibet. The Chinese indicated they did not intend to make any changes in the way Tibetans were living. On the contrary, by May 1984 they encouraged a massive immigration of Chinese to Tibet and a colossal influx of Chinese occurred. In view of that change the Dalai Lama found a better strategy for solving the Tibetan problem. In 1984 he visited the United States in an effort to convince America to support Tibet, and indeed, in July 1985, many members of the American Congress sent a letter to the Chinese officials stating their interest. It was the first time that the Dalai Lama had serious political assistance. The justice of his case was finally winning international recognition.

In September 1987 another cause for that recognition was added, the Dalai Lama had the opportunity to address the U.S. Congress. There he outlined his Five-Point Peace Plan involving the transformation of Tibet into a zone of peace. That proposal for peaceful coexistence later gave him the Nobel Prize for Peace. China, however, rejected his plan. As a result, huge demonstrations against the Chinese followed in Lhasa. "For the first time since 1959, Tibet was again headline news [worldwide],"[18] he says.

In 1988 the Dalai Lama had the opportunity to speak before the European Parliament. Again as a result, several western governments now called on the Chinese to respect human rights in Tibet and to open negotiations with the Dalai Lama on the future of Tibet. In the fall of 1988 the big news arrived. The Chinese indicated they would meet the western governments' demands and start discussions with the Dalai Lama. Full of optimism he thus nominated a team of negotiators to prepare talks with the Chinese.

In the fall of 1989 the greatest moment in the Dalai Lama's life came, he won the Nobel Peace Prize, at the age of 54. He couldn't have a greater satisfaction. But this positive season would end in 1990.

The Season after 1990

Little progress has been made on the Tibetan problem since 1990. The negotiations with China which the European governments had proposed never started. On the contrary, for security purposes China maintains at least a third of its nuclear weapons on Tibetan soil and the Chinese population in Tibet exceeds that of Tibetans. For this reason the Dalai Lama had little hope after 1990 that he would be able to return to his country in the next few years. He would have to continue living in the remote Indian town of Dharamsala, near the border with Tibet, looking at his country from afar.

Conclusion

As we've seen, the Dalai Lama's biography shows precisely the same pattern we've glimpsed in earlier alternations of seasons in the dates 1941, 1957, 1974 and 1990 which happened in the lives of Gorbachev, Mandela, Thatcher, Glenn, Taylor and Jackie Kennedy.

But another key point emerges from the Dalai Lama's biography; though he was born and raised in Asia, his life's patterns are very similar to those of people from Europe, Africa and the United States. Napoléon for example, was born and brought up in Europe, as well as Beethoven, Columbus, Verdi and others. On the other hand, Glenn and Jackie Kennedy were born and brought up in the United States of America, while Gorbachev was born and brought up in Russia and Mandela in South Africa, that is, in the southern hemisphere.

Furthermore, the Dalai Lama belongs to the Asian race, Mandela to the African one, whilst all the others were Caucasian. This reveals that the phenomenon of the alternations of seasons is *universal*, happening all over the world and in all kinds of races.

Chapter 22

Jimmy Carter

Ex-US President Jimmy Carter was of the same era as Nelson Mandela. Carter was born in 1924, Mandela in 1918. As Carter wrote in his book *An Outdoor Journal*, his childhood was a happy season. Born in the small farming town of Plains in southwest Georgia, he grew up on an outlying farm near Archery, two and a half miles from Plains. His life there was busy and happy. While "he was responsible... for managing [the farm's] commissary in the evenings"[1] (his father's landholdings were among the largest in the community), he also had his own pony, played tennis with his father or joined him on fishing trips, went to the movies and "spent many boyhood hours in his own tree house."[2] ★

Sometimes the family's handyman took him to hunt raccoons and he spent some nights with Grandmother Carter. He was also deeply attached to his nannies, one of whom he loved especially. School kept him busy and he was one of the best students in his class. Later, at Georgia Southwestern College, as well as at Georgia Institute of Technology, he got good grades and was remembered as a very intelligent student.

But the good season for Carter would end around 1941.

★ All facts and details for Carter's biography are from Kenneth E. Morris's *Jimmy Carter, American Moralist*, *University of Georgia Press, Athens, Georgia, 1996.*

The Season from 1941 onwards

As a boy, Carter worshipped his father. When "his father missed a shot when hunting, Jimmy fumbled for excuses on his behalf with the remark; 'They are sure flying high this morning.'"[3] But the situation changed in 1941–1942 when Carter was 17 or 18. In the largely African American community of Archery all his friends were black.

His father however did not allow black visitors to enter through the front door. Jimmy disagreed with his father about this and rejected his racial view. In the summer of 1943 he finally decided to leave home and left for the Naval Academy in Annapolis, Maryland, despite his parents' disapproval. He was not quite 19.

The escape brought its own problems. At the Naval Academy Carter wasn't a good student. In all his years there his leadership grades were poor. Nor did he make any close friends. He graduated in 1946 with honors. Immediately after his graduation in the summer of 1946 he married Rosalynn Smith (he was 21, she was 18).

During the first two years of his career as a commissioned officer (1946–1948), he faced an especially difficult battle with depression. He was assigned to a decrepit ship and admitted that "had he not been… obligated to serve, he would have resigned immediately."[4]

Carter was also frustrated for other reasons; in 1948 he was denied the Rhodes scholarship he had applied for, a rejection that he took hard. Although by the fall of 1948 he was accepted into the navy's submarine corps, an elite service that offered him the opportunity to be home several nights. It offered assignments in Hawaii, San Diego and back in Connecticut. His life between 1948 and 1952 had unsettling undercurrents; he "began… to doubt his ability to become a leader,"[5] his biographer Kenneth E. Morris says.

Over the Christmas holidays of 1950–1951 he had an argument with his father on the issue of race. His father supported racial segregation. Carter rejected those views. It was the last and most bitter argument between them. Two years passed without visits or real communication between the two. Early in 1953 his father was diagnosed with cancer and in July died. Over the determined opposition of his wife Carter resigned his commission in the navy to returned to Plains to take up where his father had left off. He wanted to be his own boss and to create stability in his life.

But the bad season continued, things were not as he expected. There wasn't enough of his father's estate to inherit. He acquired only the peanut warehouse but no house to live in. Furthermore, because of his racial views, he refused to join the white Citizens' Council in Plains and as a result was boycotted by the community. So he was obliged to move his family into the "government subsidized apartments for the poor."[6] The family now consisted of three children; Jack, born in 1947; James, 1950; and Jeff, 1952. This poverty-level situation lasted for 3 years, from 1954 to 1956.

From then things became surprisingly good for Carter. He now had a good income from the warehouse, an income that was almost twice the salary he had had in the navy. He was comfortable financially for the first time in his life. The bad season of 16 -17 years from 1941 to 1957 had at last ended.

The New Season from 1957 onwards

By 1957 the Carter family no longer had to live in public housing. First, they found a house and rented it and then, in 1958, the Carter family moved into a new farmhouse near the town. Three years later they acquired their own home. This was a ranch house near downtown Plains. They were living a very satisfying life; they went to dinners and dances, took trips to Atlanta and Florida, or visited restaurants and nightclubs in Albany and regularly found friends to fish or hunt with.

Carter's desire to be a leader was progressively to be fulfilled. By 1960 he was appointed chairman of the Sumter County School Board and the next year he was named chairman of its Economic Development Committee. He also became district governor of the Lions Club and later chairman of the Club's Council of Governors. In 1962 he surprised even his wife by announcing publicly that, "he intended to qualify for election to the state senate"[7], an election that he finally won after overcoming some hurdles.

During his four years at the state senate (1962–1966), Carter worked very hard and was respected by many of his colleagues. When he announced his intention to run for governor of Georgia in 1966 he was in a very good position to win. But it was too soon and lost the election. However, he took the loss as an opportunity to acquire more experience. He began organizing his campaign for the 1970 Georgia election almost immediately.

Money was no longer a problem for Carter, he was now rich and raising funds for his campaign wasn't difficult. His warehouse was now a multimillion-dollar business. During his four-year campaign for governor (1966–1970) he had many interests. At the same time, a religious reversal occurred in his life, he "gave his life to God"[8], a reversal that enabled him to feel reborn.

In 1970 Carter was elected governor of Georgia by a margin of almost 60 to 40 percent. As he himself said later, his four years as governor (1971–1974) were among the most satisfying of his life. Never again "would he display such an enormous a capacity for work… or accomplish so much."[9] He made a huge effort to reorganize the state of Georgia and was the first governor of Georgia to reform its judicial system. His life was very full.

The crowning moment came at the end of 1974 when Carter announced his candidacy for the presidency, surprising everybody. But this announcement marked the end of this good season of his life.

The Second Bad Season from 1975 onwards

Almost immediately in 1975 serious difficulties started appearing in Carter's life. First, Democratic Party leaders declared their objection to his candidacy. Then, during the primaries the following year, Carter came close to defeat. He lost almost all Western states, losing two thirds of the Midwestern states and won only a little more than half of the Eastern states. Carter's candidacy was in great danger. Almost all the political commentators predicted he would lose the election.

Yet, when he was finally elected president, in November 1976, it marked the beginning of an ordeal instead of a triumph. His victory was by a slim margin of 50.1 percent, a margin that could not produce the necessary mandate to govern successfully. The signs of an impending catastrophe appeared immediately. First, there were the president's relations with Congress. The House Speaker started by objecting to the menu the president offered to congressional leaders at their first meeting.

Therefore, almost everything Carter proposed turned to ashes. His comprehensive energy policy floundered in the Senate for months and when it passed in Congress in 1978, it had so many compromises that the president called it a partial victory. His finance reform and hospital cost containment proposals failed, as did his anti-inflation efforts (inflation rates more than doubled during his presidency). The same happened to his national health care and welfare reforms, as well as to all his domestic reform efforts. Naturally, the president was deeply frustrated by his failures.

Outside the administration, the opposition was also fierce. Labor unions openly defied the president. The 1977–1978 coal strike continued for 109 days and Carter seemed unable to solve the dispute. Though in 1978 Carter facilitated a historic peace agreement between Israel and Egypt which was signed in 1979. But even that event didn't reverse his bad season. On the contrary, they continued more fiercely.

The final blow came in November 1979 when the U.S. embassy in Iran was seized by terrorists who took 62 Americans hostage. They also burned Carter in effigy and set U.S. flags on fire "in front of waiting television cameras… which every evening brought the… images into the nation's living rooms."[10] Carter was unable to end the ordeal. When in April 1980 he approved a rescue plan it failed miserably, (his bad season didn't help) and two helicopters crashed and dead men were added to the sorrowful situation.

The crisis of the hostages ironically enabled Carter to be again nominated a candidate of his party for the next election in 1980. The bad season continued, he lost to Ronald Reagan. After leaving the White House early in 1981, Carter was, as his biographer Kenneth E. Morris says, "young enough to do something else and poor enough to need to."[11] He started his new life by building furniture for his home and he felt extremely alone.

In the next two years he built a cabin in a mountain in which all the furniture was made by him. Soon, he had to sell his peanut warehouse to pay off the debt he incurred during his presidency. In 1983, a growing public animosity toward Carter began to surface that lasted almost seven years. "An awful lot of folks in Georgia are growing deathly tired of Jimmy Carter,"[12] a local newspaper wrote in 1983, while the *Washington Post* said in 1984 that public perceptions of Carter were more negative than when he lost his reelection bid.

Also, in 1983, his beloved sister Ruth died of cancer at the age of 54 and soon his mother Lillian also died. His brother Billy died of cancer in 1988, at the age of 51 and in 1989, his other sister Gloria was diagnosed with the same form of cancer. Jimmy thus started to worry about his own health.

The Season from 1990 onward

Fortunately, early in 1990, a good season started for Carter. The signs appeared immediately. The *Washington Post* published an article that year titled "Jimmy – Come Back! All Is Forgiven!"[13] At the same time, *The Economist* asked; "Jimmy Carter for President in 1992?"[14] Meanwhile, a poll discovered that in his home state of Georgia he had a favorable approval rating with 74 percent of his fellow Georgians.

In 1991 Carter inaugurated the Atlanta Project he had inspired in an effort to combat urban poverty in the United States. By 1993 the project had had tremendous success; it had raised $32 million in private donations, instead of the $25 million that was the initial goal. By the next year Carter's return was complete. A Nebraska senator called him the "finest living ex-president,"[15] and when he appeared in bookstores to autograph copies of his book *Turning Point*, lots of people were awaiting him.

On a June Tuesday in 1994, at the age of 70, Carter was present in a ceremony in Atlanta for the unveiling of a sculpture of himself. Present were many dignitaries and his former associates. He was "being honored in life by the kind of tribute usually paid only posthumously."[16] That same summer Carter was again thrust into the international scene. In late June 1994, "he successfully diffused tensions between North and South Korea, bringing both to the negotiating table."[17] In September 1994, "he headed the negotiating team that won a peaceful transfer of power in Haiti and halted the hostile U.S. invasion there."[18]

In mid 1994 Carter's reputation was "skyrocketing,"[19] while by September 1994, a poll found that 6 in 10 Americans had a very positive opinion of him. In October 1994 *Time* magazine featured Carter on its cover. In 2002 Carter's efforts on behalf of global peace were recognized worldwide; he won the ultimate honor, the Nobel Peace Prize. At the same time, many Americans said they would also "welcome Carter's [further] involvement in domestic"[20] as well as international affairs.

Conclusion

As with all the other biographies, the good and bad seasons in Carter's life alternated in 1941, 1957, 1975 and 1990, every 16 -17 years as also happens in the lives of Gorbachev, Mandela, Thatcher, Glenn, Taylor, Jackie Kennedy Onassis and the Dalai Lama. Thus, Carter's seasons further confirm our discovery. They also confirm, however, that the last date of the alternations of our seasons is indeed the year 1990, as mentioned earlier; all the above *8* people last date of their seasonal alternations is that year 1990. This also further confirms, that so many alternations of seasons at the same dates –1941, 1957, 1974 and 1990 for so many people , mean that our discovery cannot be a mere coincidence, as mentioned earlier.

Chapter 23

Sarah Bernhardt

From Sarah Bernhardt's biography you will also see a new revelation regarding our discovery.

Sarah Bernhardt was born on October 23, 1844 in Paris, when her mother Judith was only 16. Her mother was a courtesan, while her father's name is unknown; he may have been Eduard Bernhardt, a "young French lawyer, whose name… [Judith] adopted."[1] In part because of these complexities, Sarah's childhood was the worst period of her life.*

Soon after her birth her mother sent the baby to live with a nurse, far from Paris. For the next few years the nurse's family was the only family Sarah knew. They didn't have much money and Bernhardt later recalled the house as dark and ugly. In 1852, when she was 8, Sarah was still unable to read or write. Her mother sent her to a boarding school but she felt like a prisoner there, as she says in her memoirs. The other girls "made fun of her appearance,"[2] and she developed severe bouts of illness. During her (almost) two years at that school her mother visited her only twice.

---

* *I have based Bernhardt's biography on Elizabeth Silverthorne's* Sarah Bernhardt, *Chelsea House, Philadelphia, 2004.*

In the fall of 1853 Sarah was sent to a convent school. She also hated it there and rarely saw her mother. Six years later she was withdrawn from the convent school and went to live with her mother. Sarah was so ill at that time that the doctors said she would die young. She had a persevering cough and was spitting up blood. She was so depressed that she wanted to have her coffin ready. After repeated demands her mother was forced to buy her a coffin.

But this bad season for Sarah ended abruptly within 1859.

The Good Season from 1859 onward

One afternoon in 1859 Sarah's mother took her to the Comédie Française to see a play. As her biographer Elizabeth Silverthorne says, "when the curtain slowly rose... [Sarah] thought... [she] was going to faint."[3] In fact, "it was... the curtain of my life which was rising,"[4] Sarah said later in her memoirs.

Shortly after that she decided to enter the Conservatoire (Paris Conservatory of Music and Drama, considered the finest drama school in the world) to become an actress. A brilliant season started for Sarah Bernhardt which would lead her to repeated triumphs and glory.

During the audition at the Conservatory, Bernhardt's voice charmed. She threw herself into her work and was ready to graduate two years later. At the graduation ceremony there was a competition among the students in which Bernhardt won second prize for comedy. A few days later, the Comédie Française sent her a letter asking for an interview. Bernhardt's career as an actress had begun.

She now lived with her mother and enjoyed spending time at the house of her aunt Rosine. When her aunt gave a dinner party for her, a son of Napoléon I was a guest as well as the famous Italian composer Gioacchino Rossini, "who accompanied Bernhardt on the piano as she recited a poem."[5]

The crucial moment arrived in August 1862. Bernhardt looked forward to her debut in the Comédie Française with the leading role in *Iphigénie* by Racine, the great French writer of tragedies. But because of stage fright, she became "paralyzed with fear"[6] and her performance was disappointing. After the performance she slapped another actress and the Comédie Française terminated her contract. But this didn't influence Bernhardt. Over the next four years she lived another kind of satisfying life, she acquired and discarded several lovers.

Early in 1864 she had an affair in Belgium with the Prince of Ligne Henri and she became pregnant. Enjoying her independence, she returned to Paris and moved into a flat where her son Maurice was born on December 22, 1864. She was 20 and adored Maurice.

In 1866 Bernhardt signed a contract with the Odéon Theater, one of the most famous theaters in Paris. She achieved great success in Shakespeare's *King Lear*, in Alexandre Dumas's play *Kean* (this was Alexandre Dumas the father, not the son) and in two plays by novelist George Sand. Delighted, Dumas kissed her hand after the performance and said she performed "like an angel."[7] In 1868, Bernhardt performed François Coppée's *Le Passant* and had tremendous success. While the play was to run for a few performances it lasted for 150. The critics lavished praise on her interpretation and the French emperor, Napoléon III, sent her "a magnificent brooch with the imperial initials in diamonds."[8]

In 1870 Napoléon III announced war on Prussia. While her family; mother, sisters and son went safely to Le Havre, Bernhardt stayed in Paris, transforming the Odéon Theater into a hospital where she took care for the soldiers. Later, the French government awarded her a gold medal for her efforts at the hospital. After the war ended, in 1871, the Odéon reopened and Bernhardt's appearance in several plays was well received. She was especially successful in Victor Hugo's *Ruy Blas*. The critics were effusive.

The audience, which included England's Prince of Wales, went wild and the crowds outside the theater "replaced the horses of her carriage and ran with it [as they transported her] through the streets to her apartment."[9] She had become a superstar.

After Bernhardt's success in *Ruy Blas* the director of the Comédie Française invited her to rejoin that premier theater from which she had been fired 10 years earlier at a high salary. Bernhardt had arrived. She was now living stylishly in an opulent home she built, with eight servants and two carriages and was enjoying a lavish social life. In 1874 she reached the pinnacle of success. She gave an amazing performance in Racine's Phédre at the Comédie Française. Other triumphs followed, including Alexandre Dumas's (son) *La Dame aux Camelias (The Lady of the Camelias)* and other plays.

The Bad Season from 1875 onward

From the beginning of this season, clouds in Bernhardt's relationship with the Comédie Française began to appear on the horizon and continued into the next years, despite her success in Hugo's *Hernani* in 1877. And when in 1878, Bernhardt left Paris for a few days without getting permission from the Comédie Française, as she was required to do, the theater director asked her to pay a fine. She refused and the director threatened to fire her. He kept her only because the Comédie Française was about to appear at London's Gaiety Theater and the contract would be canceled if she wasn't in the company of actors.

The Comédie Française gave its first performance in London in June 1879, with *Phédre*. But as the season was unfavorable for Bernhardt, she experienced "the worst stage fright"[10] of her life and was barely able to perform. The situation worsened shortly after that when noise and behavior problems associated with the menagerie of animals she'd accumulated in her temporary London home, including a cheetah, a monkey and a parrot led to public complaints. The manager of the Comédie Française cautioned her "to stop acting like a madwoman,"[11] while the French press criticized her behavior.

Not surprisingly Bernhardt's relations with the Comédie Française worsened. Because of her scandalous behavior the theater gave her a role she didn't like. The result was a poor performance and she received the first bad reviews of her career. Bernhardt submitted her resignation and the Comédie Française retaliated with a lawsuit which remained in the courts for years. The French press also became increasingly hostile.

Bernhardt's only choice was to leave France. Earlier she'd refused offers of a North American tour, but late in 1880 she felt she had to accept. Her performances in New York and Boston were successful but the press treated her badly, criticizing her for her excesses and exoticism. Even "a horse-drawn billboard"[12] caricaturing her appeared in the streets of Boston and followed her in many other cities. Bernhardt wanted to return to Europe immediately but her manager reminded her of her contract, so she stayed.

The bad situation continued. She was denounced by the Catholic archbishop in Montreal who forbade his congregations to see her performances. She received similar treatment from the Episcopal bishop in Chicago. The tour ended in New York in May 1881, after an exhausting trip with many brief stays in Atlanta, New Orleans, Washington, D.C., Baltimore and other cities.

Back in Paris Bernhardt found that people continued to believe her star had fallen. After waiting in vain for offers from Paris to come in, she embarked on new trips abroad. She traveled again to London, then to Italy, Greece, Switzerland, Belgium, Holland and Russia. During this period, another cause of worry was added to Bernhardt's life, she fell in love with a Greek man named Aristidis Damala, 11 years younger than her.** Damala was the son of a wealthy Greek ship owner who had moved to France. After he completed school in France the son went back to Greece in 1878 where he served as a cavalry officer, then returned to France. There he began to work as an actor but "he also became a gambler, a womanizer and a drug addict,"[13] Bernhardt's biographer Elizabeth Silverthorne says. Bernhardt ignored these and other flaws and despite her son's objections, her bad season continued and she married Damala in 1882.

The consequences soon appeared in the fall of 1882. Bernhardt purchased the Ambigu Theater in Paris where she and Damala performed in a play, *Fédora*. But Damala's performance was so bad that the whole production failed. Damala became angry and abusive. Finally he left Bernhardt for North Africa, where he enlisted in the army; she was heartbroken.

The next year, the Ambigu Theater was in a bad condition. To pay the creditors Bernhardt sold some of her jewelry. Soon after, Damala returned to Paris and Bernhardt took him back. But apparently had a serious morphine addiction, was critical and intolerant toward Bernhardt, became openly involved with a young actress and, on top of everything else, acquired major gambling debts and thought nothing of asking Bernhardt to pay these debts. She had had enough. She obtained a legal separation from him in 1883 but since she was Catholic and divorce wasn't an option.

In 1884 and 1885, Bernhardt collaborated with Jean Richepin, the French playwright and performed in several of his plays in Paris. But none was successful. Disappointed, she decided to go abroad again in 1886, this time to South America. Her 13-month tour of Uruguay, Chile, Peru, Ecuador and Panama turned out to be arduous, because the traveling conditions were

---

** *In Greek, his correct name is Damalas; in Elizabeth Silverthorne's book he is called Damala.*

often primitive. The worst disaster happened on her trip back to France. Bernhardt had a bad fall and seriously injured her right knee. She suffered unbearable pain that came and went for the rest of her life. Later, she had to have her right leg amputated above the knee.

In November 1887 Bernhardt appeared in Paris in Victorien Sardou's play *La Tosca*, which he had written for her. But the French press was highly critical, dismissing it as a play "fit only for ignorant Englishmen and American savages."[14] Thirteen years later, in 1900, the play would be developed into an opera by Giacomo Puccini, *Tosca*, which is still performed worldwide with great success.

A few weeks later, at age 23, Bernhardt's son Maurice married a Polish princess. Bernhardt was devastated, not because she disapproved of the bride, but because she feared losing her son's exclusive love. As a diversion she threw herself into her work. In the spring of 1888 she embarked on a tour that included visits to Italy, Sweden, Norway, Russia, Egypt and Turkey. Returning to France in March 1889 Bernhardt found Damala seriously ill. She did her best to care for him, but he died a few months later at the age of 34. Now a widow, she returned his body to Greece. Despite her problems with Damala she never got over his loss. She signed legal documents as "Sarah Bernhardt Damala, widow," and whenever she visited Athens, she called on his mother and took flowers to his grave.

In January 1890 Bernhardt played the role of Joan of Arc in *Jeanne d' Arc*. The role required her to fall to her injured knee repeatedly; she experienced excruciating pain and the knee became so inflamed that her doctor ordered her to stop performing. The play closed for two months.

In 1891 she decided to go on a world tour. This decision ended the bad season in which Bernhardt had been since 1875.

The New Good Season from 1892 onwards

This Bernhardt's good season started with her world tour in 1892–1893. She was a wonderful ambassador for France on this world tour. She went first to Australia, where she was given the red-carpet treatment in Melbourne, Adelaide and Sydney. She went on to New Zealand then to Hawaii and Samoa. In the United States she performed from San Francisco to Brooklyn then traveled to South America. She ended the tour in Europe, where she played from Russia to Portugal. Triumphantly returning to France in September 1893, Bernhardt was "richer by 3.5 million francs."[15]

The first thing she did with the money was to build a retreat on a small island in Brittany. A home was constructed that combined comfortable bedrooms with a dining room, salon and studio. She spent most of her time there with friends and other guests. The second thing Bernhardt did was to take over the management of the Renaissance Theater in Paris where, between 1893 and 1898 she successfully appeared in several performances. In the summer seasons of each year she continued to go to London, while in 1896 she had a brief tour of the United States.

The good season continued into the next years. In 1899, Bernhardt acquired the Nations Theater in Paris which she renamed the Théâtre Sarah Bernhardt. She renovated it, creating a luxurious apartment for herself on the premises. Between 1900 and 1904 she performed in many plays in that theater, including *La Dame aux Camelias, Tosca* and *Phédre*; they were always a huge success. Her performance as Napoléon Bonaparte's son in Edmond Rostand's *L'Aiglon (The Eagle)* was also considered a glorious success. In 1905–1906 Bernhardt had another successful American tour and in 1908 she went on her last tour of Europe.

The Season from 1909 onwards

Bernhardt's last tour of Europe ended in 1909. She had two more American tours in 1910 and 1912 but in South America she had a second terrible accident. While performing *Tosca*, she fell on stage and reinjured her right knee. She remained in bed for weeks. After returning to Paris in 1913 she couldn't walk without assistance.

In August 1914, World War I started and Bernhardt was forced to leave Paris and seek refuge in a villa near Bordeaux. In the meantime, her leg had become worse and had been put in a cast. After the removal of the cast a few months later in 1915, the worst moment in Bernhardt's life occurred; gangrene was discovered in her knee. The doctors determined that to save her life they would immediately have to amputate the leg above the knee.

Bernhardt was stoical, she knew she had no choice but she had a protracted and painful convalescence. A wheelchair was improvised to allow her to get around. It allowed her to perform some plays, in tents, hospitals and other locations during the war and travel to the United States on her last tour in 1916. But further health problems set in. She was found to have kidney problems and underwent an operation.

In 1918 Bernhardt returned to France, the war had not ended yet. She needed to continue working since she had run out of money. Between 1919 and 1921 she appeared in several plays in her wheelchair but the audiences came to see her only out of pity. At the same time her financial situation was precarious. Though she had made millions during her career, toward the end of her life "she lived on loans [and] by selling her jewelry."[16] In 1922, Bernhardt suffered worsening kidney problems and soon collapsed. On March 26, 1923, the end came, the greatest actress of the 19th century died in the arms of her son Maurice.

Conclusion

The good and bad seasons of Bernhardt's life further confirm our discovery, they alternated every 16 -17 years, just as with the other individuals' whose lives we've explored in 1859, 1875, 1892 and 1909. These dates correspond to the turning points for Hugo (1859, 1875) and Churchill (1892, 1909), who both belong to the *second* course of seasons as we've seen in their biographies. This reveals that the alternations of the good and bad seasons in the lives of individuals conforming to the second course of seasons are valid not only for men but also for women, like Bernhardt. Recall that in Margaret Thatcher's biography her alternations of seasons are quite similar to those of Gorbachev, who belongs to the *first* course of seasons.

Chapter 24

Auguste Rodin

In this chapter we further confirm of our discovery. We'll see how the good and bad seasons alternated in the life of Auguste Rodin, the great French sculptor. The few details we possess about Rodin's early years suggest that these years were bad.* Rodin's parents were poor and he was brought up in a poor section of Paris. His mother worked as a seamstress and sometimes as a maid to supplement the income of his father, a policeman.

When Rodin was 10 years old he went to school for the first time but left after three years. He said "he felt like a prisoner" there and never went again. Later, in 1857, when he was 17, he took the exams to enter the School of Fine Arts to study sculpture but was rejected. It was a humiliating experience that he never forgot. To support himself he worked for an ornament maker.

---

* *My source for Rodin's biography is William Harlan Hale's (and the editors' of Time -Life Books)* The World of Rodin, *Library of Art series, Nederland, 1976, European Edition.*

The Season from 1859 onwards

In 1859 a good season began for Rodin. While working with the ornaments and jewelry he created some masterpieces that people liked very much and he started earning better money. This situation continued for the next two to three years and in 1863 it became even better. Rodin was now earning so much money that he rented a studio for himself. At the same time he became acquainted with many famous artists, writers and other notables.

When he was 24, in 1864, Rodin acquired a girlfriend, Rose Beuret, who would remain with him for the rest of his life as both his wife and his model. The same year he was hired, at a very satisfying salary, as a designer in a famous art gallery.

Two years later he began enjoying life. He and Rose moved into a new apartment and he was receiving a better salary. His working conditions improved, he decorated, among other things, the mansion of a marquis and Rose gave birth to their first child.

In 1870, he left Paris and settled in Brussels, together with his employer and many of his colleagues, under very good working conditions. Rose followed and the couple "lived an idyllic life."[1] In 1875, at the age of 35, he was financially successful enough to be able to realize his big dream, to travel to Italy to see the great sculptures of the Renaissance. He visited Genoa, Florence, Naples and Venice. As he wrote to Rose, "he was thrilled to see Italy's great art,"[2] and he was enjoying everything.

The Bad Season from 1875 onwards

During the first two years of this season Rodin lived in Brussels. Though there he constructed his first sculpture *The Age of Bronze*, that work soon caused him huge problems. When in 1877 Rodin returned from Brussels to Paris and exhibited *The Age of Bronze*, the work caused unbelievable reactions. Rumors said that "he had used his model's body as the mold of the sculpture."[3] The great painter's worry was unbearable. The same year new worries were arrived, Rodin's beloved mother died, his father became blind and helpless and his 11-year-old son turned out to be mentally handicaped. Also, Rodin's relationship with Rose took a turn for the worse and he took up with various other women.

Rodin's misfortunes continued in 1878. That year, work he had done for another sculptor was exhibited at the Paris Salon; the other sculptor, named Laouste took credit for it. Ironically, that work won a gold medal while another work by Rodin, *The Man with the Broken Nose* (later considered a masterpiece) and exhibited at the Paris Salon under Rodin's name failed to win an award. Rodin was disconsolate.

His bad season was to continue as more disappointments were in store for him. In 1879 he entered his sculpture *Call to Arms* in a competition sponsored by the City of Paris. But the jury found no merit in that work and eliminated it even before it reached the finals of the competition. Years later, that work was installed by the French government on the battlefield of Verdun as a reminder of what happened there during World War I. The same year, Rodin began a sculpture commissioned by the French government, *The Gates of Hell* to which he would devote the next ten years. But the remuneration was almost nothing, leaving Rodin nearly destitute.

In 1880 he exhibited his work *St. John the Baptist* at the Paris Salon and won a minor award, but he had to relive the experience of being accused of using the body of his model as a mold. Many of his other works also lost favor. Disillusioned, Rodin abandoned Paris and returned to his old employer, the Sévres factory, where he decorated vases and table ornaments. Those works by Rodin later made the Sévres factory known all over the world. He was living a withdrawn and lonely life. One of his biographers says that "he was so shy that he blushed when someone addressed him,"[4] though he was a man of 40.

In 1881 Rodin went to England in an effort to find there what he had not found in France. But he didn't have any luck and returned to Paris a year later. He now lived in a poorhouse, together with Rose. His affairs with other women, models, students, servants and others understandably drove a wedge between them.

In that atmosphere, Rodin tried to work on *The Gates of Hell*, but without any success. That work, two huge gates, each 20 feet high and 12 feet wide with 180 distinctive figures, which were to form the entrance to a Decorative Arts Museum in Paris, would never be finished.

In 1884 Rodin began work on *The Burghers of Calais*, later deemed a masterpiece. Initially it created huge problems for him. When the citizens' committee of Calais saw a cast of the work in 1885, they were so enraged that they immediately asked Rodin to redo it. His life had been turned upside down. Around this time he became acquainted with a woman 20 years younger, he was 46 and she was 26, named Camille Claudel, also a sculptor. Their tumultuous relationship would last for 11 years and would cause a real storm to Rodin's life.

In 1889 the problems with *The Burghers of Calais* intensified. He had modified the statue, but the citizens' committee who ordered the work rejected the work because it had not be placed on a pedestal. The "winter" became more severe. The next year Rodin finished the statue of Victor Hugo that the French government had commissioned, the result was disastrous. The statue, representing Hugo, "naked among naked women"[5] was rejected and caused general disdain.

Rodin lost favor to such an extent that it seemed as if he had already died. That disfavor was reinforced when he completed his statue of Claude Lorrain, the painter, a short time later. The statue was considered so ugly that everyone turned against him. In 1891, Rodin began work on the statue of Honoré de Balzac, the great French novelist. But he was at a loss as to how to proceed and missed the 1892 deadline.

The New Good Season from 1892 onwards

From the beginning of this season, the people's reactions against Rodin had ceased. He set himself with enthusiasm back to work during the next years he continued Balzac's statue and he exhibited it at the Paris Salon of 1898. The statue was found by the critics and other famous people, including "Clemenceau, Lautrec, Debussy, Anatole France and others"[6] as a masterpiece, though it still displeased the public. As a result of this difference of opinion a great dispute broke out in Paris which worked to Rodin's advantage. Newspapers all over Europe reported the tumult in Paris and thus Rodin gained an international reputation.

From now on Rodin's good season continued undiminished. In 1898 Camille Claudel left him, bringing their tempestuous relationship to an end. Rodin returned to the always-faithful Rose with whom he again found peace. The next year brought him greater recognition and financial success. His works now attracted huge crowds and his earnings were correspondingly high. He even exhibited his works in Brussels and Rotterdam where the sales mounted steadily. His "wounded ego was beginning to be restored,"[7] his biographers say.

In 1900 the successes were even more impressive. At the International Exposition that opened in Paris that year Rodin erected a pavilion of his own at his own expense and so became independent of the judgment of the Exposition's various committees. He displayed all his great works in the pavilion; *The Man with the Broken Nose*, *The Burghers of Calais*, Balzac's statue, even a frame of *The Gates of Hell*. The results surpassed every expectation. The sales of his works generated huge sums and the world's most influential museums acquired his works at tremendous prices.

That situation continued for several years. Rodin was recognized as a brilliant sculptor and was honored at receptions and other events throughout Europe. For example, at a celebration in London in 1902 at which a representative of the British government was present, art students were so in awe of him that they "unhitched the horses of his carriage and pulled it themselves."[8]

In 1902 the city of Prague bought Rodin's *The Age of Bronze* and held a magnificent reception to honor him. In London the next year Rodin was again elected President of the International Society of Painters, Sculptors and Engravers. A year later the French government promoted him to the high rank of Commander of the Legion of Honor.

The greatest form of recognition came immediately after that. In 1905 the French government installed his superb work, *The Thinker*, in a place of honor in front of the Panthéon in Paris. The statue had been considered as equally "great" as all the great men of France who are "sleeping" in this mausoleum. The prices Rodin now asked for his works were fabulous and influential men from all over the world came to his Paris studio to have him make busts of them.

Among them was George Bernard Shaw, the great Irish playwright, who went for that purpose to Paris in 1906 and stayed at Rodin's studio for a month. Delighted by the results, a bust in marble, he wrote Rodin that he felt extraordinarily humble in his presence. Even more illustrious clients sought him out. In 1908, King Edward VII of England visited Rodin's Paris studio and commissioned a bust of a female favorite. Rodin's revenues at that time were staggering; while his total assets in 1900 amounted to about 20,000 francs, in 1908 he was earning around 300,000 francs *per year*.

The Season After 1908

In 1908 Rodin now 68, became acquainted with an alcoholic duchess who began to destroy his life. She isolated him from his friends, slandered them and in some cases personally drove them from his house. Rodin started drinking heavily, was often depressed and neglected his work. He was far less productive than he'd been in the past.

In this atmosphere, in 1911, Rodin made a bust of France's Prime Minister Georges Clemenceau, the man who had praised Balzac's statue 13 years earlier while others had scoffed at it. But Clemenceau rejected the bust, claiming it looked "like a Mongolian general,"[9] and asked Rodin to title it "Bust of an Unknown."[10] In 1912, a new humiliation awaited the great sculptor. He produced a statue of Vaslav Nijinsky, the famous dancer, but everyone turned against him because of rumors that Rodin had had homosexual relations with the dancer. A friend of Rodin's had found the two men "drunk and asleep on the floor, with Nijinsky on Rodin's feet."[11]

The calamities continued. The same year the government ordered Rodin to vacate the house he was living in because the government intended to use it as a public mansion. The news came as a shock; Rodin had planned to renovate the house at his own expense as a museum for his works which he would bequeath to the state. The 72-year-old Rodin could not withstand that blow; he suffered a stroke that left his left hand paralyzed.

Two years later, in 1914, World War I broke out. Frightened, Rodin left Paris for England and then sought refuge in Rome. He returned to Paris in 1915. But now he was unable to manage his affairs and began to crumble, mentally and physically. In 1916 he suffered a second stroke. The deterioration continued into the next year, Rodin found himself alone in life. His only companion, Rose, whom he had married two weeks earlier after 53 years of life with her, died. He had broken off with the alcoholic duchess several years earlier.

He now lived alone in a house the French government had permitted him to stay in until his death. In exchange, he had donated his fortune and all his works to the state. The government had already taken everything, the furniture included. The house was quite empty. In the whirlpool of the war, the public authorities neglected to supply the house with coal for heat and so, "wrapped in blankets, its aged resident"[12] had to cope as best he could.

Late in 1917, the greatest sculptor of modern times died at the age of 77, neglected and forgotten by all.

Conclusion

Rodin's biography shows that his good and bad seasons alternated in 1859, 1875, 1892 and 1908, every 16 -17 years. These dates correspond to the turning points in the lives of Verdi (1859, 1875, 1892), Picasso (1892, 1908), Hugo (1859, 1875) and Churchill (1875, 1892, 1908). Thus, Rodin's biography further confirms our discovery. Note, however, that Verdi and Picasso belong to the first course of seasons as you may recall, while Hugo and Churchill belong to the second course. Thus, from Rodin's biography, we also confirmed that the alternations of seasons every 16 -17 years at certain dates happen in both courses of seasons.

Chapter 25

Josephine, Napoléon I's Wife

As explained earlier, I decided to find at least one book with a biography of an ordinary person. After extensive research, I finally found one. It was the biography of Napoléon I's wife, Josephine, though some people may not consider her an ordinary person. As you'll see in her biography, Josephine was an insignificant woman in the early periods of her life and reduced to the role of courtesan, until the age 38. Though later her husband Napoléon did name her an empress for 5 years, she didn't become a *ruling empress* and remained in his shadow and at his mercy. Later when Napoléon divorced her, at age 46, she continued being an insignificant person until her death.

It is clear therefore, that Josephine was an ordinary woman throughout her life. However, even if we wouldn't consider her an ordinary woman, Josephine is in any case a *famous* woman.

Josephine was born in 1763 in Martinique, then a colony of France. She was a Creole, since both her parents, Joseph and Rose Tascher were French. Her baptismal name was Marie-Rose, but her parents called her Yeyette. Later, her first husband Alexandre de Beauharnais called her Rose, but her second husband, Napoléon changed it to Josephine. Until 1776, when she was 13, Yeyette's childhood in Martinique was a good season for her.

Her father was a successful sugar plantation owner. Sugar cane was produced in abundance in Martinique, making the island one of France's most important colonies. Yeyette was happy, enjoying the island's "rare beauty… [and] sparkling… turquoise ocean."[1]*

But in 1776 a bad season started for her.

The Bad Season of 16-17 Years from 1776 to 1792

In 1776 the British navy blockaded Martinique's harbors and stopped export of sugar to France. For Yeyette's family and her two sisters this was a catastrophe. The only solution for the girls was to get married. In 1777 Yeyette was only 14. However, a boy four years older named Alexandre de Beauharnais was selected by his father as a suitable husband for her. Also a Creole born in Martinique, Alexandre went to France at the age of six and at 18 he was an officer in the French army.

He wasn't a suitable husband as he loved another woman, Laure de Girardin, who was already expecting a child. Though he had to get married in order to obtain his mother's inheritance, according to the terms of the will he couldn't marry Laure since she was the wife of a naval officer. So he compromised with Yeyette. Also, Yeyette was in no hurry to get married and she didn't want to go to France. But she had no choice so late in 1779 she arrived in France accompanied by her father. Though Yeyette, like Alexandre, was unenthusiastic, they married.

Yeyette was now renamed Rose, and soon Rose's marriage turned to tragedy. Alexandre started enjoying himself, spending his newfound inheritance and going out every evening without taking his wife with

---

* *My source for Josephine's biography is Carolly Erickson's* Josephine, *St. Martin's Griffin, New York, 1998.*

him. He would return home late at night, drunk and slept until afternoon. In 1780, after almost a year of marriage he left Rose for months at a time. Their first child was born in 1781, a son named Eugene, quarrels erupted between the spouses.

In 1782 the situation worsened. Alexandre abandoned his wife who was pregnant again and went to Martinique, with Laure. There he started collecting evidence that would allow him to divorce Rose (something she soon learned about). Later, he sent Rose a letter demanding that she leave his house. When he returned to France in 1783, Rose was forced to leave the house and enter a convent that offered shelter to women suffering from marital problems. Their second child, a daughter Hortence, was already born.

Not having any other alternative, Rose decided in 1784 to seek a legal separation but being penniless she went to live with her father-in-law. When conditions in that house became unbearable and Rose continued to face tremendous financial problems, she made, in 1788 a painful decision to return to Martinique with her two children. However, as it was her bad season the situation in Martinique was worse. Her father had become a feeble man and she had to deal with the consequences of Alexander's attack on her reputation when he was in Martinique collecting evidence against her.

In 1789 the worst came. The French Revolution of July 14 of that year started in Paris when the crowds stormed the Bastille and obtained governmental power. Soon the revolutionary climate affected Martinique. Battles began between citizens and soldiers and between blacks and whites, "men were hanged… women were kidnapped."[2] Panic-stricken, Rose decided to return to France. After a torturous trip, she and her two children arrived in Paris late in 1789. But the situation there was equally bad, there was no bread or coal, the prices rose dramatically and there wasn't any money available.

The only way Rose could survive was to do the last thing she could imagine doing; to have affairs with men who could sustain her. As her biographer Carolly Erickson says, she entered a "shadow-world at the margin of respectability, populated by women whose sexual arrangements and financial survival were intertwined."[3] She was 26.

This continued through the years of 1790–1792 but soon this bad season would end.

The Good Season of 16-17 Years from 1792 to 1809

Late in 1792, the monarchy in France was abolished and in January of 1793 King Louis XVI was executed. Queen Marie Antoinette followed a few months later. A powerful Committee took the king's place and almost everybody was suspected as "an enemy of the revolution." Rose was also a suspect and to avoid arrest, she needed a "certificate of citizenship."[4] Late in 1793, the first sign of the good season that had started for her appeared. Using her acquaintances, she managed to obtain the certificate. She had survived.

In April 1794 she was arrested and spent three awful months in prison. She was released when the Committee had found nothing against her. That same year (1794), another major event occurred that drastically improved her life's conditions. While she was in prison, her husband, Alexandre de Beauharnais, then a general in the French army, had been executed as a traitor. Rose now was free to remarry.

The opportunity to remarry arrived soon. In the summer of 1795 Rose met Napoléon Bonaparte, then a brigadier general in the French army. In January 1796 Napoléon proposed to her and they were married only three months later. She was 33; he was 27. Her dream had been realized. Again she obtained a new name; Napoléon named her Josephine. Immediately after the marriage, Napoléon left Paris to become chief commander of the army of Italy. Josephine had to stay in Paris. Wanting company she continued her love affairs.

One of her lovers was a rich and influential man, Paul Barras, who helped her financially and introduced her to his wealthy friends. Finally, having plenty of money to spend, Josephine shopped and bought the newest fashions and spent hours making herself attractive, "attending [lots of] receptions and parties… [and dancing] until the early hours of the morning."[5] Another man Josephine became involved with was Hippolyte Charles, a lieutenant. He wasn't rich, on the contrary, Josephine often gave him money. She was in love with him and very happy, the only true love in her life until then.

When Napoléon learned that Josephine was unfaithful, he wrote asking her to come to Milan and she left Paris for Italy in June 1796. There, the glory awaited her. According to Josephine's biographer Carolly Erickson, "a parade of Italian notables arrived [at the Palace of Milan, where Napoléon was staying] to be presented to Madame Bonaparte…. [They were] counts and countesses, dukes and marquises,… who bowed [to Josephine]."[6] In a letter from Milan to her aunt, Josephine praised her husband's devotion, saying he treated her like a goddess.

In full glory, Josephine returned to Paris in December 1797 and she continued the kind of life she liked. She saw Hippolyte almost every day and sometimes she also saw Barras "the same day, before going home"[7] to Napoléon, who in the meantime had returned to Paris. The same situation continued when, in May 1798, Napoléon left for another campaign; to conquer Egypt. At the same time, Josephine realized a dream she'd always had; she had saved so much money that she bought a home of her own, a three-story residence, the château of Malmaison, on the banks of the Seine. By the spring of 1799, Josephine had moved in; Hippolyte stayed there as well.

In October 1799, the crucial moment arrived; Napoléon came back to Paris after almost a year and a half in Egypt. Because of his wife's infidelity he had decided to divorce her. When she went to his house, she was informed that Napoléon had ordered his porter not to let her in. In a state of panic, Josephine pushed the porter aside and rushed up to Napoléon's room. But the door was locked. She cried and begged him to let her in but in vain. She stayed there until early in the morning. When her children, Eugene and Hortence came and knocked on Napoléon's door, he unlocked the door. His face was tearstained. It took only a few moments before Napoléon, Josephine, Eugene and Hortence, all weeping "joined in an embrace."[8] Napoléon the Great had forgiven his wife. Josephine's good season had helped to this.

From that point on the culmination of this good season started in Josephine's life. Early in 1800, Napoléon became France's leading figure and moved into the Tuileries palace with Josephine. There, she stayed in the apartment of Queen Marie Antoinette and lived like a queen. She had several personal attendants and a large contingent of servants that ran the household. In 1801, Josephine now 38 wrote her mother that Napoléon made her very happy. She "lived amid the grandeur of the palace"[9] and enjoyed her life. Her love affair with Hippolyte was now over as was her affair with Barras; Napoléon had sent him away.

The situation continued into the following years 1802–1803. But in May 1804, the greatest moment arrived; Napoléon was named Emperor of France. From then on Josephine was addressed as, "Your Imperial Majesty."[10] The coronation of the new emperor was to be held in December 1804. Napoléon had decided over his brothers' objections that Josephine would be named and crowned empress along with him. At the coronation ceremony, "she knelt before her husband… [and received] the circlet from his hands… her tears flowed freely."[11] An ordinary woman had been named an empress.

From now on, Josephine lived the life of an empress. There were hundreds of balls, of open-air festivals, evenings at the theater and the opera. She spent more and more money. She spared no expense on jewelry, art, stylish clothing and elegant household objects. She continued buying even after her wardrobes were full of the most expensive gowns and other fashionable items. She had other reasons to be happy as well; in 1805 Napoléon named her son Eugene, then 23 Viceroy of Italy. The same year, Napoléon defeated the armies of Britain, Austria, Prussia and Russia and became the ruler of Europe. Sharing the grandeur and wealth of her husband, Josephine continued to experience good fortune for several more years.

In 1808, the final great moment of Josephine's good season arrived. She had always feared Napoléon would divorce her if she couldn't give him a son and heir. That fear disappeared in 1808. Napoléon decided that year to take the painful step of divorcing her and ordered that the legal preparations be set in motion. But he soon rescinded the order. His decision had caused him "spasms and... severe stomach pains."[12] Anguished, he rushed to Josephine and admitted he couldn't leave her. In what was one of the high points of Josephine's life, they had a passionate reconciliation. The possibility of divorce seemed now a thing of the past.

As a result, Josephine lived the best possible life. She bought everything she could imagine; "plants, furniture... vases... chandeliers."[13] Her house, the château of Malmaison, "was full of treasures... and in 1809 a new gallery was built to house them."[14] Though she had "more dresses... than any woman could possibly wear, she ordered more and more."[15] According to her biographer Carolly Erickson, Josephine accumulated "nearly a thousand pairs of gloves, eight hundred pairs of shoes, several thousand pairs of silk stockings,... [and] hundreds of embroidered chemises,... camisoles,... [and] nightcaps."[16] To see her guests' reactions to her wealth, she had displayed all her jewels on a large table. There were diamonds, "pearls... rubies, sapphires, emeralds and opals surpassing... any other European collection."[17]

In the same year (1809) this good season in Josephine's life ended. Late in the year 1809, a bad season would begin for Josephine, the last of her life.

The Bad Season from 1809 Onward

On the night of November 30, 1809, Napoléon invited his wife to dinner and gave her devastating news. He had decided he had to "find a wife who could provide [him] an heir to the throne."[18] In fact, he had already found someone; Marie Louise, Archduchess of Austria. Hearing the news, Josephine collapsed on the floor. Aided by a palace prefect, Napoléon carried her to her bedroom. Josephine's second marriage was over.

In December 1809 the legal formalities for the divorce got underway. In a state of melancholy, Josephine went to live at Malmaison, "wearing wide hats to hide her tearstained face."[19] She was "constantly in tears,"[20] saying she felt as if she was dead. When in 1810 Napoléon married Marie Louise, Josephine complained to her son that her house resembled a convent.

By February 1811 the economy of France had started to decline sharply. There were starving people and riots everywhere. The unrest entered Josephine's house. Her servants deceived her, stealing food, clothes and objects d'art. Josephine began to suffer from headaches and other health problems. In 1812, Russia declared war on France; Napoléon's campaign against Russia began but before Christmas of 1812 he was defeated at Moscow. France's famous Grand Armée had been destroyed. Paris was mourning and Josephine dressed in black.

By October 1813 the situation worsened; Napoléon was also defeated at Leipzig. Josephine was panic-stricken. Despite the divorce she continued to love Napoléon. When in March 1814 the Russian and Austrian armies were a few days away from Paris, Josephine was forced to leave Malmaison and go to Navarre. There she had little money and couldn't find food or coal. On March 31, the end came, the Russians and Austrians entered Paris. Napoléon was forced to resign. Trying suicide, he swallowed poison but failed. A few days later he was exiled to the island of Elba. Josephine's sorrow was unbearable.

Less than two months later her health began to deteriorate rapidly. She became feverish and when her children were called to her room on May 29, 1814, they found her unable to speak. An abbé was called to give the sacraments. A few minutes later, the woman who had become wife of an emperor, died. She was only 51.

Conclusion

As we've seen, Josephine's seasons alternated exactly as Napoléon's seasons. We have seen his in 1776, 1792 and 1809, every 16 -17 years. They conform, therefore, to the same cycle of good and bad seasons that great people's lives reveal. That fact further confirms our discovery that the good and bad season in the lives of the ordinary people alternate the same way as those of the great men and women.

The End of the Biographies

I could easily have added dozens more biographies to further confirm my theory, including biographies of more black people or Asian origin (for example Martin Luther King, or Mao Tse Tung). But since I have already cited 22 biographies I decided that the readers might find the additional ones boring or superfluous.

Chapter 26

Confirmation

As noted earlier, the conclusion arrived at is based on reliable facts. Nor is there any bias to fit my theory. All the crucial facts that shape the good and bad seasons of the people profiled in this book are widely known and cannot be disputed. I reiterate the indisputable facts are; that Margaret Thatcher became prime minister of Great Britain in 1979 and stayed in power for eleven years and that Mikhail Gorbachev was elected General Secretary of the Soviet Union in 1985, but in 1991 he resigned (as President of the Soviet Union this time), or Nelson Mandela was triumphantly released in 1990 after almost 28 years in prison, or Columbus discovered America in 1492 and he made three more trips to the New World in 1493, 1498 and 1502, or that King Henry VIII broke with the Pope of Rome in 1532 and he married Anne Boleyn the next year 1533, or that Elizabeth I of England legally became a bastard in 1536 at age 3 but she became queen in 1559. These facts cannot be disputed.

Also undeniable are the alternations of seasons that happened in the year 1990 in the lives of the famous men and women cited in this book. All the evidence confirms the theory and that I have not squeezed the lives of these people to fit that theory. Specifically; the fact that Margaret Thatcher's political career suddenly ended in 1990, since she was forced to resign as prime minister of her country, though in early 1989 she seemed she would stay in power for years to come. Even though in early 1990 Mikhail Gorbachev was elected as the all-powerful President of the Soviet Union, in the middle of 1990 his political career suddenly crashed and soon he was forced to resign.

On the other hand the fact that Nelson Mandela had an opposite shift in 1990 after almost 28 years in prison when he was suddenly triumphantly released from jail. Similarly, at the same year 1990, U.S. ex-president Jimmy Carter suddenly became (again) very popular; The *Washington Post* published an article that year titled "Jimmy, Come Back! All Is Forgiven! But as we've saw in his biography the previous ten years the public perceptions of him were extremely negative. Similar shifts of seasons in 1990 was also seen in the biographies of John Glenn, Elizabeth Taylor, Jackie Kennedy Onassis and the Dalai Lama of Tibet.

So many *indisputable* alternations of seasons therefore, in the year 1990 in the lives of so many famous people confirm that 1990 were indeed a year of seasonal alternations in the lives of famous people. That fact further confirms that our discovery is not based on unreliable or false facts.

Not a Mere Coincidence

Furthermore, the conclusion we've arrived at cannot be a coincidence. The shifts of seasons that happened not only *in the year 1990* but also in the years 1974 and 1957, for example, (that is, every 16 -17 years), in the lives of so many people, definitely confirm that the discovery is not a mere coincidence. Specifically, in addition to the shifts of seasons we've seen that happened *in 1990* in the lives of many famous people similar impressive shifts of seasons in the lives of many other people profiled in the book also happened *in 1974*, (that is, 16 -17 years before 1990).

For example, though Aristotle Onassis was the wealthiest person on earth and hadn't any health problems throughout his life, suddenly in 1974 he became seriously ill from an incurable disease and soon died. The same for Maria Callas; while she was extremely happy with her lover Onassis for the 15 years before 1974, that year she lost her precious lover and soon also died. On the other hand, a good season started for Jackie Kennedy in 1974 because of her husband Onassis's illness and his death that soon followed, she became suddenly financially independent, receiving the huge sum of $20 million plus a lifetime income of $150,000 per year.

Thatcher, though in early 1974 she was a simple member of her party and deeply disappointed, later in the same year she put her name as the candidate leader of the party and next year she was triumphantly elected. Similar shifts in 1974 can be also seen in the biographies of Gorbachev and Mandela as well as in the biographies of Glenn, Taylor, the Dalai Lama of Tibet and Carter.

As you can see there were impressive shifts for many people *in the year 1957* (that is, 16 -17 years before 1974). Onassis, for example was on his way to becoming the wealthiest person on earth, while in the previous year he was struggling with bankruptcy. Carter became financially independent in 1957 while in the previous years he lived with his family in a government subsidized apartment.

On the other hand, a bad season started in 1957 for Jackie Kennedy – her happy marriage with John Kennedy began to deteriorate that year as she learned that her husband had love affairs with many other women. Again there are similar shifts in 1957 in the biographies of Picasso, Gorbachev, Mandela and Thatcher, Glenn, Taylor and the Dalai Lama of Tibet.

So many alternations of seasons, therefore, at the same dates; 1990, 1974, 1957 for so many people (Thatcher, Gorbachev, Mandela, Carter, Onassis, Callas, Picasso, Glenn, Taylor, Jackie Kennedy Onassis, the Dalai Lama) show that our discovery cannot be a mere coincidence.

Examining Other Biographies

As was also noted earlier, all the crucial facts that shape the good and bad seasons of the people profiled in this book are widely known to all and cannot be disputed. However, in case some readers may doubt for any of these facts they can examine any other biographies they wish. Also, to further confirm these truths, they are at liberty to examine biographies of any *other people* they may decide.

For that purpose the reader must read books on complete and detailed biographies showing a person's inner state of mind, his sorrows and joys. External events alone don't tell the whole story. For example, the fact that Leonardo da Vinci painted the *Mona Lisa* in a certain year in itself doesn't tell us whether he was in a good or bad season. We need wider information of all the outer circumstances of his life that can lead us to find his mental state.

Since the books on biographies are never divided into good and bad seasons I did so by the following procedure; First, I wrote on sheets of paper the facts that are good or bad in each biography and the years in which these facts happened. Then I wrote these facts and years in chronological order. The majority of the books on biographies are not usually always written in strict chronological order. After that I separated these facts and dates every 16 -17 years in the dates we've seen in this book (for example, 1957, 1974 and 1990).

Of course the work took me much time. For each book I read I needed about one month for reading it and about half a month for writing down the facts in chronological order and separating them in the proper dates. When I tried to follow a faster way I arrived at false conclusions.

Chapter 27

Practical Use

As explained at the end of Chapter 8, my discovery is valid for all of us – not only for the famous people. Your own life will offer good and bad seasons and alternating in 16 -17 year cycles. My research extend back 500 years into the past – from 1479 to 1990 as we've seen in Chapter 8. There is no reason to think they will not continue 500 years into the future. Since our *next* alternation of seasons happened in 1990 (as we've seen in the biographies of Gorbachev, Mandela, Thatcher, Glenn, Taylor, Kennedy Onassis, the Dalai Lama and Carter), that means the last turning point of seasons in our lives lies around 2007, which will last until 2024. Then thereafter 2040, 2056, 2073.

Recall, however, that there are two opposite courses of seasons. The first and the second course. To determine your seasons you have to ascertain to which course of seasons you belong; to the first course or to the second. To do so is as follows.

First, you have to scrutinize your life "from above," over the duration of your life, not day by day. The book *Thinking Better*, [1] by psychologists David Lewis and James Green will help clarify this point. They describe a situation where two children get lost in a remote area and the authorities can't decide how to search for them, whether to send a group of rescuers to cover the area on foot or to call in helicopters to survey the terrain.

Each method has advantages and disadvantages. If the searchers choose the first method, which is time consuming, they risk bringing help too late. If they choose the second method, which is quicker, they run the risk of not being able to see the children if they are obscured by trees. Lewis and Green suggest that people who would favor the first method are pathfinder types; those who prefer the second method are helicopter pilot types. To find which seasons you belong, you have to see your life "from above", in large periods, not day by day. You have to be a helicopter pilot, not a pathfinder.

The following graphs will help in your effort to find to which course of seasons you belong. First examine whether your life's seasons alternated according to the first graph. If you find that your seasons didn't alternate according to the first graph, use the second graph.

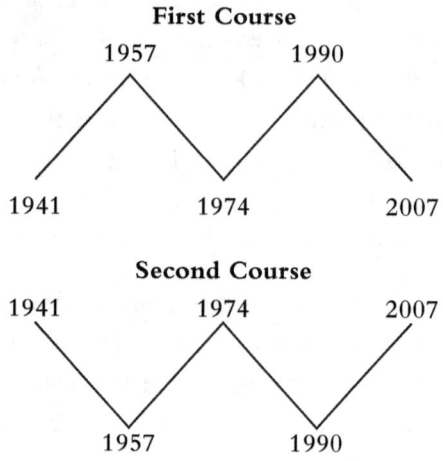

If you prefer, you can try another way. Has the period from 1990 to 2007 been good or bad compared with the years before 1990. Of course, the work for finding to which course of seasons you belong may take you a bit of time. Maybe you'll need to return after one or two days to re-examine your findings and add more details.

If despite your efforts, you cannot determine which were your good and bad seasons there is another way. You can examine how your seasons from now on. If you find that after 2007 you have a bad season in comparison with the years before 2007 that means you belong to the second course of seasons. And vice versa; if you find that after 2007 you have a good season in comparison with the previous years that means you belong to the first course of seasons.

That manner can also be used by readers who will read this book after 2024. However, you have to remember some points we've already made, specifically;

- Recall that a "good" season is a season of inner satisfaction, with successes and achievements, while a "bad" season is a season of anxiety, failure and disappointment. To use objective criteria, the main factors of a good or bad season are money, fame, love, health, etc. These criteria differ from person to person and they change with age. Although all or many of the above factors may interest a person, it is usually one of them, the most relevant, that shapes his/her good and bad seasons at a given moment. For famous Greek opera star, Maria Callas for example, love was her main pursuit after the age of 30 while her career, though equally important, came second. On the other hand, Greek tycoon Aristotle Onassis's main pursuit was money. Only later, Onassis's health became his main concern. He entered a bad season because of it, though he still remained the wealthiest person on earth.

- Also, remember that a good season is not necessarily utopia, no bad season is always a hell. There may be some bad events during a good season, as well some good events during a bad season. For example, in one of your good seasons, you may have had some problems with your health, or with your career, or a divorce may have occurred, or even death of a beloved person. These isolated events should not make you think your season has changed. It is the *overall view* of your season of 16 -17 years that counts. When Hugo was at the summer of one of his good seasons, from 1859 to 1875, he lost his wife in 1868 and his two sons in 1871 and 1873. In addition his younger daughter had been confined to a madhouse in 1872. These bad facts, however, didn't prevent him from continuing his summer; all the theaters of Paris asked to perform his works, as well as having a lot of women admirers.

- Recall that there are "spring times" and "autumns" within our good and bad seasons. Each good season starts slowly, then becomes very good and finally culminates in great satisfaction or even glory. Every bad season begins gradually, eventually becoming very bad and possibly ending in catastrophe. The first part of each *good* season resembles "springtime", while the second part resembles "summer." Likewise, the first part of each *bad* season resembles "autumn," while the second part resembles "winter." Let's use Beethoven to show this. In his bad season from 1792 to 1809 Beethoven realized he had a serious problem with his hearing. The problem worsened later and finally he became so desperate that he wanted to commit suicide. On the other hand in his good season from 1809 to 1825, Beethoven first learned to cope with his hearing problem and then at the end of this season realized tremendous success with his musical compositions.

- Keep in mind that not all of us are becoming Beethoven's or Napoleon's with the tragic or triumphant ups and downs they had in their lives. Your alternations of seasons, though clearly existing, may be less dramatic compared with those famous people.

- Finally, you have to remember that the duration of each season is something *between* 16 and 17 years. A season of your life, may have not begun exactly at the dates shown in the above graphs; it may have occurred sometime *around* those dates. The same phenomenon happens

The Seasons of our Lives

with the seasons of the year on our earth and especially with the weather we associate with each season. These seasons do not always start at the same point. Sometimes the summer starts earlier than the previous year while at other times it starts later. The same happens with the winter, autumn and spring.

Knowing Your Future Seasons

After finding to which of the two courses of seasons you belong, you will be able to foresee how your life's good and bad seasons will be in the future. By doing so you will know whether the years just ahead are likely to be good or bad for you and how long this season will last. Therefore, you can act accordingly. As noted earlier, if there is a storm on the horizon, you'll take shelter in time; if sunny days loom ahead, you'll take advantage of it before the opportunity passes. In short, you will be able to make crucial decisions regarding your career, marriage, family, relationships and all other life's issues.

Specifically, the alternations of your future good and bad seasons will be as shown in the accompanying graph.

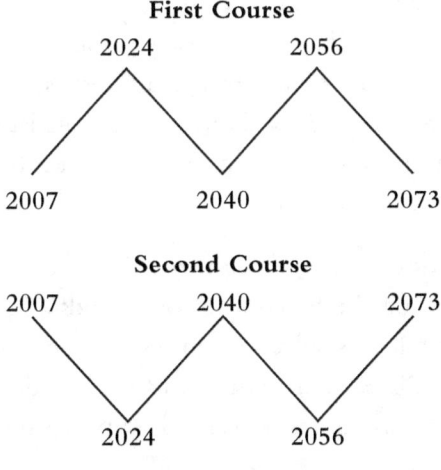

As you can see, if you belong to the first course of seasons, the years just ahead of you up to 2024 will be good; if you belong to the second course, these years will be bad.

Questions for the Future

My theory explained in this book is, of course new and as such, a new science can be born from it. New studies by other people (scientists or scholars) are absolutely necessary so that they can enable us to take greater advantages of the discovery described. Among other things, these studies must answer the following questions.

- What causes the alternations of seasons in our lives? And for what reason are there two opposite seasons? Do astronomical influences, such as unknown magnetic fields around the earth that come from the sun or other planets or even other galaxies cause the alternations of our seasons? Finding the answers to these questions may help us avoid or ameliorate ourselves against pending the bad seasons, perhaps in a similar way migratory birds leave one hemisphere during the winter and fly to the other, so that they can continually experience summer. Future generations of scientists and scholars may come up with the answer. Ancient peoples didn't know what caused the alternations of the four seasons in the earth, fall, winter, spring, summer, though they didn't deny these seasons' existence. Only thousands of years later we learned that the main cause of the four seasons in our earth is the shifting distance between the earth and the sun.

- How does that unknown cause influence the alternations of the seasons? Does it influencing the function of our minds? Consider the case of Winston Churchill. As you've seen in his biography, when World War I began in 1914, Churchill as First Lord Of The Admiralty, thought the only salvation for England was to land at Antwerp, Belgium. But no one agreed with him. Then he went alone to Antwerp, assumed leadership of a small body of sailors and ordered two divisions of inexperienced recruits to be transferred from England to Antwerp. What followed was a catastrophe. Had Churchill's state of mind been influenced by what causes the alternations of seasons in our life? The answer can help us to a greater benefit from our discovery.

- Does the conclusion at which we have arrived require some adjustments? When the great Polish astronomer, Nicholus Copernicus announced in 1543 that the earth was moving around the sun, he said that the earth's movement was in circles with the sun as their center. However, in 1609 the German astronomer Johannes Keppler discovered that the earth moves around the sun, not in circles but in elliptical orbits that have two centers, one occupied by the sun. We cannot rule out the possibility that the conclusion presented in this book may need some improvements. Despite my efforts I didn't find anyone without alternations of life's seasons. However, there may be people. There may also be a phenomenon similar to climatic seasons on earth: in Ecuador in South America where the weather is spring most of the year (with no real winter or summer). Some people may belong to a kind of "equatorial" course of season. In addition I did not find people who were excluded from the seasonal alternations as described in this book.

- Do our life's seasonal shifts of 16 -17 years apply to an entire nation or even to the entire world? What about a company, do their seasons alternate and in two opposite courses? Are the economic crises or the world's climatic changes, also governed by our discovery? I cannot answer these questions as my research only looks at the personal life of individuals. It does not apply to the lives of people in a group, like a country or a company, or even to the whole world. However, could we say that a nation's or a country's fortunes are governed by the alternations of seasons in the lives of the people's majority in that nation or country? Since there are two opposite courses of seasons, that means that during an economic crisis, for example, many people (the majority or the minority) must be in their bad season and the others at their good one. Could we say, therefore, that if the *majority* of people in a nation or country are in their good season, then their nation as an entity is also in a good season? The same question applies to our world as an entity. Also, it applies to a company; are a company's fortunes governed by the alternations of seasons, based on the *owners' seasons*? Or are they governed by the seasonal alternations in the life of its chief executive officer? All these questions need further research by other people in the future.

There are of course, many other questions to be answered. For example, should we marry a person belonging to the same course of seasons or to the opposite? Onassis and the woman he loved, Maria Callas, belonged to the same seasons and their relation was satisfactory. But Onassis and his second wife Jackie Kennedy belonged to opposite courses and their marriage was a failure. Yes, there are many questions that need answers.

Conclusion

For the moment, I hope my book has given you the means to learn whether the years just ahead are good or bad for you and how long this season will last. By knowing you can take advantage. As I explained earlier you can be daring when in a good season – fate is with you. By having the understanding of your season, you can take advantage of a good season before the opportunity passes. When you are in a good season you can take in time the necessary measures to successfully face the problems that may occur in the bad season that will follow, making provisions for the winter that will come

There are also many advantages when you are in a bad season and need not be seized by despair and pessimism –fearing that the bad season will never end. Instead anticipate the arrival of the good season, knowing that this will surely come. If your problem lies within your career in your bad season, wait to see it solved. If on the other hand, the difficulties are with your wife, husband, loved one or children you must be tolerant with all and don't despair as things will improve. The same applies in case of your being divorced. Similarly, if you have health problems in your bad season they can improve in a good season. If you have difficulties with your studies in your bad season, don't worry: this will have not any influence on your future.

When you are in a bad season remember that at the same time millions of other people around the globe are also going through a bad season. Even people we think of as being happy and successful may suffer at this moment.

In short, the ability to foresee our life's good and bad seasons changes profoundly the way we cope with our life today. Among other things, the understanding can help us to elect the right politician to govern or entrust an employee with the solution of a difficult problem if we know they are enjoying in a good season, thus operating from a position of strength. As explained a little before the end of Chapter 9, the discovery we've seen in this book radically changes the mentality and character of all people.

By use of this information, people will become more philosophical and peaceful, they will not be as quarrelsome and aggressive. On the contrary they will be tolerant, merciful and have more understanding towards others. Superficiality and imprudence will be drastically reduced.

If you want to help as many people as possible to benefit from our discovery, tell your friends to read this book and by doing so you will also have contributed to the creation of a much better world.

End Notes

2. Ludwig van Beethoven

1. Gino Pugneti's *Beethoven* published in Greek by Fytrakis Publications, Great Men of All Seasons series, Athens, 1965, (hereafter cited as P.B.), page 10.
2. P.B. 16.- **3.** P.B. 19.- **4.** P.B. 21.- **5.** P.B. 44. **6.** P.B. 44. **7.** P.B. 44. **8.** P.B. 109. **9.** P.B. 32. **10.** P.B. 57. **11.** P.B. 57. **12.** P.B. 57. **13.** P.B. 57. **14.** P.B. 57. **15.** P.B. 34. **16.** P.B. 62. **17.** P.B. 64. **18.** P.B. 53. **19.** P.B. 70. **20.** P.B. 72. **21.** P.B. 72. **22.** P.B. 75. **23.** P.B. 75

3. Giuseppe Verdi

1. Gino Pugneti's *Verdi* published in Greek by Fytrakis Publications, Great Men of All Seasons series, Athens, 1966 (hereafter cited as P.V.), page 10.
2. P.V. 10. **3.** P.V. 12. **4.** P.V. 14. **5.** P.V. 16. **6.** P.V. 16. **7.** P.V. 17. **8.** P.V. 18. **9.** P.V. 20. **10.** P.V. 25. **11.** P.V. 41. **12.** P.V. 54. **13.** P.V. 54. **14.** P.V. 56. **15.** P.V. 65. **16.** P.V. 66. **17.** P.V. 70. **18.** P.V. 70. **19.** P.V. 71. **20.** P.V. 73.

4. Pablo Picasso

1. Lael Westenbaker and the editors of Time-Life Books, *The World of Picasso*, Time-Life Books, Library of Art series, Amsterdam, 1976, European edition, (hereafter cited as T-L P), page 11.
2. T-L P 54. **3.** T-L P 57. **4.** T-L P 59. **5.** T-L P 85. **6.** T-L P 85. **7.** T-L P 106. **8.** T-L P 107. **9.** T-L P 145. **10.** T-L P 147.

5. Napoléon I

1. Mario Rivoire's *Napoléon*, published in Greek by Fytrakis Publications, The Great Men of all Seasons series, Athens, 1965 (hereafter cited as R.N.), page 10.
2. R.N. 17. **3.** R.N. 19. **4.** R.N. 19. **5.** R.N. 20. **6.** R.N. 22. **7.** R.N. 22. **8.** R.N. 24. **9.** R.N. 28. **10.** R.N. 32. **11.** R.N. 49. **12.** R.N. 51. **13.** R.N. 57. **14.** R.N. 58. **15.** R.N. 56. **16.** R.N. 60. **17.** R.N. 61. **18.** R.N. 62. **19.** R.N. 67. **20.** R.N. 72.

6. Victor Hugo

1. Cesare Giardini's *Hugo*, published in Greek by Fytrakis Publications, The Great Men of All Seasons series, Athens, 1966 (hereafter cited as G.H.), page 18
2. G.H. 18. **3.** G.H. 26. **4.** G.H. 26-27. **5.** G.H. 34. **6.** G.H. 40. **7.** G.H. 40. **8.** G.H. 40. **9.** G.H. 40. **10.** G.H. 40. **11.** G.H. 42. **12.** G.H. 47. **13.** G.H. 48. **14.** G.H. 51. **15.** G.H. 51. **16.** G.H. 67. **17.** G.H. 71. **18.** G.H. 75.

7. Winston Churchill

1. Sebastian Haffner, *Churchill*, Haus Publishing Ltd, London, 2003 (hereafter cited as H.C.), page 9.
2. H.C. 12. **3.** H.C. 13. **4.** H.C. 14. **5.** H.C. 14. **6.** H.C. 16. **7.** H.C. 16. **8.** H.C. 26. **9.** H.C. 27. **10.** H.C. 28. **11.** H.C. 35. **12.** H.C. 34. **13.** H.C. 48. **14.** H.C. 55. **15.** H.C. 57. **16.** H.C. 61. **17.** H.C. 63. **18.** H.C. 76. **19.** H.C. 91. **20.** H.C. 102. **21.** H.C. 134. **22.** H.C. 137.

10. Mikhail Gorbachev

1. Mikhail Gorbachev's *Memoirs*, New York; Doubleday, 1996, (hereafter cited as G.M.), page 29.
2. G.M. 30. **3.** G.M. 46. **4.** G.M. 49. **5.** G.M. 53. **6.** G.M. 82. **7.** G.M. 82. **8.** G.M. 83. **9.** G.M. 95. **10.** G.M. 97. **11.** G.M. 112. **12.** G.M. 115. **13.** G.M. 17. **14.** G.M. xxxiii

11. Nelson Mandela

1. Anthony Sampson's *Mandela*, Alfred A. Knopf, New York, September 1999, (hereafter cited as S.M.), page 7.
2. S.M. 10. **3.** S.M. 29. **4.** S.M. 33. **5.** S.M. 74. **6.** S.M. 82. **7.** S.M. 112. **8.** S.M. 112. **9.** S.M. 170. **10.** S.M. 173. **11.** S.M. 178. **12.** S.M. 198. **13.** S.M. 246. **14.** S.M. 253. **15.** S.M. 339. **16.** S.M. 359. **17.** S.M. 378. **18.** S.M. 447. **19.** S.M. 488. **20.** S.M. 496. **21.** S.M. 541.

12. Christopher Columbus

1. Cesare Giardini's *Columbus*, published in Greek by Fytrakis Publications, Great Men of All Seasons series, Athens, 1965 (hereafter cited as G.C.), page 35.
2. G.C. 35. **3.** G.C. 35. **4.** G.C. 43. **5.** G.C. 44. **6.** G.C. 44. **7.** G.C. 49. **8.** G.C. 57. **9.** G.C. 63. **10.** G.C. 63. **11.** G.C. 63. **12.** G.C. 65. **13.** G.C. 64. **14.** G.C. 66.

13. King Henry VIII

1. Alison Weir's *Henry VIII, The King and His Court*, Balantine Books, New York, November 2002 (hereafter cited as W.H.) page 15.
2. W.H. 85. **3.** W.H. 161. **4.** W.H. 202. **5.** W.H. 247. **6.** W.H. 242. **7.** W.H. 271. **8.** W.H. 281. **9.** W.H. 326. **10.** W.H. 331. **11.** W.H. 332. **12.** W.H. 361-362. **13.** W.H. 368. **14.** W.H. 372. **15.** W.H. 372. **16.** W.H. 36. **17.** W.H. 385. **18.** W.H. 385. **19.** W.H. 385. **20.** W.H. 419. **21.** W.H. 422. **22.** W.H. 427.

14. Margaret Thatcher

1. Libby Hughes, *Madam Prime Minister; A Biography of Margaret Thatcher* (An Authors Guild Backinprint.com Edition, Lincoln, NE, 2000, hereafter cited as M.T.), page 13.
2. M.T. 13. **3.** M.T. 36. **4.** M.T. 37. **5.** M.T. 38. **6.** M.T. 49. **7.** M.T. 51. **8.** M.T. 71. **9.** M.T. 72. **10.** M.T. 72. **11.** M.T. 73. **12.** M.T. 74. **13.** M.T. 92. **14.** M.T. 96. **15.** M.T. 97. **16.** M.T. 100. **17.** M.T. 102. **18.** M.T. 112. **19.** M.T. 118. **20.** M.T. 122. **21.** M.T. 133. **22.** M.T. 134. **23.** M.T. 134. **24.** M.T. 137-138. **25.** M.T. Addendum after page 144.

15. Queen Elizabeth I of England

1. Susan Doran's *Queen Elizabeth I*, New York University Press, 2003 (hereafter cited as Q.E.), page 16
2. Q.E. 25. **3.** Q.E. 29. **4.** Q.E. 29. **5.** Q.E. 44. **6.** Q.E. 47. **7.** Q.E. 68-69. **8.** Q.E. 69. **9.** Q.E. 77. **10.** Q.E. 88. **11.** Q.E. 89. **12.** Q.E. 90. **13.** Q.E. 118. **14.** Q.E. 120. **15.** Q.E. 120. **16.** Q.E. 120. **17.** Q.E. 128. **18.** Q.E. 128. **19.** Q.E. 132. **20.** Q.E. 134. **21.** Q.E. 134. **22.** Q.E. 134.

16. Aristotle Onassis

1. N. Fraser, P. Jacobson, M. Ottaway, L. Chester, *Aristotle Onassis*, Lippincott Co., New York, 1977, (hereafter cited as FJOC), page 4.
2. FJOC 8. **3.** FJOC 16. **4.** FJOC 16. **5.** FJOC 23. **6.** FJOC 41. **7.** FJOC 62. **8.** FJOC 103. **9.** FJOC 110. **10.** FJOC 112. **11.** FJOC 156. **12.** FJOC 183. **13.** FJOC 357.

17. John Glenn

1. John Glenn's *A Memoir*, Bantam Books, New York, Nov. 1999, (hereafter cited as G.M.), page 5.
2. G.M. 5. **3.** G.M. 17. **4.** G.M. 27. **5.** G.M. 50. **6.** G.M. 333. **7.** G.M. 342. **8.** G.M. 351. **9.** G.M. 356. **10.** G.M. 356. **11.** G.M. 356. **12.** G.M. 356. **13.** G.M. 359. **14.** G.M. 360. **15.** G.M. 360. **16.** G.M. 363. **17.** G.M. 363. **18.** G.M. 379. **19.** G.M. 385. **20.** G.M. 388. **21.** G.M. 391.

18. Elizabeth Taylor

1. Larissa Branin's *Liz, the Pictorial Biography of Elizabeth Taylor*, Courage Books, New York, 2000, (hereafter cited as B.T.), page 29.
2. B.T. 53. **3.** B.T. 60. **4.** B.T. 63. **5.** B.T. 62. **6.** B.T. 64. **7.** B.T. 67-68. **8.** B.T. 78. **9.** B.T. 80. **10.** B.T. 85. **11.** B.T. 83. **12.** B.T. 91. **13.** B.T. 73. **14.** B.T. 93. **15.** B.T. 95. **16.** B.T. 102. **17.** B.T. 105. **18.** B.T. 106. **19.** B.T. 105. **20.** B.T. 109.

19. Maria Callas

1. Anne Edwards's *Maria Callas*, St. Martin's Griffin, New York, 2003, (hereafter cited E.C.), page 25.
2. E.C. 38. 3. E.C. 63. 4. E.C. 77. 5. E.C. 87. 6. E.C. 89. 7. E.C. 98. 8. E.C. 110. 9. E.C. 121. 10. E.C. 139. 11. E.C. 142. 12. E.C. 148. 13. E.C. 158. 14. E.C. 191. 15. E.C. 206. 16. E.C. 213. 17. E.C. 228. 18. E.C. 245. 19. E.C. 272. 20. E.C. 314. 21. E.C. 314. 22. E.C. 319.

20. Jacqueline Kennedy Onassis

1. Sarah Bradford's *America's Queen*, Penguin Books, New York, 2001, (hereafter cited as B.A.Q.), page 1.
2. B.A.Q. 13. 3. B.A.Q. 31. 4. B.A.Q. 38. 5. B.A.Q. 59. 6. B.A.Q. 117. 7. B.A.Q. 120. 8. B.A.Q. 129. 9. B.A.Q. 130. 10. B.A.Q. 140. 11. B.A.Q. 149. 12. B.A.Q. 194. 13. B.A.Q. 231. 14. B.A.Q. 302. 15. B.A.Q. 315-316. 16. B.A.Q. 337. 17. B.A.Q. 357. 18. B.A.Q. 371. 19. B.A.Q. 405. 20. B.A.Q. 408. 21. B.A.Q. 411. 22. B.A.Q. 428. 23. B.A.Q. 431.

21. The Dalai Lama of Tibet

1. The Dalai Lama's Freedom in Exile, *the Autobiography of the Dalai Lama*, Harper Perennial, New York, 1990, (cited hereafter as D.L.), page 12.
2. D.L. 12. 3. D.L. 27. 4. D.L. 83. 5. D.L. 88. 6. D.L. 112. 7. D.L. 124. 8. D.L. 135. 9. D.L. 2. 10. D.L. 147. 11. D.L. 158. 12. D.L. 167. 13. D.L. 208. 14. D.L. 222. 15. D.L. 230. 16. D.L. 241. 17. D.L. 254.

22. Jimmy Carter

1. Kenneth E. Morris, *Jimmy Carter, American Moralist*, University of Georgia Press, Athens, Georgia, 1996 (hereafter cited as M.J.C.), page 49.
2. M.J.C. 50. 3. M.J.C. 68. 4. M.J.C. 103. 5. M.J.C. 106. 6. M.J.C. 115. 7. M.J.C. 123. 8. M.J.C. 157. 9. M.J.C. 199. 10. M.J.C. 276-277. 11. M.J.C. 288. 12. M.J.C. 293. 13. M.J.C. 305. 14. M.J.C. 305. 15. M.J.C. 305. 16. M.J.C. 289. 17. M.J.C. 294. 18. M.J.C. 294. 19. M.J.C. 308. 20. M.J.C. 319.

23. Sarah Bernhardt

1. Elizabeth Silverthorne's *Sarah Bernhardt*, Chelsea House, Philadelphia, 2004, (hereafter cited as S.S.B.), page 24.
2. S.S.B. 30. **3.** S.S.B. 37. **4.** S.S.B. 37. **5.** S.S.B. 42. **6.** S.S.B. 42. **7.** S.S.B. 47. **8.** S.S.B. 49. **9.** S.S.B. 55. **10.** S.S.B. 68. **11.** S.S.B. 71. **12.** S.S.B. 82. **13.** S.S.B. 87. **14.** S.S.B. 96. **15.** S.S.B. 103. **16.** S.S.B. 116.

24. Auguste Rodin

1. William Harlan Hale and the editors of Time-Life Books, *The World of Rodin*, Library of Art series, Nederland, 1976, European Edition, (hereafter cited as T-L R), page 47.
2. T-L R 50. **3.** T-L R 51. **4.** T-L R 71. **5.** T-L R 118. **6.** T-L R 122. **7.** T-L R 141. **8.** T-L R 145. **9.** T-L R 167. **10.** T-L R 167. **11.** T-L R 168. **12.** T-L R 172.

25. Josephine

1. Carolly Erickson's *Josephine*, St. Martin's Griffin, New York, 1998, (hereafter cited as E. J.), page 11.
2. E. J. 74. **3.** E. J. 82. **4.** E. J. 96. **5.** E. J. 136-137. **6.** E. J. 147-148. **7.** E. J. 177. **8.** E. J. 196. **9.** E. J. 210. **10.** E. J. 230. **11.** E. J. 239. **12.** E. J. 281. **13.** E. J. 282. **14.** E. J. 282. **15.** E. J. 282. **16.** E. J. 283. **17.** E. J. 283. **18.** E. J. 287. **19.** E. J. 294. **20.** E. J. 295.

27. Practical Use

1. Rawson, Wade Publishers, Inc., New York, 1982.

Sources

All the facts and details mentioned in the biographies cited in the book are coming from the following books:

Bradford, Sarah, *America's Queen*, The Life of Jacqueline Kennedy Onassis, Penguin Books, New York, 2001.

Branin, Larissa, *Liz, the Pictorial Biography of Elizabeth Taylor*, Courage Books, Philadelphia, Pennsylvania, 2000.

Dalai Lama, *Freedom in Exile, the Autobiography of the Dalai Lama*, Harper Perennial, New York, 1990.

Doran, Susan, *Queen Elizabeth I*, New York University Press, 2003.

Edwards, Anne, *Maria Callas*, St. Martin's Griffin, New York, 2003.

Erickson, Carolly, *Josephine*, St. Martin's Griffin, New York, 1998.

Fraser, N., Jacobson, P., Ottaway, M., Chester, L., *Aristotle Onassis*, Lippincott Co., New York, 1977.

Giardini, Cesare, *Columbus*, published in Greek by Fytrakis Publications, The Great Men of all Seasons series, Athens, 1965.

Giardini, Cesare, *Hugo*, published in Greek by Fytrakis Publications, The Great Men of All Seasons series, Athens, 1966.

Glenn, John, *A Memoir*, Bantam Books, New York, 1999.

Gorbachev, Mikhail, *Memoirs*, Bantam Books, New York, 1997.

Haffner, Sebastian, *Winston Churchill*, published in Greek by the Classical Publications Organization, Lives and Works series, Athens, 1967.

Hale, William Harlanand the editors of Time-Life Books, *The World of Rodin*, Library of Art series, Time-Life International, Nederland, 1976.

Hughes, Libby, *Madam Prime Minister*, An Authors Guild Back in print. com Edition, 2000.

Mauroisandré, *Napoléon*, published in Greek by the Classical Publications Organization, Lives and Works series, Athens, 1966.

Morris, Kenneth E., *Jimmy Carter, American Moralist*, University of Georgia Press, Athens, Georgia, 1996.

Pugneti, Gino, *Beethoven*, published in Greek by Fytrakis Publications, The Great Men of All Seasons series, Athens, 1965.

Pugneti, Gino, *Verdi*, published in Greek by Fytrakis Publications, The Great Men of All Seasons series, Athens, 1966.

Rivoire, Mario, *Napoléon*, published in Greek by Fytrakis Publications, The Great Men of All Seasons series, Athens, 1965.

Sampson, Anthony, *Mandela*, Alfred A. Knopf, New York, 1999.

Silverthrone, Elizabeth, *Sarah Bernhardt*, Chelsea House, Philadelphia, 2004.

Weir, Alison, *Henry VIII, the King and His Court*, Balantine Books, New York, November 2002.

Westenbaker, Laeland the editors of Time-Life Books, *The World of Picasso*, Library of Art series, Time-Life International, Nederland, 1976.

For further reading, the reader may also consult these books (all in English):

Ball, Stuart, *Winston Churchill*, New York University Press, 2003.

Butler, Ruth, *Rodin; The Shape of a Genius*, Yale University Press, 1993.

Castelotandré, *Napoléon; A Biography*, Rombaldi Publishers, 1971.

Cooper, Barry, *Beethoven*, Oxford Press, 2001.

Granzotto, Gianni, *Christopher Columbus, the Dream and the Obsession, A Biography*, Olympic Marketing Corporation, 1985,

Grunfeld, Frederic V., *Rodin; A Biography*, Henry Holt & Company, 1987, Haffner, Sebastian, Churchill, Haus Publishing Ltd (London), 2003.

Humes, James C., *Winston Churchill*, DK Publishing, 2003,

Josephson, Matthew, *Victor Hugo; A Biography of the Great Romantic*, Telegraph Books, 1992.

Madariaga, Salvador de, *Christopher Columbus*, Greenwood Publishing, 1979.

McLynn, Frank, *Napoléon; A Biography*, Arcade Books, 2003, O'Brian, Patrick, Pablo Ruiz Picasso; A Biography, Collins, 1976.

Phillips-Matz, Mary Jane, *Verdi; A Biography*, Oxford University Press, 1993.

Robb, Graham, *Victor Hugo; A Biography*, W.W. Norton & Company, 1999.

Solomon, Maynard, *Beethoven*, Schirmer Books, 2001.

Weaver, William, *Verdi; A Documentary* Study, W.W. Norton and Company, 1977.

Other Great Titles by Heart Space Publications

Dance of Light: a new way of understanding the Earth and all life forms

All is One : an extra ordinary book that teaches difficult concepts in a simple way!

Yogi, the Tails and Teachings of a Suburban Alpha Doggy: a delightful read illustrating the wisdom and humour that animals bring to our lives

Second Chance, Regain your Health with Tissue Salts: this book will help the full spectrum of users, from concerned parents, experienced pharmacists and health care workers

The Art of Walking: a treasure trove of knowledge, practical guidance and inspiration in lyrical prose

Know Thyself: a workbook that can become a lifeline for alife that works

Towards a Soulful Sexuality: an intelligent, thought provoking and candid new perspective of sex, age and menopause for all women.

 ***How to Write - Right!***: with this book you will become the writer you have always wanted to be

Trees, the Guardian of the Soul: a book of short stories that imparts the wisdom of the ages, appealing to all age groups

 ***The Halo and the Noose:*** a great piece of work which stimulates one to look at life differently

Hillhairyass Poems: poems and illustrations created to entertain and support young adults

 ***Guided! How to Communicate with your Spirit Guides***: Discover your soul's purpose and learn techniques to communicate with your spirit guides

he Irritable Woman's Cookbook: "cooking is like sex; you have to be in the mood", says the humorous author of this Jewish cookbook

 ***Saving your life one day at a time***: seven steps for enduring health and emotional state

The Path of Cosmic Consciousness: journey through initiation to enlightenment in the sacred Andean tradition

What if: an encounter of simple truth about life and spirituality

Paws and Listen to the Voices of the Animals: Read this book, then open your heart, free your mind and listen to the ancient wisdom of the animals that you love.

Spunky: Join me on my journey of becoming a cancer survivor, and against all odds a provincial badminton player.

Bleeding Heart: Bleeding Heart is a timeless fable about living life with passion. It will bring joy to your soul as you turn the pages ever faster.

Heart Space Publications
Australia: +61 450 260 348
South Africa: +27 11 431 1274
pat@heartspacebooks.com
www.heartspacebooks.com

www.ingramcontent.com/pod-product-compliance
Lightning Source LLC
Chambersburg PA
CBHW071957290426
44109CB00018B/2048